D1523847

SUBLIMINAL EXPLORATIONS OF PERCEPTION, DREAMS, AND FANTASIES

PSYCHOLOGICAL ISSUES

Stuart T. Hauser, *Editor*

Editorial Board

SUBLIMINAL EXPLORATIONS OF PERCEPTION, DREAMS, AND FANTASIES

THE PIONEERING CONTRIBUTIONS OF CHARLES FISHER

Selected and Edited
with an
Introduction

by
HOWARD SHEVRIN

Psychological Issues
Monograph 64

INTERNATIONAL UNIVERSITIES PRESS, Inc.
Madison, Connecticut

Library of Congress Cataloging-in-Publication Data

Fisher, Charles, 1908 Mar. 26–
    Subliminal explorations of perception, dreams, and fantasies : the pioneering contributions of Charles Fisher / selected and edited with an introduction by Howard Shevrin.
        p. cm.— (Psychological issues ; monograph 64)
    Includes bibliographical references and index.
    ISBN 0-8236-6248-9
    1. Sublimation (Psychology) 2. Subconsciousness. 3. Consciousness. 4. Dreams. 5. Perception. 6. Psychoanalysis. I. Shevrin, Howard. II. Title. III. Series.

    BF175.5.S92 F57 2003
    153.7′36—dc21

                                                                        2002024068

Manufactured in the United States of America

CONTENTS

ACKNOWLEDGMENTS

Thanks are due to the following journals for permission to reprint papers originally published by them:

Journal of the American Psychoanalytic Association
By Charles Fisher:
Dreams and Perception: The Role of Preconscious Primary Modes of Perception in Dream Formation, 2:389–445 (1954).
Dreams, Images, and Perception: A Study of Unconscious–Preconscious Relationships, 4:5–48 (1956).
A Study of the Preliminary Stages of the Construction of Dreams and Images, 5:5–60 (1957).

By Charles Fisher and I. H. Paul:
The Effect of Subliminal Visual Stimulation on Images and Dreams: A Validation Study, 7:55–83 (1959).

Psychoanalysis and Contemporary Thought
By Charles Fisher:
Further Observations on the Pötzl Phenomenon: The Effects of Subliminal Visual Stimulation on Dreams, Images, and Hallucinations, 11:3–56 (1984); originally published in *L'Evolution Psychiatrique*, 4:551–566 (1959).

Journal of Nervous and Mental Disease
By I. H. Paul and Charles Fisher:
Subliminal Visual Stimulation: A Study of Its Influence on Subsequent Images and Dreams, 129(4):315–340 (1959).

Journal of Abnormal Psychology
By Howard Shevrin and Charles Fisher:
Changes in the Effects of a Waking Subliminal Stimulus as a Function of Dreaming and Nondreaming Sleep, 72(4):362–368 (1967).

Journal of Personality
By Donald Phoenix, Lester Luborsky, Richard Rice, and Charles Fisher:
Eye Fixation Behavior as a Function of Awareness, 36(1):1–20 (1968).

I would like to acknowledge the help and support of Dr. Arnold Richards, who encouraged me to see this project through, as well as Ms. Barbara Fisher, who provided invaluable information concerning her father's professional life. Without the help of Ms. Jennifer Cho, who carried out the lion's share of the onerous work of digging out obscure references started by Ms. Colleen Hastie, this monograph would not have been completed. I also wish to acknowledge the always useful editorial suggestions given by Dr. Margaret Emery, who helped me shape the papers into a book. Lastly, I wish to thank Dr. Stuart Hauser, Editor of the *Psychological Issues* Monograph series, for his patience and unflagging encouragement.

INTRODUCTION

The history of subliminal research since the early 1960s has been a success story rare in psychology. From a handful of studies appearing in the early 1950s, mainly by psychoanalytic investigators such as Fisher, subliminal research has burgeoned into hundreds of studies in cognitive science, social psychology, personality, and neuroscience. The phenomenon itself, once challenged and considered purely artifactual, has now become a serious aspect of psychology with bearing on the role of unconscious processes in perception, memory, affect, social judgments, and prejudice. Indeed, perhaps the most influential criticism of the validity of subliminal findings, by Holender (1986), has resulted not in retrenchment of subliminal research, but in a rash of studies that has resulted in further supporting the existence of the phenomenon. At the 1995 annual meeting of the American Psychological Society, an organization of experimental psychologists, a panel was devoted to new evidence for unconscious perception contributed by two leading exponents of methodological purity in subliminal research and a member of our own research group (Panel, 1995). New methods for detecting and measuring unconscious perception were described that would have delighted Fisher by their precision and methodological unassailability, although he would have been disappointed by their meager psychodynamic content. Fisher was aware of the developing parallels between cognitive research on unconscious perception and his own work. He was hopeful that the future would prove fruitful in that regard—and it has. Psychology now appears to be on the threshold of addressing the nature of unconscious processes, not simply their existence. Fisher's research and theories, as evidenced by the papers in this monograph, have much to offer psychology.

Subliminal research is unique in another important respect. It is perhaps the only experimental method originally developed by

1

psychoanalytic researchers and thereafter adapted by psychologists
for use in understanding the preconscious stages of cognition.[1]
Charles Fisher was the pioneering psychoanalytic researcher who
introduced the subliminal method to psychoanalysis. The purpose of this volume is to bring together in one place the corpus
of Charles Fisher's subliminal investigations so that the import of
his methodological and theoretical contributions can be better
appreciated and their implications assimilated into the mainstream of psychoanalytic and psychological research. Although
Fisher's work has been summarized in two comprehensive reviews
of subliminal research (Dixon, 1971, 1981), an examination of
the psychoanalytic and cognitive literature reveals that there is
little awareness of the bearing that Fisher's research has on current questions in the field of subliminal investigation.

Khilstrom (1996), a cognitive psychologist who has made contributions to the study of unconscious processes, has noted that
research in subliminal perception would have died in the 1960s
were it not for the efforts of a small group of psychoanalytic
investigators, notably Fisher, whose research did not reach beyond a small circle, despite the fact, states Khilstrom, that the
studies met "reasonably stringent methodological standards" (p.
26). Khilstrom explains this disinterest on the part of experimental psychologists as caused by their "distrust . . . towards anything
smacking of psychoanalytic theory" (p. 26). As I will convey at a
later point in this introduction, Fisher's use of psychoanalytic
theory is tied closely to his findings, and as such would merit the
interest of empirical scientists in any discipline. By the same to-
ken, it would be incorrect to say that in the years since Fisher's
pioneering contributions that there have not been significant
methodological advances in the field of subliminal research.
Much more thinking and exploration has been devoted to methodological improvements than to theoretical issues because of
the persistent skepticism within psychology regarding anything
like the unconscious. These methodological advances have been
examined and summarized by Snodgrass (in press). Mainly they

---

[1]There was a scattering of earlier studies (Pierce and Jastrow, 1884; Sidis, 1898), but
these studies had no lasting impact. It was not until Fisher's work that laboratories at NYU
and the Menninger Foundation published subliminal studies followed by Dixon in England and then by many others as reviewed by Dixon in two books (Dixon, 1971, 1981).

have dealt with the persistent worry that consciousness has not been entirely ruled out and that the effects are therefore not truly unconscious. By and large, contemporary researchers would consider Fisher's early, more clinical studies, comprising part I of this monograph, as failing to meet current stringent standards for subliminality, but his later experimental studies, comprising part II of this monograph, as indicated by Khilstrom's evaluation, would be found acceptable. Nonetheless, the value of the early, more clinical studies should not be underestimated.

In 1919 Freud added a footnote to the fifth edition of *The Interpretation of Dreams* (1900), its uncharacteristic length conveying the importance it held for the author. Fisher quotes this footnote in chapter 1 at the very outset of his subliminal researches. In this footnote, Freud, no great advocate of experimentation, singled out the experimental work of O. Pötzl, a Viennese sensory physiologist, in which he had demonstrated how consciously unperceived elements of a briefly flashed picture returned in dreams, having undergone the transformations Freud had himself only recently discovered. Freud states, "The questions raised by Pötzl's experiments go far beyond the sphere of dream interpretation as dealt with in the present volume" (1900, p. 182).

Like a seed buried in rich soil but lacking a knowing hand to tend it, the promise in this footnote languished unfulfilled for over 30 years. It was Charles Fisher who saw its promise and brought it to fruition. In his hands, the seedling grew and burst into bloom. As an investigator, Fisher incorporated the sensitivity of the clinician and the ingenuity of the true explorer, creating experiments of singular richness. Fisher has been practically alone in his exploration of transferences in the experimental situation and the bearing of these transferences on the highly individual ways in which subliminal perceptions are almost immediately transformed according to the laws of the primary process. Fisher hypothesized that dream work begins at the moment at which the subliminal stimulus has been flashed. According to this view, the unnoticed subliminal elements are not stored until the night and then reworked in the dream; rather, unconscious fantasy and conflict, condensation, displacement, and symbol formation are ever at work. Our dreams begin behind our eyes in full daylight.

Fisher suggested a revision of Freud's "picket fence" model for dream formation. He suggested that topographic regression did not begin in sleep, but was already in full progress during the day. This revision of dream formation is more clearly in accord with clinical observations, insofar as we know from slips, symptoms, and the transference itself that the primary process is continuously at work, although its visible influences appear only sporadically during the day as well as at night.

Fisher's subliminal research and theorizing have contributed to a radical rethinking of the role of the unconscious (comprising the preconscious and the dynamic unconscious) in mental life. It can now be argued on the basis of considerable experimental evidence that all psychological processes begin in an unconscious phase and that consciousness itself is a later and optional stage (see Shevrin and Dickman [1980] for a further development of this position). Freud did not quite make up his mind on this point, at times arguing that perception was first conscious, and at times arguing that perception starts in an unconscious phase. The evidence from subliminal perception research provides strong support for the position that all psychological processes begin unconsciously. The preconscious is given a new importance as a mediating way station for most psychological processes. In Fisher's model, the preconscious is the port of entry for external stimuli where they can be immediately shunted into consciousness or be drawn into repression or the dynamic unconscious. It is in the preconscious that dreams begin, as well as symptoms, slips, and developing transferences. Fisher's pioneering efforts in this field have yet to be fully appreciated.

From the papers collected in this monograph some eight propositions can be derived that capture the essence of Fisher's originality and his claim to enduring importance to psychoanalysis and psychology. These propositions are briefly described below, following which a fuller rendering of their implications will be provided.

1. All stimulation goes through an initial preconscious phase. Preconscious processes assume a role of considerable importance both with respect to consciousness and the dynamic

unconscious. As such, the preconscious is pivotal in understanding the conceptual relationship between cognitive psychology and psychoanalysis, between underlying psychological processes and clinically relevant phenomena.

2. Consciousness is a later and optional stage. An enormous amount of psychological activity goes on prior to consciousness, some, all or none of which may in fact become conscious. Certain lawful relationships describe the conditions under which one or another of these eventualities is likely to occur.

3. The full effects of a subliminal stimulus are a function of the personal history and unconscious conflicts of the subject. This view challenges the automatic processing hypothesis of some cognitive psychologists and underscores the importance of unconscious motivational dynamics, defenses, and character organization in understanding the fate of subliminal stimuli, as well as increasing the important methological value of subliminal stimuli as means of exploring the dynamic unconscious.

4. The relationship to the experimenter plays a significant role in the influence of a subliminal stimulus. Transferential issues play an important role in understanding how a subliminal stimulus effects psychological processes. These issues are largely ignored in most subliminal investigations, yet are of crucial importance in understanding exactly how a subliminal stimulus will be processed.

5. The nature of a subliminal effect is in part determined by the responses used to detect it. In most psychological investigations employing subliminal stimuli, responses are highly structured, purely cognitive, and lacking in personal relevance. However, subliminal effects can be detected in such altered states of consciousness as accompany dreaming, fantasizing, and imagining and are of significant personal relevance.

6. Dream work and fantasy formation involving subliminal stimuli occur immediately after subliminal exposure. The mind functions as a multilayered, dynamic organization so that perception, dream work, and fantasy formation are constantly interacting with each other and occurring in close proximity

to actual stimulation. Responses attuned to these different levels of mental functioning can reveal subliminal influences (see 5 above).

7. The principles of mental organization effecting a subliminal stimulus can be qualitatively different from those effecting a supraliminal stimulus. The concepts of primary and secondary process are especially valuable in understanding how a subliminal stimulus is processed. Indeed, with the use of subliminal stimuli, primary process influences on perception itself can be demonstrated with important implications for cognitive psychology.

8. Subliminal findings fit with psychoanalytic structural theory and make possible a better incorporation of the topographic model into structural theory. In particular, the role of the preconscious can be more fully clarified and conceptualized on the basis of subliminal findings than is currently the case.

Before examining each of these propositions in greater detail, something should be said about Fisher's style and practice as an investigator. Fisher began his research career in the Ranson Institute of Neurology at Northwestern University Medical School. When still a graduate student he succeeded in localizing the lesion in the anterior hypothalamus causing diabetes insipidus. As with Freud's early research as a neurologist, Fisher's discovery required painstaking examination of laboratory preparations. The research resulted in a book Fisher coauthored with Ingram and Ransom, *Diabetes Insipidus and the Neurohormonal Control of Water Balance* (1938). The approach of the research physiologist is to observe carefully the effects of an invasive manipulation on several systematically monitored laboratory animals. Given that each animal is of a known genetic strain and its laboratory environment controlled, it is reasonable that a generalization can be made from a few specimens. Fisher carried over this approach to his research on subliminal perception. As in his neurophysiological investigations, each patient or subject was carefully examined and counted as an experiment. Similarly, a patient or subject was considered to be a control if the manipulation was absent. Each case spoke for itself, and to Fisher each case spoke volumes. He was a master at elucidating intriguing possibilities in his rich, multifaceted data. These empirically stunning early studies, done on the model of his earlier neurophysiological investigations, are presented in part I. They contain a wealth of suggestive illustrations and imaginative constructions that will be drawn upon in the detailed consideration of the eight propositions below.

When Fisher realized that psychological researchers did not play by the same rules as physiological investigators, and that several convincing cases and a few individual controls were not sufficient to persuade his psychological colleagues, he then entered upon a series of productive collaborations with psychologists who provided this experimental know-how. These studies comprise part II. They were uniformly successful and were among the first subliminal experiments to include systematic controls, objective and reliable judgments, and suitable statistics. Interestingly, in the two studies with Paul (chapters 5 and 6), Fisher proved to be the judge with the best hit rate for determining subliminal influences. The total immersion in phenomena he practiced as a physiological researcher poring over his slides and as an analyst listening to his patients stood him in good stead as an investigator of subliminal processes.

I will now proceed with an examination of each of the eight propositions.

All Stimulation Goes Through an Initial Preconscious Phase

The term *preconscious* is meaningful only in a psychoanalytic context and stands in contradistinction to consciousness, on the one hand, and the dynamic unconscious, on the other. To cognitive psychologists, for example, there are only conscious and unconscious processes. Yet there is agreement that all stimulation goes through an initial nonconscious phase prior to consciousness, no matter what it might be called or how it might be conceptualized. For example, a word first activates a semantic network of associates before becoming conscious. This can be demonstrated by presenting an associate of the word immediately afterward. The reaction time to the associate will be much faster than if it had been presented first, indicating that it had been already activated preconsciously by the first word.

However, it should be noted that during the roughly 60 years (1910–1970) of academic dominance by behaviorism, neither consciousness nor the unconscious was accorded scientific status. The very concept of a mental process was disallowed. Since the 1970s, psychology has freed itself from its behaviorist straitjacket. First, the notion of a mental process as an internal event that could be reported on (*introspected,* in an older yet still apt terminology) was found acceptable and necessary; then the notion of consciousness reappeared very much in its nineteenth-century garb; and finally the necessity for an unconscious mental life was gradually acknowledged (Shevrin and Dickman, 1980). The important role that unconscious processes are now playing in cognitive psychology is psychoanalytically speaking limited to purely cognitive, nondynamic, nonconflictual processes, although research in social cognitive psychology and social psychology have extended interest to the influence of unconscious affect (Murphy and Zajonc, 1993) and even unconscious motivation (Bargh and Ferguson, 2000), but still very much in a nonconflictual context.

The cognitive unconscious differs in several fundamental ways from the preconscious that Fisher, in particular, has stressed. For Fisher the preconscious is a busy way station between consciousness and the dynamic unconscious. As presented in his model (see chapter 3), all perceptual stimuli, subliminal and supraliminal, first register preconsciously, where interaction occurs selectively with preconsciously stored memory traces resulting in recognition; at the same time, dynamically unconscious wishes and their related memory traces also interact with preconscious registrations. Indeed, Fisher took the position that only through "piggybacking" on some preconscious registration can dynamically unconscious contents achieve conscious representation. He cites Freud (1915) in this regard who maintained that the unconscious cannot be directly known and is always inferred from some overt manifestation, usually in some transformed guise. Fisher pointed out that the phenomenon of transference, so fundamental in psychoanalysis, was already present in this "transfer" from an unconscious wish to a preconscious registration: The past in the form of a wish and its associated memories assimilate the preconscious registration, thus imposing the past on the present, the essence of transference. Fisher cited many examples of how preconscious registrations are drawn into and endowed with conflictual, infantile significance. In one image, for example, the subject utilized a corner of a subliminal star stimulus that had a point missing by transforming it into two spread thighs with an unclear hermaphroditic genital. The image related to a childhood memory of watching a small girl spreading her thighs and urinating. "Hermaphrodite" and "point missing" were connected with the subject's observation of the small girl's missing penis (see chapter 3). In our discussion of the seventh proposition we will examine further the relationship between recent discoveries in the brain processing of visual stimuli and the nature of preconscious registration bearing on the kind of fragmentation of the subliminal stimulus found in the previous example.

Once registered preconsciously, according to Fisher's model, the stimulus can undergo two radically different fates: If of supraliminal intensity, it will customarily be delivered directly into consciousness after making contact with appropriate preconscious memory traces; if of subliminal intensity, it will more likely be subject to dynamic unconscious processes following which it can be delivered "indirectly" into consciousness by way of dreams, images, hallucinations, and free associations. By "indirectly," Fisher meant that the originally preconsciously registered content can become conscious in some form but will not be recognized as such. There will be no way to recover the original registration as a perception of a particular stimulus. In this important respect, as Tulving noted, Fisher anticipated the contemporary cognitive distinction between explicit and implicit memory. The "recovered" subliminal registration is in cognitive terms an implicit memory insofar as the individual cannot identify or experience the recovered content as the true memory of the original registration. The only explicit memory is of the portion of the original stimulus of which the person was initially aware.

The notion of stimulus registration, or encoding in cognitive terminology, was also of theoretical importance to Fisher. He favored a strict definition of perception according to which perception occurs only as long as the perceptual stimulus is present. As soon as the stimulus disappears we are no longer dealing with perception but with a memory of a perception. Thus subliminal perception lasts only as long as the brief stimulus presentation, the rest is memory and memory transformations involving processes of recognition and dynamic unconscious influences. Nevertheless, despite the brevity of the perceptual process the actual registration, or encoding, is of photographic accuracy. Only in this way could Fisher account for the way in which details of the subliminal stimulus were accurately embedded in dreams and images. For example, the corners of a star forming the number 4 would be repetitively reproduced in an image (see chapter 3, p. 142–148). In addition, clear associations to the idea of star, such as comets, would also appear in indirect recoveries (see chapter 3, p. 148–154). From findings such as these it seemed reasonable to infer that accurate registration of the subliminal stimulus had occurred. In much recent research, some of it in our laboratory, results support Fisher's hypothesis that highly accurate registrations can occur with only the briefest stimulation. We have shown that at 1 msec, far faster than the 100 msec exposure time generally used by Fisher, faces, individual words, and brief phrases can be shown to have subliminal effects (Shevrin, 1973; Snodgrass, Shevrin, and Kopka, 1993; Wong, Shevrin, and Williams, 1994; Shevrin, Bond, Brakel, Hertel, and Williams, 1996).

There is one last, but quite important property of the preconscious, concerning its role as the locus of various fragmentations and transformations of the subliminal registration, that will be taken up in detail under the seventh proposition below.

Consciousness Is a Later and Optional Stage

From the preceding discussion of the important role played by preconscious registration which, for Fisher, applies both to supraliminal and subliminal stimuli, the role of consciousness can readily be inferred: It is in fact a later and optional stage in stimulus processing. Within Fisher's model, it is entirely possible for a clearly supraliminal stimulus, measured by its intensity, to register preconsciously and never become directly conscious. Its fate in this respect would depend on the particular unconscious wishes acting upon it preconsciously. Negative hallucinations provide examples of this outcome. Brakel (1989a,b) has contributed two illuminating reports on negative hallucinations encountered in psychotherapy.

For Fisher, consciousness must be unambiguously distinguished from its contents. When he described how preconscious registrations appear in consciousness in some "delayed" manner, he meant that they do not immediately appear in consciousness as is true of most stimuli, but might appear that night in a dream. But in addition to being "delayed," Fisher also refers to their "indirect" appearance in consciousness, by which he meant that when the preconscious registrations appear in dreams and images they are not recognized as belonging to the actual subliminal stimulus. In fact, Fisher has reported that his subjects usually reacted with surprise when they were confronted with the stimulus above threshold and even when they were struck by evident similarities between the stimulus and their dreams and images. Becoming aware of these parallels does not awaken an actual memory of the stimulus. As Shevrin and Luborsky (1958) have shown, reminiscence effects are possible as long as the subject is engaged in the task of recalling the *stimulus*, so that the newly recovered elements are retrieved as part of the perceived stimulus. But once the recovered elements have been incorporated into a dream or image, it no longer seems possible for subjects to refer the recovered elements back to the original stimulus spontaneously. It is also possible, as Fisher has reported, that the initially perceived parts of the stimulus (at 100 msec, the duration employed by Fisher, some parts of the stimulus are usually perceived) can already reveal the intrusion of dynamically unconscious influences. The subject believes he is describing the stimulus when in fact the account is infiltrated with unconscious contents. Thus, one young male subject described the Three Kings picture (see chapter 1, p. 55) as depicting three young women in bathing suits whose significance only became apparent in the subject's later associations. From examples like these, Fisher inferred that Pötzl's "law of exclusion," according to which there was a dissociation between what became conscious initially and what would be recovered indirectly in dreams, was subject to some important exceptions that his model could account for.

In the light of these considerations consciousness as a later and optional stage refers to what the subject is conscious of as a perception of the stimulus. All else relating to the stimulus is recovered "indirectly," meaning simply that the subject is unaware of any relationship between these "indirectly" recovered contents to the previous conscious perception of the stimulus. Rather, the subject believes that these "indirectly" recovered contents are part of the dream, image, or association through which the recovery occurred.

The Impact of a Subliminal Stimulus as a Function of the Personal History and Unconscious Conflicts of the Subject

Perhaps the most decisive difference between Fisher's approach to subliminal perception and contemporary investigations by most psychologists is the important role assigned by Fisher to the personal history and unconscious conflicts of his subjects. For the experimental psychologist, the focus of investigation is a particular function (i.e., perception, memory) considered to work in the same way across individuals. Individual variability belongs to error. For Fisher, on the other hand, individual variability was at the heart of the investigation. Implicitly he took the position that a given function can best be understood in the full context of its interaction with other functions. Each of these approaches has its strengths and weaknesses. In fact, Fisher undertook both approaches. In part I are found studies based on essentially a case history method; in part II are found a series of purely experimental studies.

His theoretical model, however, was designed to be a comprehensive account of the main functional interactions between preconscious registration, dynamic unconscious influence, and indirect conscious retrieval. Almost by definition, dynamic unconscious influences have to be individualized; they cannot be convincingly studied generically. The challenge posed by Fisher's clinically rich early studies was to design a study in which dynamically individualized unconscious conflicts could be incorporated into a conventional experimental model involving sufficient numbers of subjects and suitable controls. This has been attempted with some success and owes its inspiration to Fisher's early studies (Shevrin, Bond et al., 1996)[2]. We have been able to demonstrate that brain responses show a different pattern depending on whether stimuli related to a particular person's unconscious conflict are presented subliminally or supraliminally; this difference in pattern does not appear for stimuli related to conscious symptom experience hypothesized to be caused by the unconscious conflict nor for totally unrelated control stimuli. Moreover, the differences in pattern can be explained as due to the operation of inhibitory or repressive processes. The inclusion of individualized unconscious conflict points the way to a variety of other variables that can be incorporated into subliminal investigations that do not pose the same practical difficulties as the assessment of unconscious conflict, but which highlight the role of individual differences. In several experiments we have introduced different instructions or strategies the subject is to follow in retrieving subliminal registrations, as well as to establish the subject's preferences for these different strategies. We have found that subliminal effects are a function of these preferences and strategies. Subjects who prefer a strategy encouraging them to relax and let a word come to mind show above chance effects, while perhaps more surprisingly, subjects who prefer a strategy encouraging them to base their guesses on exactly what they can see in the tachistoscope perform significantly below chance when asked to follow the more relaxed strategy. They not only cannot allow themselves to benefit from the relaxed strategy, but appear to inhibit correct responses. Moreover, this inhibition occurs entirely unconsciously and thus may provide an experimental model for intrapsychic defenses. This finding has been replicated six times in our laboratory (Snodgrass, Shevrin, and Kopka, 1993; Snodgrass and Shevrin, submitted) and twice elsewhere by Van Selst and

---

[2]It is of interest to note that George Klein, codirector at the time of the influential Research Center for Mental Health at New York University, in an unpublished discussion given in 1956 to The New York Psychoanalytic Society of Fisher's presentation of a version of one paper constituting chapter 1 recommended that in future studies stimuli should be tailored in advance to known and specified conflicts in order to determine more exactly the impact of the stimulus and the nature of its ultimate reemergence in altered states of consciousness. This unpublished discussion only came into the author's hands when he began to work on this monograph long after the investigation of unconscious conflict had been completed and a preliminary report published (Shevrin, Williams et al., 1992). In these and other ways George Klein demonstrated his foresight as well as insight.

Merikle (1993). Just as Fisher had anticipated (see chapter 6), these findings underscore the importance of individual differences in subliminal effects. In further support of Fisher's emphasis on individual differences, it is noteworthy that in a recent report of a blue ribbon panel of leading cognitive psychologists, the importance of individual differences was underscored and their absence identified as a significant limitation of much cognitive research (Brewer and Luce, 1998).

For many psychologists, unconscious processes are considered to be automatic in nature and involuntary (Shiffrin and Schneider, 1977); they behave like habitual actions. Intentional acts are solely conscious (Bargh, 1989).[3] There is no place in this conception for unconscious motivation and defense, or even for the simultaneous influence of conscious factors, such as strategies and preferences, on subliminal processes. If a subject's preference for a more relaxed strategy increases subliminal effects, it means that an apparently automatic unconscious process has been effected by consciousness and is thus not really automatic. Similarly, if an unconsciously operating defense can determine what is available consciously, as in the research cited previously (Snodgrass, Shevrin, and Kopka, 1993), then unconscious processes cannot be said to be automatic in the sense defined by Shiffrin and Schneider (1977). Again, it is important to note that not all psychologists subscribe to the automatic–controlled distinction. Allport (1989), after citing numerous studies failing to confirm the theory, offers an alternate model much closer to Fisher's ideas and in general to a psychoanalytic perspective in which motivational influence can be exercised unconsciously (see Shevrin, Bond et al. [1996, chapter 3] for an in-depth discussion of these issues).

THE RELATIONSHIP TO THE EXPERIMENTER PLAYS A SIGNIFICANT ROLE IN THE INFLUENCE OF A SUBLIMINAL STIMULUS

Fisher posed a question that has generally not been addressed in subliminal studies: Of all the stimuli, subliminal and supraliminal,

---

[3] It is a mark of the continued growth of the field as it appears to move more in the direction of psychoanalytic ideas, that Bargh has more recently changed his mind and

to which a subject has been exposed during the day, why should the experimenter's subliminal stimulus exercise such a predominant influence on the subject's images and dreams? Fisher's answer was to invoke the role of transference. To a psychoanalyst transference is ubiquitous. Fisher cited numerous examples of how his subjects incorporated some view of him into their reported dreams and images, as well as elements of the experimental room, and even stimuli glimpsed along the subject's route as he accompanied them to the laboratory. He cited instances in which subjects invested the experiment with voyeuristic significance, not too surprising in view of the very nature of the experiment. It should also be mentioned that most of Fisher's early subjects were patients at Mt. Sinai Hospital, New York, where he was an important figure as a physician on the staff. It was Fisher's hypothesis that these transferences served to set apart the subliminal stimulus from most of the other stimuli encountered elsewhere during the day.

Only in his early, more clinical studies would it be possible to identify these transferences; in his later, more experimental studies no reference is made to transferential phenomena and in this respect they are no different from countless other subliminal studies done since. Nevertheless, if Fisher is correct, transferences must be at work in these experiments as well, although they cannot be discerned. The role of transference in subliminal research remains to be more fully understood. In fact, the role of transferences in all experimental research remains essentially unchartered although there is convincing evidence that it is present. I have explored this whole issue elsewhere (Shevrin, in press).

THE NATURE OF A SUBLIMINAL EFFECT IS IN PART DETERMINED BY THE
RESPONSES USED TO DETECT IT

In psychological research, precision of measurement and tightness of control are most often bought at the expense of the full

---

has agreed on the basis of new evidence from his laboratory that motivation can in fact be unconscious (see Bargh and Ferguson, 2000), although he stops short of implicating unconscious conflict.

richness of the phenomenon under investigation. Yet it must also be noted that opting for the full richness of the phenomenon runs the risk of not being able to establish with convincing certainty any one aspect of the phenomenon. As noted above, in the evolution of his subliminal research, Fisher moved from quasi-clinical to fully experimental studies, but in neither of these types of studies did Fisher abandon the open-ended nature of the responses used to obtain subliminal recoveries. In most studies he followed Pötzl in asking subjects for dream reports the day following exposure to the subliminal stimulus. In others he initially adapted the Allers and Teler (Pötzl, Allers, and Teler, 1960) technique of asking for word associations to key stimulus-related words, and then asked for images that might have occurred during the word association task. He abandoned the combined word association and image technique, concluding that the stimulus-related word given to elicit the new word association and image could serve as a contaminating suggestion. He then simply asked subjects to close their eyes and describe and then draw the first image that came to mind. He discovered that images obtained within minutes of stimulus exposure could contain rich recoveries of the consciously unseen stimulus. As will be further elaborated with respect to the sixth proposition, this finding was of particular importance for Fisher.

There is a decided contrast between the open-ended responses used by Fisher and the highly structured, purely cognitive responses used in most cognitive subliminal experiments. In subliminal priming studies, for example, a word is rendered subliminal and its effect on a supraliminal word estimated by a reaction time. If the subliminal word is a close associate of the supraliminal word, or target, then the time taken to decide that it is a word (lexical decision task) will be shorter than if the target is unrelated. Much of interest can be learned with these cognitive approaches, not the least of which is to establish unambiguously the existence of a subliminal effect by way of an easily measured and reliable measure; but the psychological poverty of the response limits how much one can learn about the full range of unconscious processing going on subliminally. Moreover, the presence of a simpler and sparer subliminal effect in cognitive studies may not mean that no richer subliminal effects are present; rather that these responses cannot tap them. For example, Greenwald, Draine, and Abrams (1996) have argued that subliminal effects are over within 100 msec and leave no memory trace of themselves. They based these conclusions on a priming procedure employing neutral stimuli in which maximum subliminal effects were found when the response to the supraliminal stimulus occurred within 100 msec of the subliminal priming stimulus. But their results may be limited to their procedure. In Fisher's research as well as our own, subliminal effects have been found days afterwards, and certainly many seconds afterwards. In the Snodgrass, Shevrin, and Kopka (1993) research, the inhibition effects were found in the order of several seconds after stimulus exposure. In the Shevrin and Fisher study reported in chapter 7, subliminal effects were found hours later, and in a recently completed anesthesia study (Bunce et al., 2001) subliminal effects from stimuli presented during general anesthesia were detected a day later in keeping with the findings from the Pötzl procedure itself when subliminal influences were found in dreams reported a day later.

DREAM WORK AND FANTASY FORMATION INVOLVING SUBLIMINAL STIMULI OCCUR IMMEDIATELY AFTER SUBLIMINAL EXPOSURE

Perhaps Fisher's finest contribution to psychoanalytic theory is his proposed revision of the theory of dream formation. It is particularly notable because it is based on his empirical research, one of the few if not the only significant theoretical revision not derived entirely from clinical experience. Yet he makes out a convincing case, combining subliminal empirical findings and systematic theoretical analysis. The exegesis of these issues is mainly presented by Fisher in one paper, "Study of the Preliminary Stages of the Construction of Dreams" (chapter 3).

This revision has its starting point in his empirical findings. Fisher discovered that his subjects' images were in many respects as dreamlike in nature as their dreams. And yet these images were obtained only minutes after the exposure of the subliminal stimulus. These images appeared to contain evidence for the activation of powerful unconscious wishes and dreamlike primary process condensations. They appeared to be as capable as dreams in eliciting rich, personally meaningful memories and associations. The reader is referred to chapter 2, pp. 00 to 00, for an extended example. In that particular case, even the subject's initial impression of the subliminal stimulus already manifested the influence of unconscious forces. The stimulus was a colored photograph of two Siamese cats and a parakeet perched between them. Following the 1/100 sec exposure, the subject reported seeing two animals resembling dogs or pigs. However, when she attempted to draw the dogs or pigs, the animals turned out to look like peculiar combinations of mammal-like bodies and bird-like heads and tails. Although the subject was an artist, she complained that she had to draw the animals that way almost compulsively despite her intention to do otherwise. This condensation of mammal and bird was a harbinger of what would further develop in her images. In one image, she imagined a watchdog, but again when she attempted to draw the dog it turned out to look like a bird very much like the parakeet in the subliminal picture (see Figure 2.13, p. 114). She became increasingly frustrated by her inability to draw an animal that did not also look like a bird. When the picture was reexposed supraliminally she immediately saw the connection between the parakeet and her birdlike animals. But she also reported meaningful childhood associations to the parakeet in the picture involving a vicious watchdog and pigeons. Fisher summarizes what can be learned from this subject's productions: "The picture of the two cats and the parakeet reactivated deep-seated oral–sadistic material based on the idea that cats prey upon birds. There was a compulsive emergence, in spite of the subject's intentions, of an aggressively oral bird–mammal creature. There were many fusions and condensations of the cats with the bird, evidently related to unconscious conflicts having to do with eating and being eaten" (chapter 2, p. 117).

On the basis of such evidence, Fisher hypothesized that dream-like influences were already at work during the day. He reasoned that these images were sampling the current of preconscious registrations that provide the source for the day residues drawn upon by dreams. In addition to the "indifferent" perceptions cited by Freud, which were fleetingly in consciousness and could often be

remembered as such, Fisher argued that a multitude of preconscious registrations never in consciousness during the day provided the main source of day residues. These day residues had
already been influenced by unconscious wishes and revealed primary process transformations. They were, in a sense, ready-made
dream contents primed to be taken advantage of during the night
when another current of unconscious influence would play upon
them, and stitch them into the developing dream fabric. If this
view were correct, then Freud's "picket fence" model, in which
both a progressive and regressive movement of dream wishes were
posited, was no longer necessary (see chapter 3, p. 183, Figure
3.24) and was in fact unable to explain how day residues entered
the dream. This problem was created in Freud's model by the
assumption that during the night unconscious forces were barred
by censorship from gaining entry into the preconscious, having
then to surrender their progressive course toward consciousness
and turn back toward earlier memories and images. Once these
had been activated, the presumed intensity of their condensed
status could activate perceptual experience giving rise to the hallucinated character of dreams. But, Fisher argued, in this model
there appeared to be no way in which unconscious wishes could
make contact with the preconsciously registered day residues.
Fisher then substituted his own model (see chapter 3, Figure 3.26,
p. 187), which does accommodate the role of day residues as
already shaped by unconscious forces at the time of their initial
registration. Once this transfer has occurred, the already dreamlike day residues are withdrawn from any later progressive course
into daytime consciousness as a perception or memory of a perception and, instead, are available during the night for incorporation in dreams. But as Fisher's research has also shown, these
same preconsciously registered and unconsciously transformed
day residues can also be incorporated into daytime images.

Fisher's updating of Freud's model accords well with another
body of data responses to projective tests. For example, Rorschach
responses lend themselves to interpretation in terms of unconscious influences interacting with the subject's efforts to describe
what the blot looks like. In the case of Rorschach blot, it is its
ambiguity that parallels functionally the brevity of subliminal stiu-
mulation. If Fisher's model is correct, the Rorschach blot first

registers preconsciously where it is peculiarly prone to unconscious influences because of its structural ambiguity. Were the
blot well structured perceptually, given its supraliminal intensity,
it would quickly be delivered into consciousness largely unchanged. Similarly, Fisher's model may help us recast our understanding of the free association process. By assuming a prone
posture without any clear focus of attention, the stimuli that do
register are not as clearly articulated and bound to each other,
and are thus more subject to unconscious influences. Again, it is
important to emphasize that these stimuli all register initially at
a preconscious level. The dots on the ceiling or the sun shining
in the window noted in passing by the patient on the couch appear to more readily engage feelings and memories only tangen-
tially related to the actual conscious stimuli. Thus inattention
may serve the same purpose as stimulus ambiguity and stimulus
brevity. What they all assume is that the initial preconscious registrations will be more subject to the transfer of unconscious influences prior to their becoming conscious in one state or another.

THE PRINCIPLES OF MENTAL ORGANIZATION EFFECTING A SUBLIMINAL STIMULUS CAN BE QUALITATIVELY DIFFERENT FROM THOSE EFFECTING A SUPRALIMINAL STIMULUS

This proposition is already strongly implied by the previous
proposition dealing with the transfer of unconscious influences
to preconscious registrations. The various transformations of the
preconscious registrations described by Fisher are particularly
striking because they are all in a visual modality, and can thus be
seen and followed through a series of responses, including images
and dreams. Occasionally, Fisher cites a transformation that affects the meaning of a stimulus rather than its perceptual character, and this he will refer to as apperception rather than
perception. Fisher's reliance on drawings is particularly noteworthy, because drawings not only allow for convenient identification
of visual forms, but often what appears in the drawings cannot at
all be inferred from the verbal account of the image (viz., the

birdlike animals example above). In an interesting paper in this regard, Brakel has shown how drawings of dreams can be incorporated usefully in analytic practice, taking advantage of their richer incorporation of dream features (1993).

The question arises as to the mechanism by which these various fragmentations, rotations, and fusions of preconscious registrations takes place. Fisher suggested that these are already occurring preconsciously and are a function of the registration process rather than of any defensive distortion. His argument is that the unconscious influences play upon and use the already diffusely organized preconscious registrations. Pötzl advanced a similar idea when he argued that early stages of perception are inherently fragmentary and only a later "abstracting" process resulted in the unified perception of ordinary consciousness.

In the years since Fisher's work, much has been learned about the nature of visual perception based on animal research and human lesion studies. The results describe a visual system whose operation depends initially on feature detection processes spread over thirty or more individual subsystems giving rise to a veritable mosaic of individual parts that then have to be integrated. This parallel and distributed functioning of the visual system on a piecemeal basis raises the question as to how the individual fragments are "bound" together to form a unitary percept. Reiser, in his seminal book, *Memory in Mind and Brain* (1990), provides an eloquent account of this process in neuroanatomical terms:

> First, neural impulses are routed through multiple separate stations where different aspects of image characteristics (size, shape, texture, color) are separately analyzed. As visual information is sequentially processed, moving forward along the pathway, individual neurons have progressively wider "views." Individual neurons in the striate cortex [the visual sensory center in the occipital lobe], like individual cells in the retina, "see" only discrete features of objects and partial "views." By the time final stations of the inferior temporal lobe are reached, however, individual neurons "see" whole objects and scenes in which all the physical properties of objects (size, shape, color, and texture) that have

been separately processed along the way have now been assembled
and can be seen together [pp. 111–112].

This modern account, based on the most recent discoveries,
sounds in outline not too dissimilar from Pötzl's 1917 account
of a visual "abstracting" process serving to integrate the more
primitive levels of perception found in patients with brain lesions,
in the hallucinations of Korsakoff patients, and in the delayed
recovery in dreams of subliminal registrations. If one were to
articulate both Pötzl's and Fisher's formulations with the account
provided by Reiser, it would suggest that preconscious registrations are characterized by the "tiny discrete features" of objects
and their later unification. The "transformations" of preconscious registrations revealed in images and dreams are not subsequent to this process of "binding" into unitary objects, but are
prior to this unification; they are the product of the premature
arrival into consciousness of perceptual features. Unconscious influences are transferred onto these features before they are integrated into whole objects. From this vantage point, the primary
process, at least as present in the visual modality, is a function of
the perceptual process and not of defensive operations.

Although a case can be made for the perceptual basis of primary process visual transformations, it does not exclude the possibility that other types of primary process transformations can
affect the whole object itself and its meaning. Fisher cites a number of such examples. The subliminal verbal stimulus, star, can
result in images of meteors and comet tails, suggesting that the
meaning of the word has been activated as well as its associates.
In experiments using a rebus stimulus, a picture of a pen pointed
at a knee forming the word *penny,* Shevrin has shown that primary
process transformations of the words *pen* and *knee* can result in
subliminal effects in the form of clang associations and associations to the rebus condensation itself (Shevrin, 1973; see also
chapter 7). The conclusion one must reach is that preconscious
processes can be fluid and fragmentary at different levels of organization, from the concrete perceptual to the abstract conceptual.
Perhaps this is the hallmark of preconscious processes and constitutes their unique role in mental life, a role that Fisher's contributions have helped to bring to the fore.

SUBLIMINAL FINDINGS FIT WITH PSYCHOANALYTIC STRUCTURAL
THEORY AND MAKE POSSIBLE A BETTER INCORPORATION OF THE
TOPOGRAPHIC MODEL IN STRUCTURAL THEORY

Freud developed three different models over the years in his efforts to account for his clinical findings: the early topographic
model, the successor systems model, and the final structural
model. Each was introduced in order to deal with a particular
conceptual problem. The early topographic model was in some
ways the simplest; it described the status of a mental content solely
in terms of its relationship to consciousness. Thus an idea could
be in consciousness, or it could be preconscious and readily enter
consciousness, or it could be unconscious and be kept from entering either the preconscious or consciousness by some defense
mechanism. This model left out a good deal; in particular it left
out of consideration the nature of the mental processes characterizing the conscious, preconscious, and unconscious status of an
idea. In order to accommodate these considerations, Freud
shifted to a systems model in which the purely adjectival, lower
case use of the terms *conscious, preconscious,* and *unconscious* simply intended to modify the status of an idea, was replaced with
the upper case nouns, *Conscious, Preconscious,* and *Unconscious,*
in order to denote that now more than the status of an idea with
respect to consciousness was involved. In addition, each system
was characterized by different functions and mental processes.
For example, the secondary process held sway in Consciousness,
and the primary process in the Unconscious. But in time it became apparent that this systems model was not on all fours. For
example, defenses that had been assigned to the system Consciousness were in fact in the adjectival sense unconscious in their
operation. It was to deal with this kind of problem that Freud
introduced the structural model of id, ego, and superego. The
ego was defined to possess certain unique functions such as reality
testing, but could also possess unconscious functions such as defenses. But where and in what systematic way could the earlier
topographic model find a place? Some decided that it really no
longer had a place (Arlow and Brenner, 1964) and had been
superseded by the structural model. If this were indeed the case,

how could subliminal findings be incorporated with the renewed importance they give to preconscious processes? Interestingly, in only a few places in his writings on subliminal perception, does Fisher use the terms *ego*, *id*, and *superego;* instead he talks about *preconscious registration, unconscious wishes and memories, delayed delivery into consciousness,* and so on. Are the two models incompatible, or is Fisher describing phenomena at some lower level of abstraction than is applicable to functions at the level of id, ego, or superego? Or do subliminal findings offer an opportunity to reconsider our conception of the structural model and to bring it more into line with how the mind operates at its actual working level? Now that we know more about how perception works and how supraliminal and subliminal stimuli register, how can these operations be incorporated into the structural model? Certainly they are not solely ego functions or id operations. Fisher's subliminal findings strongly suggest that the mind is organized in interacting, dynamic cells in which id, ego, and superego functions are intimately entwined forming compromise formations to which ongoing conscious, preconscious, and unconscious processes contribute. Each image obtained in one of Fisher's subliminal experiments is derived from the operation of these interacting dynamic cells. It would be quite misleading and incomplete to refer to such an image solely as an ego function. Rather, it is the product of a complex interaction of many functions including those of the id and superego. Nor is it sufficient to refer to the image simply as a compromise formation because that does not inform us of the process by which it was created. When we undertake to describe that process we must then invoke the role, not only of conscious and unconscious processes, but in particular of preconscious processes about which Fisher has done so much to advance our understanding.[4]

In sum, when we consider the full import of these eight propositions we are left with the strong impression that Fisher's contributions reach out in a number of directions: toward contemporary psychology, sensory neurophysiology, and psychoanalysis. The

---

[4]For a more extended consideration of the way in which the topographic model can be incorporated into the structural model based on recent subliminal experimental findings, the reader is referred to chapter 12 of *Conscious and Unconscious Processes: Psychodynamic, Cognitive, and Neurophysiological Convergences* (Shevrin, Bond et al., 1996).

neurophysiologist he started out to be finds a noteworthy place in the psychoanalyst and experimental psychologist he became.

ORGANIZATION OF THE MONOGRAPH

The monograph is divided into two groups of papers covering a period from 1957 to 1968. The four papers in part I are empirical and clinical in nature in contradistinction to the four papers in part II that are reports of formal experiments. These latter papers constitute the culmination of Fisher's subliminal research insofar as they benefit from many of the insights gained in the empirical studies, which are now put to more rigorous experimental test.

Part I is devoted to four pioneering studies, three of which were published in the *Journal of the American Psychoanalytic Association*, and the fourth in a psychoanalytic journal devoted to theory and interdisciplinary studies, *Psychoanalysis and Contemporary Thought*. This last paper has the further distinction of having originally been published some 25 years before, in 1963, in the French journal *L'Evolution Psychiatrique* and was now published in English for the first time as a tribute to Fisher. Leo Goldberger, the editor of the journal, stated in his introduction to the paper, "We not only wish to honor our distinguished colleague, but also to affirm the contemporary relevance of his seminal contributions to the subliminal field of research" (p. 3). In the years since that statement was made, the relevance of Charles Fisher's work in view of the mounting importance of subliminal perception research in psychology and neuroscience has if anything increased.

Part II is devoted to four carefully designed experimental studies undertaken in collaboration with several different psychologists who had become interested in Fisher's research, marking the beginning of his growing influence beyond psychoanalysis. In the two studies with Irving Paul (chapters 5 and 6), psychologists at the New York University Research Center for Mental Health were recruited as independent judges and contributed substantially to the positive outcome of the research. With the exception of the first experiment with Paul (chapter 5), which appeared in the same journal as Fisher's previous reports, the *Journal of the American Psychoanalytic Association*, the three other experiments appeared in nonpsychoanalytic journals, attesting to the spreading interest among nonanalytic researchers in Fisher's work. The second study with Paul appeared in the *Journal of Nervous and Mental Disease*, whose readership reaches across a broad spectrum of psychiatrists, clinical psychologists, and social workers; the third study (chapter 7), a collaboration with Howard Shevrin, appeared in the *Journal of Abnormal Psychology*, and the fourth study (chapter 8), done in collaboration with Lester Luborsky, Richard Rice, and Donald Phoenix, appeared in the *Journal of Personality*. These latter two journals are still leading periodicals in their respective fields in psychology.

REFERENCES

Allport, A. (1989), Visual attention. In: *Foundations of Cognitive Science*, ed. M. I. Posner. Cambridge, MA: MIT Press, pp. 631–638.

Arlow, J. A., & Brenner, C. (1964), *Psychoanalytic Concepts and the Structural Theory*. New York: International Universities Press.

Bargh, J. A. (1989), Conditional automaticity: Varieties of autonomic influence on social perception and cognition. In: *Unintended Thought*, ed. J. S. Uleman & J. A. Bargh. New York: Guilford Press, pp. 3–51.

———— Ferguson, M. J. (2000), Beyond behaviorism: On the automaticity of higher mental processes. *Psychol. Bull.*, 126(6):925–945.

Brakel, L. (1989a), Understanding negative hallucination: Toward a developmental classification of disturbances in reality awareness. *J. Amer. Psychoanal. Assn.*, 37(2):437–463.

———— (1989b), Negative hallucinations, other irretrievable experiences and two functions of consciousness. *Internat. J. PsychoAnal.*, 70:461–479.

———— (1993), Shall drawing become part of free association: Proposal for a modification in psychoanalytic technique. *J. Amer. Psychoanal. Assn.*, 41(2):359–394.

Brewer, M. B., & Luce, R. D. (1998), Basic research in psychological science. *Amer. Psycholog. Soc. Observer*, Report 6:3–39.

Bunce, S. C., Kleinsorge, S., Villa, K., Kishwaha, R., Szocik, J., Brakel, L. A. S., & Shevrin, H. (2001), Neurophysiological evidence for implicit memory formation under general anesthesia. Paper presented at the 5th International Conference on Memory, Awareness, and Consciousness, June 1–3, New York City.

Dixon, N. F. (1971), *Subliminal Perception: The Nature of a Controversy*. London: McGraw-Hill.

———— (1981), *Preconscious Processing*. London: John Wiley.

Fisher, C., Ingram, H., & Ransom, J. (1938), *Diabetes Insipidus and the Neurohormonal Control of Water Balance*. Ann Arbor, MI: Edwards.

Freud, S. (1900), The Interpretation of Dreams. *Standard Edition*, 4&5. London: Hogarth Press, 1953.

———— (1915), The unconscious. *Standard Edition*, 14:159–204. London: Hogarth Press, 1957.

Greenwald, S. G., Draine, S. C., & Abrams, R. L. (1996), Three cognitive markers of unconscious semantic activation. *Science*, 273:1699–1702.

Holender, D. (1986), Semantic activation without conscious identification in dichotic listening, parafoveal vision, and visual masking: A survey and appraisal. *Behav. & Brain Sci.*, 9(1):1–66.

Khilstrom, J. F. (1996), Perception without awareness of what is perceived, learning without awareness of what is learned. In: *The Science of Consciousness: Psychological, Neuropsychological and Clinical Reviews*, ed. M. Velmans. London: Routledge, pp. 23–46.

Murphy, S. T., & Zajonc, R. B. (1993), Affect, cognition, and awareness. Affective priming with optimal and suboptimal stimulus exposure. *J. Personal. & Soc. Psychol.*, 64:723–739.

Panel (1995), Unconscious perception at the objective threshold. Participants: A. Greenwald, E., Reingold, & M. Snodgrass; chair and discussant, H. Shevrin. American Psychological Society Meeting, July 1, New York City.

Pierce, C. S., & Jastrow, J. (1884), On small differences in sensation. *Mem. Nat. Acad. Sciences*, 3:73–83.

Pötzl, O., Allers, R., & Teler, J. (1960), On the utilization of unnoticed impressions in association. In: Preconscious Stimulation in Dreams, Associations and Images: Classical Studies. *Psychological Issues*, Monogr. 7, Vol. 2. New York: International Universities Press.

Reiser, M. (1990), *Memory in Mind and Brain*. New York: Basic Books.

Shevrin, H. (1973), Brain wave correlates of subliminal stimulation, unconscious attention, primary- and secondary-process thinking and repressiveness. In: Psychoanalytic Research: Three Approaches to the Study of Subliminal Processes, ed. M. Mayman. *Psychological Issues*, Monogr. 30. New York: International Universities Press, pp. 56–87.

———— (in press), Commentary on experimental psychology and psychoanalysis: What we can learn from a century of misunderstanding. *Neuro-Psychoanal.*, 2(2):255–264.

———— Bond, J. A., Brakel, L. A. W., Hertel, R. K., & Williams, W. J. (1996), *Conscious and Unconscious Processes: Psychodynamic, Cognitive and Neurophysiological Convergences*. New York: Guilford Press.

———— Dickman, S. (1980), The psychological unconscious: A necessary assumption for all psychological theory? *Amer. Psychologist*, 35:421–434.

———— Luborsky, L. (1958), The measurement of preconscious perception in dreams and images: An investigation of the Portal phenomena. *J. Abnorm. & Soc. Psychol.*, 56:285–294.

———— Williams, W. J., Marshall, R. E., Hertel, R. K., Bond, J. A., & Brakel, L. A. W. (1992), Event-related potential indicators of the dynamic unconscious. *Consciousness & Cognit.*, 1:340–366.

Shiffrin, R. M., & Schneider, W. (1977), Controlled and automatic information processing. II Perceptual learning, automatic attending, a general theory. *Psychol. Rev.*, 84:127–190.

Sidis, B. (1898), *The Psychology of Suggestion.* New York: Appleton.

Snodgrass, M., & Shevrin, H. (submitted), Reliable unconscious inhibition.

—————— —————— Kopka, M. (1993), The mediation of intentional judgments by unconscious perceptions: The influences of task strategy, task preference, word meaning, and motivation. *Consciousness & Cognit.,* 2:169–193.

Van Selst, M., & Merikle, P. (1993), Perception below the objective threshold? *Consciousness & Cognit.,* 2:194–203.

Wong, P. S., Shevrin, H., & Williams, W. (1994), Conscious and nonconscious processes: An ERP index of an anticipatory response in a conditioning paradigm using visually masked stimuli. *Psychophysiology,* 1:87–101.

PART I

EMPIRICAL–CLINICAL STUDIES

Considering the value and importance of these groundbreaking explorations to the development of the field of subliminal research, as well as to psychoanalytic theory, it is unfortunate that the conception of science to which most psychologists subscribe is still so closely tied to formal experimentation and a largely outmoded philosophy of science based on a strict operationalism, a view that disparages the commonsense observation, speculation, and imagination so important in the early hypothesis-generating phase of scientific exploration of any new phenomenon. It is well known that initially scientific hypotheses, in a new field in particular, arise from ordinary experience and informal observation. The scientist open to this phase develops the "prepared mind" spoken of by Pasteur as the precursor of discoveries and their ultimate demonstration. If in addition, we keep in mind that as an experienced psychoanalyst, Fisher was immersed daily in the intimate, inner workings of his patients' life experiences, then it should not come as any surprise that he was able to be sensitive to so much in his research subjects' dreams and images.

As noted in the Introduction, Fisher came to psychoanalysis and to his psychoanalytic investigations following a productive career in a highly respected physiological laboratory during which he collaborated with some of the brightest lights in physiology of the time, scientists who had made pioneering contributions that still remain landmarks to this day. I stress this fact in order to underscore that Fisher was no scientific neophyte when

he began his subliminal investigations. We must suppose he delib-
erately chose an empirical approach, closer in spirit to his earlier
physiological investigations, in which innovative variations in procedure, careful observation of individual cases, clinical sensitivity
to transference, and a profound knowledge of psychoanalytic theory were allowed full play. By opening himself up to the entire
range of phenomena that his procedures were capable of evoking,
he developed an intimate knowledge of these phenomena which
paid off in his later more formal experimental studies. A good
illustration of this is provided by the interesting finding, reported
in chapter 6, that of all the judges, it was Fisher who was consistently superior in identifying subliminal influences in images and
dreams. The stimuli used in the experimental studies were win-
nowed and refined from experience with a range of stimuli in
these early empirical–clinical studies in which Fisher had immersed himself. One can cite another example of how these earlier empirical–clinical studies gave rise to hypotheses tested in the
later experimental studies. It was the hypothesis that the figure–ground organization of perception did not apply to subliminal registrations, a hypothesis tested in the two experiments done
in collaboration with Paul (chapters 5 and 6) by using the Rubens
Double Profile stimulus.

In almost all of Fisher's subliminal studies stimuli were exposed
for 1/100 sec and delivered by a slide projector with a mechanical
shutter affixed to it. The stimulus was projected on a screen some
dozen feet from the subjects and covered an area of approximately 2 by 2 ft. Luminance (the light reflected from the stimulus
to the subject's eyes) is rarely mentioned so we do not know
how bright the stimulus was, an important factor in determining
subliminality. But Fisher relied on a fairly good criterion for establishing subliminality—the psychophysical method of ascending
limits. At the end of each procedure he started by exposing the
stimulus at 1/100 sec, asked what the subject saw, almost always
the report was of a flash of light, then he increased the time by
increments until the subject first reported seeing something—the
detection threshold—and then he further increased the time until the subject could clearly identify the stimulus—the identification threshold. Generally, identification would occur at about a

second and Fisher would infer that the stimulus had been presented approximately 100 times below the subject's identification threshold.

By contemporary methodological standards Fisher's stimuli
were very likely at the subjective threshold as distinguished from
the objective threshold. The subjective threshold is defined as
the exposure time at which the subject decides that nothing was
seen while very likely something was in consciousness, but failed
to meet the subject's own criterion for something being conscious. Subjects vary considerably in their personal criterion for
accepting something as conscious. In a personal communication,
George Klein once told the writer of a subject to whom he was
exposing a triangle using the method of ascending limits. The
subject was reporting seeing nothing even though the exposure
time had exceeded one second. Finally Klein in exasperation
asked the subject if he was seeing a triangle, to which the subject
replied, "Yes, but that's nothing.

Because classical psychophysical methods, such as the method
of ascending limits, confound the subjective criterion for consciousness of a stimulus with true sensitivity, or actual awareness
of a stimulus, a new method has been devised based on signal
detection theory (SDT). The basic procedure calls for a stimulus
to be compared with a no-stimulus condition. The subject is asked
after each exposure to say whether he or she detected something
or not. Stimulus and no-stimulus conditions are interspersed randomly but in equal numbers. A measure of sensitivity is devised
by comparing the number of hits (correct guesses) with the number of false alarms (incorrect guesses). If the measure of sensitivity does not depart significantly from zero then the stimuli are
being exposed at the objective threshold, meaning that the subject could not detect the difference between a stimulus and a no-
stimulus condition. There is considerable controversy in the field
as to whether subliminal effects can be obtained at the objective
threshold. Most contemporary subliminal studies still rely on the
subjective threshold so that Fisher is not out of step in this regard.
Nevertheless, Snodgrass (in press) has concluded following a
careful evaluation of the literature that objective threshold findings exist (see Snodgrass, Shevrin, and Kopka [1993] for one such
study and its replication by Van Selst and Merikle [1993]), and

that the effects at the objective threshold may be different from those obtained at the subjective threshold. Specifically, that inhibitory processes can be demonstrated at the objective threshold that are absent at the subjective threshold, suggesting that subliminal effects at the objective threshold may be occurring at a deeper unconscious level. This supposition is further supported by findings on the subliminal activation of unconscious conflict at the objective threshold reported by Shevrin, Bond et al. (1996).

Yet Fisher obtained evidence for similar activations of unconscious conflicts with stimuli that were at the subjective threshold. This apparent inconsistency can be resolved if it is borne in mind that Fisher obtained his results from dream reports and descriptions of spontaneous visual imagery, whereas most contemporary experiments at the subjective threshold rely on such psychologically "empty" responses as reaction times, word-stem completions, and deciding if a word or a nonword had been presented. These responses are part of a standard priming procedure in which the subliminal stimulus is presented and is quickly followed by a supraliminal stimulus either bearing some relationship to the subliminal stimulus, or none at all. As contrasted with Fisher, no rich account of an image or dream is ever obtained. It is thus likely that the more deeply unconscious effects emerge because of the nature of the response, even though the stimulus has been delivered at the subjective threshold. It further suggests that the initial depth of stimulus registration can be compensated for by the extent to which the response obtained samples the full richness of interaction between preconscious registration and dynamic unconscious influences. It should be remembered that even at the subjective threshold the stimulus still registers preconsciously. This supposition is lent some considerable support from an experiment described in chapter 7 in which the effects of a subliminal stimulus presented at the subjective threshold is tracked following REM sleep awakenings and stage 2 N-REM awakenings. The results demonstrated that the same subliminal stimulus exercised strikingly different influences depending on the sleep rate. More primitive primary process transformations emerged after REM dream awakenings, and more rational secondary process transformations emerged after N-REM awakenings.

One other significant difference between Fisher's subliminal method and most contemporary experiments needs to be noted. In most contemporary experiments, the subliminal stimulus is exposed on a computer screen and is quickly "masked" by a stimulus usually containing randomly dispersed letters. This "masking stimulus" is then followed by a target stimulus that the subliminal stimulus may or may not influence in some hypothesized manner. This method is referred to as *backward masking*. The method is based on the observation that if a stimulus, ordinarily seen if presented alone, is followed quickly enough by another stimulus exposed for a longer time, that subjects will report no awareness of the "masked" stimulus. This method has the advantage of convenience insofar as computers can be programmed to present stimuli automatically. The main disadvantage of the method is that, because of constraints imposed by the mechanics of the computer screen, the stimulus cannot be exposed for less than 17 msec. The result is that all backward masking experiments are at the subjective threshold. In our own work we use a Dodge-type tachistoscope that makes it possible to expose a stimulus reliably at 1 msec, thus readily achieving below objective threshold exposures without backward masking being necessary.

The succession of chapters in part I follows not only a chronological progression but also documents the evolution of Fisher's thinking about the complex processes involved in subliminal perception. Chapter 1 is a replication of the original Pötzl method, tracking the effects of a complex picture on subsequently reported dreams. Chapter 2 is a replication of the Allers and Teler method of tracking subliminal effects in images obtained in response to word associations related to the unseen parts of the picture. Chapter 3 abandons the word association part of the Allers and Teler procedure and simply relies on freely evoked images following the stimulus presentation. He also begins to explore the methodological advantages of employing simple stimuli such as numbers and geometrical figures in place of the complex visual scenes previously used. It is in this chapter that Fisher presents his modification of Freud's "picket fence" model of dreaming, described briefly in the Introduction. In all three chapters he emphasizes the importance of obtaining drawings as well as descriptions of images and dreams, demonstrating how many of the most striking recoveries were revealed in the drawings only (see Brakel [1993] for a defense of the clinical use of dream drawings). Chapter 4 is something of a summing up of these early studies as well as a report of several new efforts. In this chapter Fisher reports on the influence of LSD on subliminal effects in an effort to replicate the Pötzl findings that subliminal effects are found in hallucinations. He also conducted an experiment with a woman suffering from almost total organic blindness that might be considered the first report of the blindsight phenomenon (Weiskrantz, 1995). This subject also suffered from hallucinations. The effects of the Rubens Double Profile stimulus could be detected in her hallucinations in which she reported seeing a Janus-faced soldier. Chapter 4 is also notable for the first effort to follow the effects of the same stimuli presented both subliminally and supraliminally. Finally, in a characteristic burst of theoretical creativity, Fisher identifies how modern artists such as Picasso had intuitive access to the early stages of perceptual processing only revealed through subliminal registrations.

After reading the four studies comprising part I, the reader will be better prepared to appreciate how the experimental studies in part II built on and extended the discoveries described in part I, and in this manner the reader will have traversed the same path followed by Fisher himself.

REFERENCES

Brakel, L. (1993), Shall drawing become part of free association: Proposal for a modification in psychoanalytic technique. *J. Amer. Psychoanal. Assn.*, 41(2):359–394.

Shevrin, H., Bond, J. A., Brakel, L. A. W., Hertel, R. K., & Williams, W. J. (1996), *Conscious and Unconscious Processes: Psychodynamic, Cognitive, and Neurophysiological Convergences.* New York: Guilford Press.

Snodgrass, M. (in press), *Unconscious Perception: Theory, Method, Evidence.* Amsterdam: John Benjamins.

———— Shevrin, H., & Kopka, M. (1993), The mediation of intentional judgments by unconscious perceptions: The influences of task strategy, task preference, word meaning, and motivation. *Consciousness & Cognit.*, 2:169–193.

Van Selst, M., & Merikle, P. (1993), Perception below the objective threshold? *Consciousness & Cognit.*, 2:194–203.

Weiskranz, L. (1995), Blindsight: Conscious vs. unconscious aspects. In: *Scale in Conscious Experience: Is the Brain Too Important to be Left to Specialists to Study*, ed. J. King. Hillsdale, NJ: Lawrence Erlbaum.

1

DREAMS AND PERCEPTION: THE ROLE OF PRECONSCIOUS AND PRIMARY MODES OF PERCEPTION IN DREAM FORMATION (1954)

CHARLES FISHER

In 1919 Freud added the following footnote to the section on day residues in *The Interpretation of Dreams* (1900):

> An important contribution to the part played by recent material in the construction of dreams has been made by Pötzl (1917) in a paper which carries a wealth of implications. In a series of experiments Pötzl required the subjects to make a drawing of what they had consciously noted of a picture exposed to their view in a tachistoscope (an instrument for exposing an object to view for an extremely short time). He then turned his attention to the dreams dreamt by the subjects during the following night and required them once more to make drawings of appropriate portions of these dreams. It was shown unmistakably that those details of the exposed picture which had not been noted by the subject provided material for the construction of the dream, whereas those details which had been consciously perceived and recorded in the drawing made after the exposure did not recur in the manifest content of the dream. The material that was taken over by the dream-work was modified by it for the purposes of dream

construction in its familiar "arbitrary" (or, more properly, "auto-cratic") manner. The questions raised by Pötzl's experiment go far beyond the sphere of dream-interpretation as dealt with in the present volume. In passing, it is worth remarking on the contrast between this new method of studying the formation of dreams experimentally and the earlier, crude technique for introducing into the dream stimuli which interrupted the subject's sleep [note 2, pp. 180–181].

I have not been able to find any further reference by Freud to Pötzl's work. It would be most interesting to know what Freud considered the "wealth of implications" of this investigation to be, and why he thought the questions raised by it went far beyond the sphere of dream interpretation as dealt with in *The Interpretation of Dreams*. The only attempt at repetition of the work was made by Malamud (1934) and Malamud and Linder (1931), who employed a modified technique without using the tachistoscope. They confirmed some of Pötzl's more important findings, but failed to see the broader implications of the results.

I am presenting some of his findings and preliminary results of my repetition of his work for the following reasons:

1. Although Pötzl's work has been recognized as a study of repression in apperception (Rapaport, 1951) and as throwing light on the relationship between dream images and visual distortions in various pathological states, it has never been integrated into psychoanalytic theory or brought into relation with Freud's psychology of the dream process.
2. Pötzl's findings would appear to necessitate a very great expansion of the role of day residues in the process of dream formation, more especially of the visual percepts associated with day residue experiences.
3. These findings indicate that a form of preconscious visual perception plays a significant role in dream formation. This form of perception, appearing in normal individuals, seems to be identical with a primitive perceptual process found in certain abnormal states, such as visual agnosias and hallucinations. It also appears to be closely related to the type of perception found in eidetic imagery.

4. Pötzl's findings suggest the need for an amplification of certain parts of Freud's psychology of the dream process, as set forth in chapter 7 of *The Interpretation of Dreams*, especially the processes going on in that part of Freud's hypothetical psychic apparatus which he called the P (perception) system.

I became interested in Pötzl's work during the course of an investigation on the nature of suggestion (Fisher, 1953a,b). In this investigation an attempt was made to influence dream production by direct suggestion in various therapeutic and nontherapeutic relationships, Pötzl was not an analyst and, working in 1917, did not have a sufficient appreciation of transference or the influence of suggestion. He did not attempt to answer the question why his subjects dreamed about the tachistoscopically exposed picture, which represented a day residue lasting 1/100 sec, in preference to countless other visual experiences occurring on the same day. It occurred to me that Pötzl's instruction to his subjects to record any dreams that occurred the night following the experiment may have been interpreted as a command to dream about the picture. My own investigation has proven this to be the case. However, the present paper will not be concerned primarily with the problem of suggestion but with the implications of Pötzl's work for the psychology of the dream process and the theory of perception.

METHOD

This investigation was carried out in the Department of Psychiatry at Mount Sinai Hospital. Eighteen patients on the psychosomatic ward were used as subjects. Most of these were used in only one experiment; in a few instances in two experiments. In addition, six staff physicians volunteered to act as subjects. For the most part the patients on the psychosomatic ward suffer from serious ailments, such as ulcerative colitis, asthma, anorexia nervosa, etc. Before commencing an experiment, I had a brief interview with each patient for the purpose of establishing rapport. I then solicited their voluntary cooperation, noting that the experiments were not intended to have any therapeutic effect and were being carried out solely in the interests of my work. With regard to the nature of the experiments, I told them simply that I was going to expose a picture on a screen and ask them to describe and make a drawing of what they had seen, and stated that when the experiments were completed I would explain them in greater detail.

In some of the early experiments the experimental room was located some distance from the ward in another building; it was reached by a walk which took several minutes through a series of corridors. On the day of the experiment I accompanied the subject from the ward to the experimental room. When we arrived, the subject was requested to fix his eyes on a screen and told that at the count of three a picture would be flashed on it. The tachistoscope consisted of an ordinary SVE projector with a Rafex camera shutter attachment which permitted exposures as brief as 1/200 sec. In later experiments the experimental room was located on the ward.

After tachistoscopic exposure, the subject was asked to describe verbally and then to make a drawing of what he had seen. He was then instructed to remember and to write down the next morning any dreams he had that night. It will be noted that at no time was the subject specifically commanded to dream. If the next morning the subject brought a dream, an attempt was made to obtain spontaneous free associations, followed by a request for associations to as many specific elements in the dream as possible. The subject was then asked to make drawings of specific visual scenes from his dream.

This procedure duplicates exactly that followed by Pötzl. Several additions were made to this technique. In the early experiments the subject was taken on a walk from the ward to the experimental room, using the same route as the day before, and was instructed to tell me of anything he saw on the way or in the experimental room that reminded him of his dream. In the later experiments the subject was asked if anything in the experimental room reminded him of his dream. On arrival in the experimental room, the picture that had been tachistoscopically exposed was projected on the screen so that it could be examined at length, and the subject was instructed to report anything in the picture that reminded him of his dream. In a number of control experiments a picture other than the one that had been tachistoscopically exposed was put on the screen and the subject was asked if anything in it reminded him of his dream.

In these experiments four colored pictures of landscapes or street scenes were used for tachistoscopic exposure. In five experiments, instead of exposing a picture, four words were printed on a slide and exposed tachistoscopically for 1/200 sec. Pötzl exposed the pictures in his experiments for 1/100 sec. This exposure period was used in most of the experiments, but in some instances 1/200 sec was used. In several experiments the exposure period was increased to 30 sec, in repetition of the method used by Malamud (1934).

RESULTS

I will present the results of 6 experiments out of a total of more than 30. The results were quite uniform, and these 6 experiments are representative. In the first 2 experiments it will be shown that extensive visual elements of the tachistoscopically exposed pictures appeared in the manifest content of the subsequent dreams and these elements did not show much distortion. In the second 2 experiments a similar result was obtained, but the visual elements taken from the pictures underwent rather extensive distortion. In all instances the visual elements of the pictures which appeared in the manifest content of the dreams were not consciously seen during tachistoscopic exposure. In the fifth experiment I will report the results of an experiment involving the tachistoscopic exposure of words rather than pictures, and in the sixth the results following the exposure of a picture for 30 sec.

EXPERIMENT I

The subject, J, used in this experiment, was a 28-year-old college graduate, a social worker, who was on the psychosomatic ward because of a severe ileitis which she had developed 3 years prior

Legend to Figure 1.1

Figure 1.1: *The Three Kings.* This is a black-and-white drawing of the original colored picture. In the original the sky is blue, the sandstone figures are clay colored, and the two men in the foreground are wearing dark blue shirts and trousers. The man on the left is wearing a white hat. The shrubs in the foreground are a light greenish yellow.

This picture was used for tachistoscopic exposure in experiments I, II, and III. In experiment I the "king" on the right became Ruth M, the other two kings were incorporated into the dream images of the two men on the pile. The small knob on the head of the middle king was condensed with the painter's cap, and the surgical cap. The linear structure on the head of the king on the right probably formed the bangs of Ruth M. The colored pile of coal is represented by the mound on which the two torsos of the kings on the left rest.

In experiment II the two men dressed in blue shorts and shirts in the dream represent a condensation of the two men in the picture with a vague outline on the mound between them. The vague outline shown in the drawing in a much clearer manner than it appears in the original colored picture consists of an upraised right arm, to the right of which a head can be made out. The subject stated that there were two men, one on either side of the burst of dirt. Actually the outline of a single figure with an upraised arm can be more easily made out, the area of the burst of dirt representing the head. It may be that the subject was reluctant to see this, since it would mean that he was shot in the head. The blue shirt and shorts were displaced from the men in the picture to the figure or figures contained in the vague outline.

In experiment III the "blue jacket" which the subject wore in the dream is taken from the man on the left; the subject became identified with this man. The man on the right represents the man in the red convertible. The two men are displaced upward in the dream, the one on the left to a position between the two cars, the one on the right into the red convertible (see Figures 1.9, 1.11). The middle figure is represented by the blonde in the dream.

Figure 1.1. (For legend to Figure 1.1, see page 42.)

to admission. She was a tense, anxious subject, very cooperative and eager to please. She had serious emotional problems.

Response to Tachistoscopic Exposure

A picture which I shall call the "Three Kings," was tachistoscopically exposed for 1/100 sec (Figure 1.1). This picture shows three large humanlike figures carved out of sandstone by natural erosion in the desert of Utah. A fourth moundlike structure is seen to the left, and in the foreground two men in blue shirts are looking at the kings.

The subject manifested a great deal of anxiety about "looking," complained of her vision, of blinking, and expressed the fear that the picture might "shock" her. After exposure she stated, "That's Moslem, Indian. All I saw was the top half. I saw a gold color like I used in painting recently. The sky was very blue, not *shocking* blue. The top of the dome had a sharp spire. It's not logical to assume there were windows in it, but I get dark, vertical lines. There was nothing on the dome, but there were vertical lines on the bottom. I didn't see the *bottom,* but I caught the lines and projected them onto the dome."

The subject drew what she had seen as shown in Figure 1:2. The spired dome and the lines at the bottom which represent the windows are indicated. In the light of subsequent events, it will be noted that the subject was clearly frightened about looking at something shocking. She made a distinction between the "top" and the "bottom"; evidently there was something about the "bottom" that she avoided.

Dreams of the Night Following Tachistoscopic Exposure

The subject described and drew her dream as though it were a picture, the events in the dream having a temporal and spatial distribution. The action started in the lower right corner of the picture and proceeded to the upper left corner.

> Something went on here [pointing to the lower right corner], but off the picture, something about swimming. I had committed *a crime in the water.* I was given a ticket by a policeman. Then I was walking along a path in the country. I saw a girl in pajamas standing on top of a pile. Her hair was long and disarranged and she

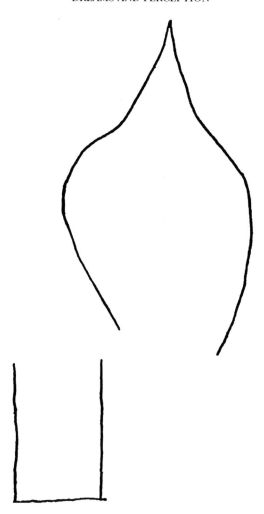

Figure 1.2. *Experiment I.* Subject J's drawing of what she saw after tachistoscopic exposure of Figure 1.1. It shows a dome with a spire. The open rectangle below represents the window which the subject experienced as if it were in the dome, although she saw it below.

wore no makeup. I said to myself, "Is that Ruth M?" I had her confused with Milly [another patient on the ward], although I knew it was Ruth M. I was looking for someone. Then I came to the place I was looking for. It was a pile of coal, blending beautiful colors, red, purple, and blue. There were two men on top of the pile. I could see them from their torsos up. One's face was well defined, the other not. The first was E's husband [another patient on the ward]. He was wearing a white shirt and had a ruddy, sunburned complexion, a red nose, and wore a housepainter's cap. I told him about my problem in the water. I felt an injustice had been done to me. He sympathized and said, "I'd get a lawyer. They do that too much around here," meaning giving tickets. I asked him if he could get me one. I began to climb up the pile. It was precipitous. I was surprised I didn't slip. My body was flattened against the pile. I didn't get to the top. I awoke nauseous, loggy, and sick and asked the nurse to call the doctor.

Associations to Dream

To the crime in the water the subject associated the fact that the day before she had masturbated in the bathtub and felt very guilty about it. Ruth M was a close friend whom the subject envied for her beauty, health, husband, and child. Confusing Ruth M with Milly, a very ill patient with a gastrointestinal disease, related to her hostile wishes toward her friend. In her associations she also expressed wishes that Ruth M might die of cancer. This brought out the subject's own fears about cancer. Her ileitis and cancer fears began following an operation for a perirectal fistula. The first doctor who operated on her fistula "butchered" her; he took his "pound of flesh." Her buttocks were completely mutilated. Once after the operation *she took a mirror and looked at her buttocks.* She almost fainted at the sight of all the raw flesh. It was painted with gentian violet and was all *red, purple, and blue.* The patient connected this with the colored pile of coal in the dream. The word *pile* she associated with "piles." Her mutilated buttocks were undoubtedly the "shocking" sight at the "bottom" which she unconsciously hinted at in her comments before the exposure of the picture. The coal reminded the subject of the blackness of the pubic hair when she looked at herself in the mirror. It also associated to the words *finster-eigen,* meaning "black eyes"—that is, she got *black before her eyes* and almost fainted when she saw her mutilated buttocks. The colors of the pile of coal also were associated with the colors she had used in copying a painting of a nude by Modigliani. She thought the climbing up the pile was connected with a desire to attain the "voluptuousness" of this nude.

The subject thought that E's husband was attractive and wished she could be married to him. He reminded her of the boy with whom she had her first love affair. The sunburned, ruddy face and red nose were connected with the fact that at the time I was quite sunburned and E's husband, therefore, represented me. She connected the painter's cap with the surgical cap worn by Dr. M, who operated on her fistula successfully the second time, and for whom she had a great affection, in contrast to Dr. W, who butchered her. The lawyer was associated to the idea that she was going to sue Dr. W for malpractice.

The Drawings

The subject made the drawing shown in Figure 1.3 to illustrate her dream. As already noted, the events in the dream transpired in sequence from the lower right-hand corner to the upper left, as the subject walked along the path shown in the drawing. The "crime in the water" took place, she noted, outside the frame of the picture. Although at this point the subject was completely unaware that the three figures and their location on "piles" closely resembled the three kings in the picture, the most cursory inspection reveals this to be true. The figure on the right represents Ruth M, and is drawn as a total human figure with arms and legs. It can be seen that the figure on the right in the picture of the three kings could be imagined to be a complete human figure, while the kings on the left show only the torsos. The painter's cap on the middle figure is to be noted and the pathway which closely resembles an outline in the foreground of the picture of the three kings.

Results of Reexamination of the Tachistoscopically Exposed Picture and Revisiting the Experimental Setting

When the subject was taken through the corridors which led to the experimental room, she behaved in a very interesting manner. She stopped periodically, with an abstracted air, and with an attitude of surprise pointed to a number of objects and structures which reminded her of elements in her dream. First, she pointed to a sign, high up on a wall in the corridor, which read "Harris Memorial," and said that she must have seen it out of the corner of her eye on the day of the experiment. She said that Ruth M's

Figure 1.3. *Experiment I.* Subject J's drawing of her dream. The three figures and their location on piles closely resemble the general outline of the three kings in Figure 1.1. Ruth M is represented by the king on the right, the two men in the dream by the two kings on the left. The four vertical lines probably represent the two men in blue in the picture. The pathway was taken from rather obscure outlines in the foreground of Figure 1.1. The mound on which the torsos of the two men rest was the colored pile of coal in the dream.

married name was "Harris," that is, her full name was Ruth M. Harris. After 50 ft further down the corridor she stopped and pointed to a candy vending machine along the wall. Various candy bars were exposed through little windows, and one of these was labeled "Baby Ruth." This again she had noted in passing in a very fleeting manner. She believed she had combined the sign and the candy bar label to form the concepts of Ruth Harris and

Ruth Harris's baby, since the dream dealt with her envy of Ruth's baby. When we got to the room just off the experimental room, she pointed to a man who was in the process of painting. This man wore a painter's cap. She thought this was the painter's cap she had put on the figure of E's husband.

When the picture of the three kings was reexamined, it took a minute or so before she grasped with an attitude of great surprise that it so closely resembled the drawing of her dream. She readily confirmed the identity between the three figures in her drawing and the three kings. She thought she had combined three structures to form the painter's cap; the actual cap the painter wore, the white hat on the male figure to the left in the picture, and the little knob on the head of the middle king. One final detail: There happened to be in the center of the screen, on which the pictures were exposed, a small red cross. This cross coincided in location with the nose region of the middle king when it was flashed on the screen. The subject felt that this was one factor in causing the nose of E's husband to appear as red, since he corresponded to the middle king.

Interpretation and Comment

I believe that this dream can be structured around several unconscious wishes activated by the experimental *situation, procedure,* and *instructions,* and that it is basically a transference dream.

1. *The wish to get well:* The dream opens with the commission of the crime in the water, that is, the "crime" of masturbation, the subject's guilt, and the threat of punishment, e.g., the ticket from the policeman. Her illness, the fistula, and the subsequent mutilation of her buttocks are conceived of as the punishment for her masturbation. She ultimately appeals to the man with the painter's cap, E's husband, who represents me, for help. He is sympathetic and advises her to get a lawyer. The lawyer connects with her preoccupation with suing the doctor who mutilated her for malpractice. All this expresses her wish for restitution by me of the bodily organs damaged by masturbation. At the deepest unconscious level her illness is probably conceived of as castration.

2. *Voyeuristic–exhibitionistic wishes:* It seems probable that an experiment in which the subject is asked to look at, describe, and

draw a picture stirs up unconscious voyeuristic and exhibitionistic impulses. As noted, from the beginning this subject manifested great anxiety about looking, and was afraid of seeing something shocking at the "bottom"; she therefore excluded the bottom of the picture from conscious perception. This undoubtedly relates to the memory, reactivated by the dream, of looking at her mutilated "bottom" in the mirror. The dream also expresses hostile, rivalrous, and oedipal wishes involving Ruth M and E.

EXPERIMENT II

The following experiment took place under unusual circumstances. During a lecture to a group of psychiatrists, I demonstrated the tachistoscope by exposing the picture of the three kings for 1/100 sec. Several days later one of the physicians present came to me and reported the following:

Response to Tachistoscopic Exposure
I saw something that looked like Cambodian temple ruins in the jungle. There were three towers like Cambodian temples. They were yellow orange against a blue sky (Figure 1.4)

Dream of the Night Following Tachistoscopic Exposure

> There was an outcropping of rock, a little hill about 20 ft high, in a desert area. The hill was fairly level, but on the left one particular rock was standing detached and a little higher than the others. The desert floor rose up to the rocks. The people were standing on the sloping area; they were wearing blue shorts and blue short-sleeved shirts. A sequence of film was being made and characters were fleeing across the desert, running up over the hill while being shot at. One of the people, myself, is aware that the bullet is a real one and not a blank. The bullet struck in the middle of the hill, between the two people. I am one of the two people on the slope. A whole camera crew was behind us shooting the picture.

The Drawings
The subject made the drawing shown in Figure 1.5 to illustrate the dream. The desert scene is portrayed with the outcropping

Figure 1.4. *Experiment II.* Subject's drawing of what he saw following tachistoscopic exposure of Figure 1.1. The drawing represents three Cambodian temples.

Figure 1.5. *Experiment II.* Subject's drawing of his dream. It can be seen how closely the drawing resembles the lower half of Figure 1.1. The outcropping of rock in the dream is taken from the fourth mound, far to the left in the picture. The two men in blue are seen running over the hill, the one on the left with upraised left arm. The dot between them shows where the bullet struck.

of rock and the rock on the left which is somewhat higher than the rest. The two men are shown on the slope, the one on the left representing the subject. The dot between them shows where the bullet struck. The subject stressed that in the dream his left arm was upraised. He drew another picture to illustrate this (Figure 1.6).

It seemed evident that the drawings conformed very neatly to the lower part of the exposed picture which had not been consciously perceived. The rock which was higher than the others corresponded to the fourth mound in the picture. The two men in blue shorts and shirts corresponded to the two men in the

Figure 1.6. *Experiment II.* Subject's drawing of the man on the left in Figure 1.5, who represents himself. The upraised right arm can be seen to resemble very closely the arm shown in Figure 1.1 between the two men.

picture, both of whom are in blue. One is shown with his sleeve rolled up, from which the idea of the short-sleeved shirts was probably taken.

Results of Reexamination

The subject confirmed the above conjectures with certain exceptions. The man on the left who stood for the subject, was taken from a difficult-to-see outline in the middle of the picture. On close examination one can see the outline of an upraised right arm (on the mound between the two men) having the same visual form as the arm in the drawing (Figure 1.6). A head, torso, and a right arm appear to be connected with the vague outline in the picture (Figure 1.1). The subject saw this outline as two men, with the region that looks like a head representing the spot where the bullet had struck, as though the dirt was scattered. It seems probable that the vague outline which represented the two men to the subject was fused with the forms of the two men in blue in the picture.

During the lecture an assistant was operating a projector to show lantern slides. The subject felt that the idea of a camera crew behind him was connected with this. The shot in the dream, and the burst of dirt, related to the burst of the picture on the screen. The clicking of the shutter on the projector became the sound of the bullet which was described by the subject as not being loud in the dream. In the dream there was a whole camera crew with a director. The director who ordered the shooting probably represents me.

Comment

If a composite is made of Figure 1.4 and Figure 1.5, we obtain an outline drawing that conforms very nicely with the picture of the three kings (Figure 1.7). There are several points of interest. The transformation of the sound of the shutter into the sound

Figure 1.7. *Experiment II.* A composite of Figures 1.4 and 1.5, which combines what the subject saw consciously during exposure of the picture, and what was seen preconsciously and formed the manifest content of the dream. It can be seen how closely the composite resembles an outline drawing of Figure 1.1.

of the bullet indicates how preconscious auditory percepts may be incorporated into the dream from events surrounding the experiment, in the same manner in which visual percepts are dealt with. The subject's insistence that the vague outline represented two men rather than one, may be a manifestation of resistance to the idea that if it represented one man, himself, then the bullet would have struck him in the head. In his version the bullet struck between the two men and did not hit either of them. The subject described the movement of the dream as taking place from right to left, e.g., the men fled over the hill in this direction. He believed that this was the direction of his eye movements during the original tachistoscopic exposure.

EXPERIMENT III

The subject, R, was a 17-year-old Puerto Rican boy who was admitted to the hospital because of asthma from which he had suffered since the age of 13 months. His most recent attack of asthma was precipitated by a suicide attempt on the part of his alcoholic father. For a period prior to hospitalization the patient had been addicted to marijuana and heroin. He could not remember dreaming for at least 5 years.

Response to Tachistoscopic Exposure
    The picture of the three kings was exposed for 1/100 sec. The subject stated, "I saw three blond girls in bathing suits like on a beach. One of them was taking a photo with a camera."
    He then made the drawing of this scene as shown in Figure 1.8. Note that the drawing of the girls corresponds in perspective and spatial relationships to the three kings. The girls are somewhat masculine in appearance, narrow-hipped, without hands, with bras outlining the breasts and, especially the middle figure, showing an almost phalliclike triangle at the crotch.

Dream of the Night Following Tachistoscopic Exposure

    I had gone home. There was some kind of party there. Then I was going to some hotel. I was following a man who was in a red

Figure 1.8. *Experiment III*. Subject's drawing after tachistoscopic exposure of Figure 1.1. The three girls have approximately the same spatial
relationships as the three kings. Note the girl on the right holding a
camera to her eye.

convertible down a street. I was supposed to watch him; somebody
was paying me to watch him. He was running away from home. I
was outside the hotel which was called the Pigle Hotel, watching
this man talking to a blonde who was standing alongside the car.
He drove away. All this time I was in pajamas and was wearing a
blue jacket. Then I was inside the hotel. I took my jacket off and
started to talk to a lady at a desk about the man I was supposed to
watch, and I told her to call the police and tell them to send me
a car, that the guy I was following had a car and I could not follow
him on foot. The lady at the desk had a mean-looking face. All of
a sudden I saw my aunt through the glass door outside. My main
worry was that my aunt would see me in pajamas. I wanted to hide.

Associations to Dream

The subject's associations centered around his separation from
his mother and feelings that she preferred his younger brother.
The aunt and godmother are mother substitutes. The Pigle Hotel
connected with the hotel at which the patient had stayed 5 years
before when he returned to Puerto Rico with his aunt and was
separated from his mother for several years.

The Drawings

The subject was asked to make drawings of the dream scene showing himself watching the man in the red convertible talking to the blonde (Figure 1.9), of the Pigle Hotel (Figure 1.10), and of his godmother (Figure 1.11). I wish to emphasize that the subject was completely unaware that any of these drawings or any aspect of his dream were related to the tachistoscopically exposed picture or to the scenes surrounding the experiment.

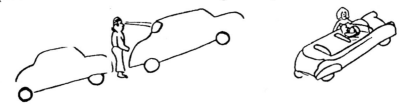

Figure 1.9. *Experiment III.* Subject's drawing of himself in the dream watching the man in the red convertible. The spatial relationship of the two men in blue and the middle king resemble those of the two men and the girl in the dream, if the dream figures are thought of as displaced upward, the man on the right into the red convertible, represented by the breast region of the middle king, and the man on the left, with whom the subject is identified, between the other two cars. The subject is shown in his blue jacket standing between the two cars, the two lines leading from his eyes indicating that he was looking through the rear window of the car at the man in the red convertible talking to the blonde. The red convertible is taken from the outline of the breast region of the middle king. The convertible plus the head of the blonde standing next to it equal the middle king. By displacement into the convertible the man in blue on the right is brought into close spatial relationship with the breast of the girl.

Results of Reexamination of the Tachistoscopically Exposed Picture and Revisiting the Experimental Setting

As he walked through the corridors to the experimental room, his eye periodically fell on something that caused him to pause, look puzzled, fall into a sort of abstracted state, and then point out that the object or structure related to something in the dream. He pointed out a series of structures which he had fused together in a composite to form the image of the Pigle Hotel, as shown in

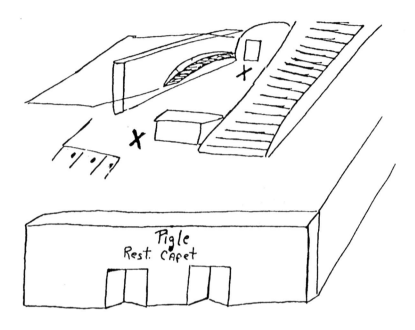

Figure 1.10. *Experiment III.* Subject's drawing of the "Pigle Hotel." The latter is composed of various architectural structures taken from the hospital. The "restaurant-cafeteria" was derived from the hospital cafeteria. The "X" in front of the hotel shows the spot where the aunt was standing when the subject saw her through the glass door. At the time the subject was standing at the spot indicated by the "X" between the telephone booths and the desk at the left of the foot of the staircase. The woman who looked like his godmother was sitting at the desk. The "X" at the rear indicates the door under the archway through which the subject left the hotel in his dream after he had retrieved his blue jacket.

Figure 1.10. The words *Restaurant-Cafeteria* on the front of the dream hotel were related to the hospital cafeteria which he had fleetingly noticed the day before on walking along the corridor. The doors of the hotel, the courtyard, the desk, the arch, the stairway and the telephone stalls in the dream picture all had

Figure 1.11. *Experiment III.* On the left is subject's drawing of his godmother. It appears to be a condensation of the two kings shown in the
drawing. The bulging hair line in front resembles a similar structure on
the king on the right. The bun in the back may represent a displacement
downward of the knob on the head of the same king. The chin and
nose of the godmother appear to resemble corresponding structures on
the king to the left. The visual forms from which the subject constructed
the three cars shown in Figure 1.9 are labeled in the drawing I, II, and
III. Outlines I and II are taken from corresponding shadows in Figure
1.1. They represent the cars between which the subject was standing in
the dream. Outline III is the breast region of the middle king and in
the dream it becomes the red convertible.

their exact counterparts in actual structures he had seen. Although these were widely separated in space, they were fused in
the dream to form a composite.

　　The subject was very puzzled by the word *Pigle* and was unable
to produce any associations to it. However, during the reexamination period the following material came to light. He noted a fish
bowl containing some tiny fish in a room just off the experimental
room. The day before he had noted them casually and had
thought of them as *pigmy fish.* He thought that Pigle had something to do with pigmy. Then he noticed a cartoon pinned to the
wall which showed a psychiatrist sitting behind a couch on which
reclined a baseball umpire in full regalia. He had fleetingly noted
this cartoon the day before. The umpire was saying to the somewhat bored psychiatrist, "And then Phil Rizzuto got up to bat."
The subject pointed out that Phil Rizzuto was a very small man,
a pigmy ball player, and that the name *Phil* had something to do

with Pigle. It appeared that "Pigle" represents a condensation of the words *Phil* and *pigmy*; by substitution of the fourth letter of Phil for the fourth letter in pigmy the word *pigly* is derived.

When the picture of the three kings was exposed on the screen, the subject quickly spotted the blue shirt on the man to the left and identified it as the blue jacket he was wearing in the dream. He noted that the spatial relationships between the two men and the middle king duplicated his drawing of himself in relation to the man in the red convertible and the blond girl. His drawing of this scene is shown in Figure 1.9. The subject portrays himself standing between the two cars on the left, looking through the rear window of one of the cars toward the man in the red convertible. As the visual source of the red convertible, the subject pointed to the area on the middle king corresponding to the breast region. This is shown in Figure 1.11, which is an outline drawing of the picture of the three kings. As the source of the two cars between which he was standing, the subject pointed to two obscure outlines, labeled I and II in the slide. The source of the red convertible is labeled III. It can be seen that these configurations more than vaguely resemble the outlines of the cars. Through a series of transpositions of figures and spatial rearrangement of structures a significant portion of the picture of the three kings was transformed into the dream scene of the patient watching the man in the red convertible. This came about by elevating the man in the blue shirt with whom the subject is identified in the dream through the blue jacket, to a position between the two small cars. At the same time the man on the right was elevated to a position within the convertible, bringing his head into close proximity to the breast region of the middle king. It can be seen that the head of the girl seen alongside of and behind the car (Figure 1.9), when combined with the outline of the convertible, resembles the head and chest region of the middle king.

The profile figure that the subject made of his godmother (Figure 1.11) appears to be a condensation of the profiles of the two kings on the left. The nose, chin, and mouth region of the godmother resemble that of the figure on the left, while the protruding hair in front more nearly resembles a corresponding outline of the middle king. If the triangular structure on top of the head of the middle king is displaced backward, it takes up the position of the bun on the head of the godmother.

Interpretation and Comment

The first striking characteristic of the material is the abundance of voyeuristic and exhibitionistic references. This was already evident before any dreams were produced, in the response to the exposure of the picture. The subject saw three girls clad in shorts and bras, one of whom was taking a picture. This probably has some connection with the cameralike appearance of the tachistoscopic apparatus and the exposure of a picture on a screen, and represents a projection of the subject's own voyeurism. It is highly probable that the participation in an experiment in which the subject is asked to look at, describe, and draw a picture stirs up unconscious voyeuristic and exhibitionistic conflicts. The dream, in its manifest content, is centrally concerned with watching and exposure, e.g., watching the man in the red convertible, fear that the aunt would see him in his pajamas, etc. The second aspect of the material that is noteworthy is that it deals largely with the idea of a boy leaving home, with feelings of rejection by the mother and jealousy of the younger brother. Third, the dream revolves around three female figures, the aunt, the blonde, and the godmother, who represent various aspects of the mother image and become connected with the images of the three kings in the picture.

I come now to the very remarkable transformation of the outline of the breast region of the middle king into the red convertible. Ordinarily a car has the symbolic meaning of a penis, which it probably has here also, but it clearly seems to represent "breast" in addition. The rearrangement of structures in this scene results in the bringing of the head of the man in the car into close proximity to the breast region of the blonde. It may be suggested that the "man in the car" has the meaning of the "car in the man," that is, the breast in the mouth. The validity of the equation—red convertible equals breast—obtains support from an entirely independent source. It was found that the subject had pinned above his bed the pictures of six convertible cars; to the left of these he had put the pictures of the torsos of three pinup girls, all of them showing the breasts half-exposed.

The dream takes place in the setting of the Pigle Hotel which is represented as a cafeteria, reminds the subject of the hotel in which he stayed when he was separated from his mother, and is equated with the hospital. The Pigle Hotel relates to the subject's pigmylike feelings, inferiority, helplessness, and dependency, and his oral strivings toward the mother. The word *Pigle* connects with his feelings of smallness as against me, the psychiatrist, and refers back to "Phil," the cartoon of the umpire and the analyst, and the tiny fish.

The evidence indicates that in this experiment the transference relationship is the chief motivating force for the dream, that the experimental situation, the experimental procedure, and the content of the experimental instructions aroused in the subject at least three major unconscious wishes.

1. *The wish to get well:* It is necessary to imagine the position of this boy in the hospital in relation to me. With his serious chronic illness and tragic, unhappy background, a doctor asks him to cooperate in an experiment. Even though he is told that the experiment is not intended to cure him, he unconsciously develops magical wishes toward the doctor who has been nice to him. These take the form of a wish to go home, to be well, to have a new chest, to obtain the maternal breast-penis, which is represented by the red convertible, itself derived from the breast region. It may be remarked that the patient had a marked pigeon breast, that he was preoccupied with it, and that he engaged in exercises in an attempt to change it. That is, his illness was represented to him by the deformed chest. In the dream the patient goes to his godmother and asks her to get him a red convertible so that he can follow the other man. Associations indicated that I was identified with the godmother.

The dream, then, basically expresses the subject's unconscious wish for restitution of the breast-penis by the mother, whom he blames for his illness. But this wish stirs up all his oedipal and sibling rivalry conflicts. It is these that are portrayed in the dream by the triangle of the two men and the blonde. This is why the dream material deals so largely with the idea of a boy leaving home and of his painful separation from his mother, while his little brother remained with her. The dream also expresses the wish for a red convertible, like the rival's, so that he can possess mother.

The idea expressed in the dream that he was being paid to watch the man in the red convertible probably also is connected with his magical wishes to be rewarded for participation in the experiment. It was, after all, I who asked him to watch the man in the car, that is, to look at the picture.

2. *Voyeuristic-exhibitionistic wishes:* The abundance of voyeuristic and exhibitionistic material evidently relates to the primal scene, conceived of in oral terms. The dream opens with the subject going home where he finds a "party" going on. The triangular arrangement of the subject, the man in the convertible, and the blonde, is connected with oral envy and wishes for the breast, and represents the primal scene.

3. *Wishes produced by the suggestion to dream:* The oral nature of the dream may in part have been due to the transference meaning to the subject of being given a suggestion to dream. I have reported evidence elsewhere (1953a,b) that the suggestion to dream has transference implications, and that the subject reacts unconsciously as if the suggestion represents an oral incorporation.

EXPERIMENT IV

A picture of the Tower of London was exposed to the subject, a physician, for 1/100 sec (see Figure 1.12).[1]

Response to Tachistoscopic Exposure
On the left the subject saw a red, cylindrical-shaped structure, extending up two thirds the height of the picture. It looked like a barrel or silo. The remainder of the picture was seen as green trees and shrubbery extending the length of the picture. The silo-shaped structure was bright red, except for some streaks in it of a lighter color (Figure 1.13).

---

[1]Closer examination of the drawing reveals that it shows not the Tower of London, but the Horse Guards in Whitehall. In a seemingly universally shared error, both Fisher and all his subjects (as well as this writer) thought the drawing to be of the Tower of London. In our notation, we will follow psychic rather than external reality and continue referring to the drawing as the Tower of London.

Figure 1.12. *(For legend to Figure 1.12, see page 64.)*

Legend to Figure 1.12

Figure 1.12: *The Tower of London.* This is a black-and-white reproduction of a Kodachrome. Certain details—the hole in the sentry box, the guardsman's hat, the chin strap—appear more clearly in the drawing than in the original. In the original the sentry is wearing a brilliant red coat which has a white belt, white trimming at the cuffs, white buttons down the front; the epaulettes are black with white trimming. He is wearing a black guardsman's hat with a white chin strap; his trousers are black. The sentry box is a deep black. The man in the center foreground is wearing a black suit and a dark gray fedora hat. The sky is blue with white clouds. The towers and buildings in the background are various shades of white, gray, and black.

In experiment IV the dream scene which involves the dark man riding in the back seat of a car, and which was characterized by a dense feeling of blackness, relates to the guard standing in front of the sentry box. The upper part of the sentry box, which is very black in the picture, represents the back seat of the car (see Figure 1.14). The circular hole in the back of the sentry box at the level of the guard's head represents the window in the back of the car in the dream. The black trousers of the guard are so poorly defined in the picture that this may have helped in their elimination from the dream image of the man in the car, who is drawn in Figure 1.14 without legs. The epaulettes and the chin strap are to be noted since they played a significant role in the dream. The black hussar's hat disappears into the black background of the sentry box and its outlines can hardly be detected in the original. Note the man in the fedora hat to the right in about the center foreground of the picture. It was this fedora hat that was displaced onto the man in the back seat of the car. The white sidewalk behind the fence became the road in the dream which, however, was reversed in direction.

Dream of the Night Following Tachistoscopic Exposure

Something about the police, about cruelty, riding in a car. Making a right turn, presumably in an auto, but there is no auto. Somebody was being made to sit in a certain way as if hoisted up in the back. His shoulders were being pulled up, hunched up. The back seat

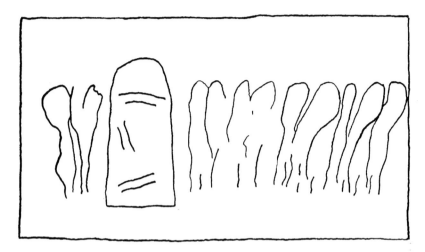

Figure 1.13. *Experiment IV*. Subject's drawing of what he saw following tachistoscopic exposure of Figure 1.12. The structure on the left represents the silo, surrounded on either side by shrubbery.

of the car where the man was sitting was very dark and black. The man was dark, Italian looking. He was wearing a very black fedora hat.

The Drawings

The subject made a drawing showing the road and then one showing the back seat of the car (Figure 1.14), with the man sitting in it. He made marks at the shoulders indicating the hoisting and hunching of the figure, as though he were being pulled up from the shoulders. He drew the fedora in profile, seeing it with a sort of downsweep at the brim. The man is sitting on the seat, indicated by the dividing horizontal line. The subject had no wish to make legs or arms on the figure, nor to put features on his face. At the end he felt a strong compulsion to put an oval-shaped window in the drawing to indicate the back window of the car.

Associations to Dream

The idea of the "police" was connected with the Mafia and the secret police. The entire scene was Italian. The man in the

Figure 1.14. *Experiment IV.* Subject's drawing of his dream. The small drawing on the right represents the road on which the car turned in the dream. It is a reversal of the form of the sidewalk in Figure 1.12, which curves in the opposite direction. The main drawing shows the dark, Italian-looking man sitting in the back seat of the car. The rectangular back seat area of the car was taken from the dark black sentry box behind the guard. The elliptical window in the rear corresponds to the round hole in the back of the sentry box and shows the same spatial relationship to the man. The drawing of the dream image of the back seat of the car is much broader than the corresponding area of the black sentry box, as if it were stretched out to the right along with the window which is elliptical instead of round. The dark man represents the guard before the sentry box. The markings on his shoulders which were drawn to show the point at which he was hoisted correspond to the guard's epaulettes. The fedora hat was displaced from the man in the foreground in Figure 1.12, seen to the right of the sentry box.

car was Italian and looked like Sacco or Vanzetti. Some injustice was being done. The subject said Sacco and Vanzetti were hanged but corrected this to electrocuted. The hoisting up by the shoulders of the man in the car had to do with the idea of his being hanged. The subject also thought of a recent item in the papers about a Yugoslav who refused to have his eyes bandaged when he was shot to death for antigovernment activity.

Results of Reexamination of the Tachistoscopically Exposed Picture
    The subject did not recognize the picture as the Tower of London, but continued to think of an Italian scene. He immediately

noted the guard in the red coat and the great black guardsman's hat standing in front of the sentry box. He pointed out that the box was very black and that this was like the back of the car. The drawing of the man in the back seat was taken from the outline of the trunk and head of the guard. The places at the shoulders which were drawn to represent the points of hoisting corresponded to the epaulettes on the guard. The black hat was a condensation of the hussar's hat and the fedora hat of the man to the right, seen in profile. The guard faces front, the man in the fedora is seen in profile. The subject felt that this was why he could not put features on the man in his drawing. The window in the car corresponds to the hole in the back of the sentry box, seen in identical spatial relationship to the man. The idea of hanging came from the white chin strap of the guard's hat. The hanging, however, was displaced to a hoisting from the shoulders. The road corresponds to a white walk inside the gate behind and to the right of the sentry box, but it curves in the opposite direction, from left to right.

Comment

The subject did not recognize the picture as the Tower of London during the reexamination, but thought of it as Italian. The only thing he knew about the Tower was that it was a place where executions were carried out. Since the dream was centrally concerned with execution, the possibility remains that the picture was preconsciously recognized as the Tower of London. The subject had certainly at some time seen pictures of the Tower.

The displacement of the fedora from the man on the right to the figure in the car is of interest. The displacement of the idea of "hanging" from the chin strap to the epaulettes is also striking. It suggests that the chin strap must have been apperceived, but did not appear in visual form in the manifest dream.

The manifest content of the dream was largely composed of preconsciously perceived elements in the picture. But it must be noted that the area of the silolike structure which was consciously perceived also contains the chief preconscious percepts which got into the dream. This suggests that structures in the picture undergo double registration, a conscious and a preconscious one, the latter much more detailed and photographic and destined for incorporation into the manifest content of the dream. The eye movements during tachistoscopic exposure were evidently from right to left. The road was reversed in direction. It is possible that during the sweep of the eyes from right to left the fedora hat was carried and displaced to the guard's head.

I shall not enter into an interpretation of this dream. The dream was heralded by the perception of the silo during the tachistoscopic exposure. Both the black sentry box (the back of the car) and the silo were thought of as coffinlike, containing dead material. The execution by hanging related to oral–sadistic death fantasies. The absence of arms and legs on the figure was connected with the idea of being "drawn and quartered" as part of the execution. The blackness of the subject's dream image of the back seat of the car was associated with the "dark" childhood memory of the ride to his mother's funeral and with her coffin. The memory involved a depressive identification with the mother.

Experiment V

The incident of the preconscious perception of the words *Harris* and *Baby Ruth* in experiment I suggested the idea of experimenting with the tachistoscopic exposure of words instead of pictures, something which Pötzl did not attempt. The following is a report of one such experiment:

Three words and a three-figure number were tachistoscopically exposed to the subject, a physician, for 1/200 sec; the words were arranged on the slide in the following manner:

EX*IT*

246   MINK

STAR

This exposure was so rapid that the subject recognized only several letters in two of the words, but could not identify any of them. That night he had a dream, the chief association to which concerned the idea of "8 automobile accidents." Although it was not conclusively demonstrated, there is a strong possibility that the subject extended the arithmetical progression 2-4-6 to 8, and that the association was somehow related to the preconscious perception of the numbers. The next night the subject had another dream, one of the principal parts of which involved a "guitar." On reexamination of the exposed words the subject immediately felt that they had something to do with the word *guitar.* He believed that he had used the "6" as a "G," taken the "it" from "exit" and the "tar" from "star" to compose the word *gittar,* which is the phonetic equivalent of *guitar.* I might add that another day residue involved an actual guitar that the subject owned, suggesting that the verbal image had activated the visual image.

It will be noted that the "gittar" dream occurred on the second night following tachistoscopic exposure. I have a considerable amount of evidence that the preconscious visual percepts in these experiments are active in dream formation for at least 48 hours, and possibly longer.

Another subject who failed to consciously perceive the number 246 after exposure of the same slide for 1/200 sec, had a dream which involved a scene in which he was "adding cubes" of ice to a custard. It appeared that the number 246 was converted into a dream image of "adding cubes" on the basis that a cube is a structure with four sides one way around plus two sides, that is, it is a 2-4-6 sided figure. Also the arithmetical progression of 2-4-6 contributed to the idea of adding cubes. This subject was a very good mathematician.

A more direct appearance in the dream of a preconsciously perceived word is illustrated in the following experiment. A female subject failed to consciously note the word *mink* when the same slide was exposed for 1/200 sec. In the manifest content of the subsequent dream there appeared a girl friend whose husband had given her the nickname *Mink* because her sexual proclivities resembled those of the animal of the same name.

EXPERIMENT VI

In this nontachistoscopic experiment a picture was exposed to the subject, an intelligent young girl, for 30 sec. The picture was of a Coney Island sideshow and street scene. Across the front of the sideshow was a large sign reading "$1000 Reward If You Fail To See The Bear Girl Alive." A quite prominent picture of the Bear Girl was shown above the sign. In spite of the prolonged exposure of 30 sec the subject failed to note the Bear Girl. That night she dreamed that she was nude to the waist and trying to fasten her bra. She drew a picture of this scene, as shown in Figure 1.15. The dream figure is shown on the left, the Bear Girl, as she appeared in the exposed picture, on the right. The resemblance between the two pictures is striking, and there is little doubt that the dream image was based on the picture of the Bear Girl. The dream figure was rotated about 180 degrees. The suitcase the dreamer was carrying was taken from the right end of the sign on which the words, "The Bear Girl Alive," can be seen. The identical angles of the sign and suitcase are striking. The left hind leg of the bearskin approaching the sign corresponds to the right hand of the dream figure holding the suitcase. The left hand of the dreamer is shown fastening the bra; this corresponds to the forepaws of the bearskin on either side of the breasts of the Bear Girl. The idea of the Bear Girl was converted in the dream into a "bare" or "nude" girl.

DISCUSSION

The results of this investigation confirm and extend Pötzl's findings. They have many implications and raise many problems, only a few of which can be discussed at this time.

It has been shown that in the process of preconscious visual perception under discussion, an enormous amount of intricate visual material is selected out of the perceptual field and registered psychically in amazingly brief time intervals, such as 1/100 or 1/200 sec. The process of registration may take place in an almost photographic way, an excellent example being the epaulettes, the oval window, and the fedora hat in experiment IV. Just as impressive as the accuracy of registration is the distortion undergone by some of the preconscious visual percepts. These take the form of fragmentation, spatial dislocation, condensation

Figure 1.15. *Experiment VI.* The dream figure, of the subject trying to fasten her bra, is shown on the left, the "Bear Girl," as she appeared in the exposed picture, on the right. The dream figure was rotated about 180 degrees as compared with the "Bear Girl." The suitcase the dreamer was carrying was taken from the right end of the sign on which the words, "The Bear Girl Alive," can be seen. The identical angles of the sign and suitcase are striking. The left hind leg of the Bear Girl approaching the sign corresponds to the right hand of the dream figure holding the suitcase. The left hand of the dreamer is shown fastening the bra: This corresponds to the forepaws of the bearskin on either side of the breasts of the "Bear Girl." The idea of the "Bear Girl" was converted in the dream into a "bare" or "nude" girl.

and composite formation, symbolic transformation, spatial reversals and rotations. I refer to such spatial dislocations as resulted in the dream image of the subject in experiment III, watching the man in the red convertible.

The manner in which the dream work handles preconscious

visual percepts is of great interest. Several different kinds of transformations can be detected. In many instances the percept retains the meaning of the object image denoted by it. For example, the percept of a hat taken from the exposed picture will appear in the dream as a hat, as in experiment IV, even though accompanied by a spatial displacement. In almost all the experiments the percepts of the human figures in the pictures appeared in the dreams as images of human figures. Very often the subject identified himself with one of these figures, and it was a common occurrence for the experimenter to be represented in some kind of condensation with the visual percept of a human figure from the exposed pictures.

In other instances the preconscious visual percept was not treated as representative of a thought element or of an object but as an object itself. Fliess (1953) has remarked that for purposes of dream speech the dreamer treats verbal day residues in the manner of a schizophrenic; a word image in the speech of the day before is not conceived as representative of a thought element or of an object, but as an object itself. Many of the preconscious visual percepts were treated in the same way as Fliess has indicated for word images. Thus, in experiment IV, the epaulettes appeared in the dream, not as epaulettes, but as points of attachment for the hoisting having to do with the image of the execution by hanging. In the same experiment the black sentry box in the picture appeared in the dream as the back seat of the car. In other experiments an elephant became transformed into a fireplace, a sign board into a suitcase, and a stool into a bed, etc.

Because the visual percepts are treated as concrete objects they may be fragmented, torn apart, and mutilated in the arbitrary manner that Freud (1900) has described as happening to the auditory percepts that go into making up the speech of dreams. Thus, the symbolic transformation of the cars in experiment III from visual structures torn out of their context depended upon such arbitrary treatment.

The experiments with the tachistoscopic exposure of words also revealed the same kinds of transformations. In some experiments the object denoted by the word appeared in visual form in the dream, e.g., the transformation of Baby Ruth Harris into Ruth M in experiment I. In another experiment the exposure of the word *book* resulted in a dream image of a book. In other experiments the exposed words were treated in an arbitrary manner, as concrete objects; a good example is to be found in experiment V in which the appearance of the guitar in the dream was related to the word *gittar,* formed out of letters torn from context.

I believe that what Freud said about speeches and verbal material in dreams has to be extended to include the visual structure of dreams. He was always insistent that speeches in dreams were taken from auditory percepts of the day before. He showed how the dream dealt with these in the most arbitrary fashion, tore them from their context, mutilating them, accepting one fragment, rejecting another, and often fitting them together in a novel manner. He stated that *the dream work cannot create a new speech* (1900). It is somewhat puzzling why he did not apply the same formulation to visual percepts. Earlier I indicated that Freud's description of the manner in which the dream treats auditory percepts applies equally well to the treatment that has been demonstrated for visual percepts in these experiments. He indicated that when verbal ideas in the day residues are recent, actual fragments of perceptions, and not the expression of thoughts, they are treated like concrete ideas and become subject to the influence of condensation and displacement.

In the sense in which Freud used the phrase, it is entirely possible that the dream work cannot compose a new visual structure any more than it can a new speech.

Although Freud was well aware of the existence of multiple day residues for any given dream and even defined the dream as "the unconscious working over of preconscious thought processes" (1940, p. 50), his discussion of day residues cannot give an adequate idea of the degree to which the structure of a dream may be anchored in the visual *percepts* of the day before. In many of the experiments every single detail of the visual structure of the dream could be traced to preconscious visual percepts of the day before.

Freud considered the chief accomplishment of the dream work to be the transformation of the latent thoughts, as expressed in words, into perceptual forms, most commonly into visual images, and he constructed his hypothetical model of the psychic apparatus for the express purpose of explaining this transformation. He stated that our thoughts originated in such perceptual forms; their earliest material and the first stages in their development consisted of sense impressions or memory pictures of these. It was later that words were attached to these pictures and then connected so as to form thoughts. The dream work subjects our thoughts to a regressive process and retraces the steps in their development; in the course of this regression all new acquisitions won during the development of memory pictures into thoughts must necessarily fall away. As Freud (1900) put it, in regression the fabric of the dream thoughts is resolved into its raw material. By raw material Freud clearly means perceptual forms.

In this account of the transformation of the dream thoughts into perceptual forms, Freud appears to take into account only memory pictures *from the past;* this is what is meant by retracing the steps in development of the dream thoughts. But this formulation does not take into sufficient account the empirically proven fact that the visual images of the manifest content of the dream extensively incorporate percepts associated with current day residues. I believe this difficulty can be resolved if we expand Freud's formulation that an unconscious idea cannot enter consciousness unless it is "covered" or "screened" by a preconscious day residue to include the notion that the memory pictures connected with the unconscious idea cannot attain consciousness unless they are covered or screened by preconscious sensory percepts associated with the day residue.

The results of this investigation indicate that memory pictures from the past do not appear in dreams unless they are "covered" by recent sensory percepts. Even, for example, when a figure from the past does appear in the dream, it can be demonstrated that fusion or condensation with a figure in the tachistoscopically exposed picture or with a visual percept from the scenes surrounding the experiment has taken place. Such a demonstration can only take place under experimental conditions which include control of the field of the day residues.

One of the chief functions of day residues, then, is to provide the perceptual material out of which the visual and auditory images of the manifest content of the dream are composed, and to provide a "cover" so that memory pictures from the past can be aroused to hallucinatory intensity. The need for day residues in dream formation may be due to the fact that only recent impressions have the capacity to be aroused to hallucinatory intensity. This possibility receives support from a recent investigation by Narusi and Obonai (1953). They found that recent visual percepts underwent progressive decompositions and fusions, quite like the distortions noted in Pötzl's experiments, but that after two days they could no longer be aroused to hallucinatory intensity. This corresponds with what we know about the capacity of percepts associated with day residues to enter into dreams, that is, they must not be older than a day or two.

In stating that a memory picture from the past has to be "screened" or "covered" by a recent percept, I do not mean to imply that the manifest visual structure of the dream is an identical copy of the tachistoscopically exposed picture. Even though the picture may impose itself upon the manifest structure of the dream in a very striking way, as in experiments I and II, differences between them can be demonstrated. These differences are brought about by fusion and condensation between visual percepts from the picture and memory pictures from the past. Thus, in experiment IV the dream scene of the man riding in the back seat of the car was derived from the black sentry box and the guard in the exposed picture, but the two visual structures were not identical. The blackness of the dream image was derived from the blackness of the sentry box condensed with the "black" memory of the ride to the maternal funeral. The shape of the car was based on that of the upper part of the sentry box, but more nearly corresponded to the actual shape of the back seat of the car derived from the childhood memory. Sometimes the memory picture from the past is carefully disguised, and at other times it intrudes itself into the manifest content more sharply, but in all these experimental dreams a recent percept appears to have been utilized as a "cover." In experiment I the painter's cap was condensed with the memory image of the surgeon's cap, and the colored pile of coal with the memory of the mutilated buttocks. In all these examples the relationship between the recent percept and the memory from the past seems to have been one of association by similarity.

I have called the type of perception involved in these experiments *preconscious* because, although the percepts are taken in and registered outside of awareness, they are capable of being made conscious. Kris (1950) has pointed out that preconscious is what is capable of becoming conscious easily and under conditions which frequently arise. It is different from unconscious processes in the case of which such a transformation is difficult, can only come about with considerable expenditure of energy, or may never occur. Kris (1950) states that:

> [N]ot all preconscious processes reach consciousness with equal ease. Some can only be recaptured with considerable effort. Second, preconscious mental processes are extremely different from each other both in content and in the kind of thought processes used; they cover continua reaching from purposeful reflection to fantasy, and from logical formulation to dream-like imagery [p. 542].

It may be noted that the preconscious percepts under consideration belong to the class that are not recaptured easily. Kris pointed out that when preconscious material emerges into consciousness, the reaction varies greatly. The process may not be noticed—the usual reaction if the preconscious process is readily available to consciousness. But emergence into consciousness can be accompanied by strong emotional reactions. Such was the case with the subjects in these experiments, many of whom showed great astonishment and wonder when they recognized their dream images after confrontation with the tachistoscopically exposed pictures.

However useful the usual process of free association may be in ordinary therapeutic dream analysis, I believe it is incapable of reviving the preconscious visual percepts revealed in these experiments. It has been shown what a large share these visual percepts have in building up the visual structure of a dream. Everyone is aware how many dreams or parts of dreams leave us baffled and how even very freely associating patients cannot produce the material which would clarify these obscurities. The evidence suggests that these preconscious visual percepts can be recalled only after a process of confrontation. Even after the subjects make their drawings, which so clearly resemble the visual structures of the exposed pictures, they have no awareness of any relationship between them. Only after confrontation and comparison with the

original and then, at times, after prolonged search, do the subjects note the similarities. Pötzl pointed out how apt the subjects
were to forget what they had drawn. The kind of confrontation
used here is possible only in an experimental setup and by virtue
of the control that the experimenter has over the sources of the
day residues. Not only are the preconscious visual percepts taken
from the tachistoscopically exposed pictures, but, as has been
shown, they are also taken from all the scenes that surround the
experiment. Actually the visual percepts are mostly structured
around the transference situation. It is by virtue of this control
over the visual perceptual field of the day residues and through
the control of the dream process itself, through the giving of an
indirect suggestion to dream, that one is able to track down the
preconsciously perceived visual day residues. In contrast to this,
Fliess (1953) has remarked that perhaps the only day residue
sometimes available to the analyst and unavailable to the patient
is an element of a previous analytic hour, which in the dreamer
has become (re-)repressed.

Pötzl's most important finding was that those parts of the tachistoscopically exposed pictures which were consciously perceived
did not appear in the subsequent dreams; those parts which were
preconsciously perceived did. This is not strictly true, although it
is correct to say that the main part of the visual structure of the
dream may be built up from the preconscious percepts. In a good
many instances, however, there is a double registration: Some of
the visual structures are registered twice, once consciously, once
preconsciously. The preconscious percept is registered with much
greater accuracy and involves details not appearing in the conscious percept. For example, in experiment IV, the guard and the
sentry box were consciously perceived as a silo, but preconsciously
there was registration of many of the details of the figure of the
guard and the structure of the sentry box.

There is also the implication in Pötzl's 1917 paper that consciously perceived elements do not appear in dreams. This, of
course, is not the case, since it is a matter of daily analytic observation that consciously perceived and remembered day residues
may enter into the formation of the visual structure of the manifest content of dreams. What Pötzl's work does show is the extent
to which preconsciously perceived elements may enter into the

same process. As opposed to the conscious percepts, the preconscious percepts appear to be connected with more deeply repressed material.

The evidence that the preconscious percepts appear in the manifest content of the dream is as follows: First, the drawings that the subjects make of the dream scenes frequently so closely resemble structures in the exposed picture that the resemblance is evident without reexamination of the picture. Second, the subjects themselves are able to point out the resemblance when they reexamine the pictures or the scenes surrounding the experiment. The discovery of the resemblance is accompanied by a sense of recognition, a feeling of surprise and even of shock. Third, the structures that are pointed out during the reexamination have the proper form, spatial location, and color in relation to the dream images, unless, of course, these are distorted due to displacements, condensations, and other primary process mechanisms.

I have carried out a number of control experiments in which the subject was given for reexamination, not the tachistoscopically exposed picture, but another one. In these experiments the subject failed to recognize elements of the dream in the picture. In other control experiments I have presented the subject with three pictures, among which was the one exposed, and asked him which one reminded him of his dream. In these experiments the subject was able to select the correct picture.

I have carried out several experiments on myself, and can affirm the feeling of recognition and surprise when the picture is reexamined and certain structures are spotted. The subjective experience of tachistoscopic dreaming is very impressive. When one makes drawings of the dream scenes, they seem to come out of the pencil, almost like automatic writing—the pencil draws by itself. Along with the automatic quality there is a compulsive need to put in or omit certain elements.

It will be recalled that in both experiments I and III, that which the subjects perceived consciously after tachistoscopic exposure appeared to have some connection with their subsequent dreams. In seeing the three girls in bathing suits, one holding a camera as though taking a picture, the subject hinted at the voyeuristic–exhibitionistic nature of the dream to come. It might be suggested that what he saw represented a defense (projection) against his own voyeuristic impulses, and that for this reason he was able to permit these particular percepts to enter consciousness. Similarly, Subject J's avoidance of the "bottom" of the picture and her seeing only the spired dome, represented her defense against looking at her own castrated "bottom." She was able to permit the dome to enter consciousness because it represented the penis which she so much wanted to see when she looked at her "bottom" in the mirror. Pötzl also pointed out that there was some connection between what was consciously seen and the subsequent dream.

I have not paid special attention to the spoken word in these experimental dreams, and have not been able to track them down to their day residue sources. As is well known, Freud (1900) was insistent that the spoken word was always connected with verbal day residues of the preceding day, although, as has been discussed, he did not extend this principle to cover visual images in the dream. The results of experiment II, involving the click of the shutter and the "shot" in the dream, suggest that preconsciously perceived auditory percepts may play the same role in dreams as preconsciously perceived visual percepts.

One of the important additions I made to Pötzl's technique was the attempt at systematic reexamination, not only of the tachistoscopically exposed picture, but also of all the visual scenes surrounding the experiment. It has been shown that many visual elements from these scenes are preconsciously perceived and appear in the pictorial form of the dream. Nevertheless, the dreams do appear to be structured principally about the preconsciously perceived portions of the exposed pictures, the visual elements from the surrounding scenes playing a secondary role. The question arises why this should be so, since this brief 1/100 sec exposure is simply one visual impression among thousands of others that occur in any given day. Pötzl explicitly denied that suggestion played a role in his experiments, but he did not carry out the simple control experiment necessary to demonstrate his contention. Such a control experiment would require the presentation of the picture tachistoscopically *without* the subsequent instruction to record the dreams of the following night. Utilizing Pötzl's technique, I have found that in 18 out of 21 experiments, my subjects produced and remembered dreams on the night of

the experiment; many of these subjects had not remembered
dreams for months or years. In control experiments 8 of these
same subjects failed to dream if no instructions were given to
record dreams following exposure of the pictures. These results
indicate that the instruction to record dreams functions as an
indirect but highly effective suggestion to dream and is interpreted as a command to dream about the pictures.

In a number of instances the subjects dreamed about the pictures even when no instructions were given. I believe that the
explanation for the specific structuring about the pictures lies in
the fact that all these dreams are transference dreams and that
the transference preempts the dream process. The experimental
situation, procedure, and instructions activate unconscious wishes
in relation to the experimenter, which are most intensely aroused
at the moment of tachistoscopic exposure, come closest to the sur-
face at this instant, organize the preconsciously perceived visual
field, and prepare the percepts then and there which are later to
be included in the dream. For example, the hospitalized patients
develop certain unconscious wishes connected with the hope of
some magical repayment from the experimenter for cooperation
in the experiment. These unconscious wishes are most intense at
the moment of tachistoscopic exposure, because *this* is the experiment upon which they are based. The preconsciously perceived visual percepts from the pictures, therefore, receive the most intense
cathexis from the unconscious and are drawn into the dream
process.

It may be postulated that those percepts which touch on the
unconscious wish, and the anxieties and conflicts associated with
it, are drawn out of conscious perception, and that a selective and
organizing function of the ego may be involved in this process, as
will be discussed later. If we take experiment III as an example,
we can conceive of this process taking place as follows: At the
moment of tachistoscopic exposure the subject's wish to get well,
represented in the unconscious as a wish for oral restitution of
the breast and/or penis, arouses his oedipal and sibling rivalry
conflicts. As a consequence, he preconsciously perceives (represses) the image of the two men in the lower part of the picture
because these two figures, in conjunction with the three female

figures taken from the "kings," are suitable to represent the triangular oedipal and sibling rivalry conflicts. In the dream the subject becomes identified with one of these men, the rival with the other. It is further postulated that simultaneously with the preconscious perception of these figures, the percepts are subjected to the work of the primary process and the distorting effects of the dream work begin.

The above formulation involves a circular argument since it assumes that because a percept is excluded from consciousness, an active, central, selective process is involved. There are a number of methodological difficulties present in demonstrating this. When a complex picture is exposed for 1/100 sec, a large part of it may be excluded from consciousness, not because of a selective process, but because the perceptual task confronting the subject is beyond his perceptual capacities. Another complicating factor is that more visually prominent structures may be consciously perceived, while less prominent ones are excluded from consciousness. Although the fact of preconscious perception and the important role that preconscious percepts may play in dream formation has been decisively demonstrated, further investigation will be needed to determine the relative influence of central and field factors in preconscious perception. The idea that an active, selective, central process does go on receives support from the experiments with prolonged, 30 sec exposures (see experiment VI, Malamud [1934], and Malamud and Linder [1931]), in which it can be shown that even visually prominent structures may be excluded from conscious perception.

Rosen (1954) has raised the objection that the distortion of the preconscious visual percepts is a consequence of the tachistoscopic nature of the experiment, and has stressed the importance of attention cathexis and temporal span of image presentation. He suggests that subliminal perceptual data with insufficient attention cathexis to reach consciousness in the waking state, due to the brevity of the visual presentation and the consequent attenuation of the necessary attention cathexis to raise these percepts to the level of consciousness, can nevertheless gain the necessary charge for this purpose by borrowing energy from the primary process during sleep. Although the problem of attention cathexis and temporal span needs careful investigation, I do not believe it is the crucial factor in the results obtained. The use of the tachistoscope may enhance the distortion of the percepts, but is not a necessary factor in producing them, as shown by the results of the experiments with prolonged exposure times in which the same types of distortion occur. I do not believe it can be legitimately argued, as Rosen does, that in the one case the perceptual distortions are due to the tachistoscope, and in the other to the assumption that increased temporal span allows time for mobilization of defenses, since in both instances the same types of distortions occur. We cannot assume a priori that defenses, e.g., an active, central, selective process, equivalent to the mechanism of repression, takes time to be mobilized and cannot occur in $1/100$ sec, since too little is known about the speed of mobilization of ego defensive functions.

The problem arises as to whether the primitive perceptual process revealed in these experiments plays a role in normal, spontaneous dream formation. It seems unlikely that the experimental situation and procedure add anything new to nature, but they may well exaggerate and caricature certain processes that go on normally. Some of the findings, such as the incident with the words *Baby Ruth Harris,* suggest that natural tachistoscopiclike processes play a role in normal dreaming. The experimental procedure may also load the process of dream formation in the direction of the utilization of external visual percepts, since the indirect suggestion to record dreams acts as a command to dream about the exposed picture. However, there is no reason to deny the possibility that at least some normal dreams may make use of external visual percepts, especially preconscious ones, in a very similar manner. Also, it is worth pointing out that several subjects structured their dreams around preconscious percepts derived from the exposed picture even when no suggestion was made to dream.

We need to investigate the role played in dream formation by mental images (associated with what Freud called trains of thought) not based on immediate external perception. Mental images may serve the same function as percepts. Schilder (1942) has pointed out that there is no absolute difference between an image and a percept. The possibility that verbal, optic, or other imagery may be condensed with preconscious percepts in the formation of the manifest content of the dream needs further exploration. In the 16 hours of the average person's waking day there are more than 5 million 1/100 sec intervals, so that an enormous amount of preconscious visual perceptual material is potentially available for dream formation.

Pötzl was a neurologist who undertook his dream experiments not primarily out of interest in the psychology of the dream process, but because he was concerned with visual perception, especially in relation to visual agnosia. He started out with the observation that patients with visual agnosia develop peculiar perceptual impairments. For example, such a patient was shown a bouquet of roses from which a strikingly long asparagus stem stood out. He apprehended only a red rose. Now the bouquet was removed and the patient was asked to establish the color of the collar insignia of some officers who were present. He brought the collar of one of them into his residual visual field and said, "A green necktie pin." This is a correct delayed delivery of a form impression but without reference to its content. Such belatedly developed images are like dream images capable of all kinds of condensations. It is clear that the asparagus was not consciously perceived, but was registered preconsciously and then belatedly appeared in consciousness in the form of the green necktie pin. In an earlier investigation, Pötzl showed that patients with alcoholic hallucinosis excluded from their hallucinations those parts of tachistoscopically exposed pictures that were consciously perceived, but the less the picture was comprehended, the richer became the hallucinations. The hallucinations showed all the characteristics which Freud had demonstrated for the dream. Pötzl was also influenced by work on eidetic images which showed that elements of the stimulus picture may be present in the eidetic image which were not recognized by the subject at the time of exposure, that is, they were preconsciously perceived.

   Pötzl concluded that the visual percepts of indirect vision come to full clarity of form in a delayed and partial manner. He believed that a similar evolutionary process is present in normal subjects, but is held in check by what he called a "central abstraction process." He postulated that in one condition, namely the dreams of normal persons, the abstraction process is excluded, and the primitive, visual evolutionary process is released. He decided to study the formation of dreams with the same tachistoscopic technique he had utilized in his investigation of experimental hallucination formation.

I would like to say a few words about eidetic imagery. Kluever (1934a,b) defines eidetic images as visual, auditory, tactile, etc., phenomena which assume perceptual character and which, like positive or negative afterimages, appear and are seen in perceived space. The object which is first viewed on a screen for a brief period may be eidetically reproduced with almost photographic fidelity. Thus, an eidetic child may without special effort reproduce symbols taken from the Phoenician alphabet. In contrast to this, there is another kind of eidetic imagery, known as the fragmentary type, in which the images undergo all kinds of distortions. Kluever (1934a,b) and Schilder (1926, 1942) have described the following kinds of changes in these images: (1) the stimulus picture is fragmented; (2) the fragments may undergo rotational displacements, translocations of shapes, colors, directions, and movement; (3) there may be changes in size; (4) the transposed material may be elaborated and condensed freely; and (5) elements of the stimulus object may be present in the eidetic image but are not recognized by the subject (this last means that they were preconsciously perceived). It can be seen that eidetic images have the same characteristics which have been mentioned as belonging to the type of preconscious perception revealed in the dream experiments, namely, photographic accuracy combined with great distortion. As an example of the photographic accuracy and preconscious nature of eidetic imagery the following experiment described by Urbantschitsch (1907), the discoverer of eidetic imagery, may be described. He moved a card on which was written a six-figure number quickly across the eyes of a subject. The subject perceived nothing but lines, but was able to recover the number eidetically. This experiment is very much like Subject J's preconscious perception of the words *Harris* and *Baby Ruth*, and comparable to the dream experiments in which words were exposed for 1/200 sec. The types of distortion described by Kluever and Schilder are identical with the spatial rotations, displacements, fragmentations, and condensations undergone by the preconscious visual percepts in the dream experiments.

In making analogies between eidetic imagery, the perceptual distortions in visual agnosia, and the type of preconscious perception involved in dream formation, the possibility presents itself that the distortions found in dream images may occur during the process of perception or in close temporal relation to it. Schilder (1942) states that attitudes of perceiving and representing are not sharply differentiated from one another and that they show intermediate steps; he classes eidetic imagery as such an intermediate step. Jaensch (Schilder, 1942) believed that eidetic images stand between perception and representation.

I would like now to discuss further the possibility that the distortion in dreams may take place in much closer relation to the perceptual process than has been generally conceived. I believe that most analysts are of the opinion that distortion in dreams occurs during the state of sleep, and that Freud was of this opinion too, although in several places he hinted that this was not entirely the case. He pointed out that an unconscious idea is quite incapable of entering into the preconscious and that it can exert its influence only by establishing contact with a harmless idea already belonging to the preconscious, to which it transfers its intensity and by which it allows itself to be *screened*. This is the fact of transference. The transference may leave the idea from the preconscious unaltered or it may force upon this some *modification* derived from the content of the transferred idea. It will be noted that Freud always spoke of unconscious ideas, thoughts, or chains of thought and not of percepts. Further, Freud did not amplify what he meant by "some modification" derived from the content of the transferred idea nor discuss its possible nature or extent. He remarked, however, that the way to distortion was paved by the "transference" of the wish onto recent material.

In this connection certain formulations of Betlheim and Hartmann (1951) are of importance. In their well-known investigation, these authors told stories with erotic content to patients with Korsakoff's syndrome and asked them to repeat them. In the repetition the patients' stories were distorted and symbolically transformed. Betlheim and Hartmann raised the question of how the representation of the memory traces in these cases was to be conceived. They suggested the possibility that in certain cases and for certain contents *even the registration of memories may take place in symbolic form.* They referred to the work of Pötzl in support of this contention and recalled Freud's assertion that at early levels of development the symbol and what it symbolizes are identical.

I believe that the idea, advanced by Betlheim and Hartmann, namely, that the registration of memories may take place in symbolic form, may have a far wider application. I wish to suggest that such registration may be a normal mechanism, occurring in everyone, during the process of dream formation. The preconscious visual percepts discovered by Pötzl may be subjected, not only to symbolic transformation, but to working over by *all of the mechanisms of the primary process.* These transformed percepts may be registered as memory traces and later reactivated in the regression to perception at night. The process of perception, working over by the unconscious wish and the primary process, and the registration as memory trace, may go on practically simultaneously.

In discussing Schilder's concept of the sphere, Rapaport (1951) pointed out that it is much like Freud's primary process. The difference is that Schilder observed mechanisms attributed to the primary process operating not only on material of the unconscious, but also on material on the fringe of consciousness. The mechanisms of the primary process may not be as exclusive to the unconscious as has been thought, according to Rapaport.

In considering the chronological relations of the dream processes, Freud (1900, 1915) divides them into three stages. In the first, the unconscious wish links itself up with the day's residues and effects a "transference" onto them. This first portion of the dream work has already begun *during the day,* under the control of the preconscious. Freud also stated that the "transference" may not occur until a state of sleep has been established. A wish now arises which seeks to force its way along the normal path taken by thought processes, through the preconscious to consciousness. But it comes up against the censorship which is still functioning and to the influence of which it now submits. At this point it takes on the distortion for which the way has already been paved by the "transference" of the wish onto the recent material.

Its further advance is halted by the sleeping state of the preconscious. The dream process consequently enters on a regressive path and is led along that path by the attraction exercised on it by groups of memories. In the course of its regressive path the dream process acquires the attribute of representability. It now has completed the second portion of its zig-zag journey, which probably proceeds all through the night. The first portion was a progressive one, leading from the unconscious scenes or fantasies to the preconscious; the second portion led from the frontier of the censorship back again to perception. When the content of the dream process has become perceptual, it succeeds in drawing attention to itself and in being noticed by consciousness.

There is as yet no direct proof that the preconscious visual percepts are subjected to distortion by the dream work at the moment at which the "transference" of the unconscious wish to them takes place. The only evidence is by analogy with Betlheim and Hartmann's (1951) findings in Korsakoff's syndrome and Pötzl (1917) and Schilder's (1953) findings in visual agnosia, eidetic imagery, and alcoholic hallucinosis. On the other hand, the assumption that all the distortion in dreams goes on during the second stage of the dream process at night has not been demonstrated either. Recently two Japanese investigators, Narusi and Obonai (1953), in a brilliant investigation on the decomposition and fusion of mental images, have demonstrated that transformations in preconscious visual percepts take place immediately after perception. Under deep hypnosis they conditioned the sight of a simple geometrical pattern to the sound of a buzzer. They were able subsequently to arouse the mental image of the figure to hallucinatory intensity by sounding the buzzer. They found that these images underwent progressive decompositions, fusions, fragmentations, displacements, and distortions quite like those noted in Pötzl's experiments. These transformations began immediately after perception and went on for about 2 days, after which the images could no longer be aroused to hallucinatory intensity. These findings raise the question of whether we are dealing here with the natural process of decay and evolution of the mental images; that is, something inherent in the memory traces that underlie them. The transformations that occur in these mental images appear to be simplified versions of primary process mechanisms. We are therefore presented with two alternatives: The primary process mechanisms may reside in these natural transformations and the dream work makes use of them for its own purpose. Or some force which we call the primary process may itself bring about these transformations in the mental images. Further investigation will be needed to elucidate this problem.

In summary, it can be said that the process of dream distortion which Freud ascribed mainly to the second stage may have to be extended to include the first stage of the dream process. Freud equated the Pcpt. system with Cs., but it is clear that Pcpt. also belongs to the system Pcs. He stated that in normal thinking in the waking state the regressive movement never extends beyond the mnemic images; it does not succeed in producing hallucinatory revival of the perceptual images. Although this is true, it is abundantly evident from Pötzl's work that the unconscious wish does regressively influence the perceptual process, but not to the degree of hallucinatory revival.

Many years ago, both Pötzl (1917) and Schilder (1953) formulated the idea that perception developed in stages. Pötzl spoke of an "evolutionary process" and Schilder (1953) stated that the processes of visual perception and apprehension have many part apparatuses, which play into forming the final Gestalt. Each of these part apparatuses consists of hierarchically arranged part functions. Present-day investigators in the field of perception, such as Hebb (1949), have only recently begun to formulate similar conceptions. I refer also to the so-called functionalist school of investigators in the field of perception, which includes Bruner, Werner, Postman, Klein, Brunswik, Frenkel-Brunswik, Krech, McCleary, McGinnies, Witkin, Miller, and others (Blake and Ramsey, 1949; Bruner and Krech, 1949). Among these academic psychologists, perception has moved into a central place, and very active research is going on in which perception has become a meeting ground of general experimental and clinical–social psychology. In the foreground of these investigations is the relation between personality and perception. There has been a shift due to the growing recognition of the projective nature of perception, to the recognition that "the perceived world pattern mirrors the organized need pattern within" (Bruner and Krech, 1949).

In connection with the conception of preconscious perception, the functionalist school has produced evidence that discriminatory perceptual activity can go on below the threshold for conscious recognition. Evidence of this sort has been reported by Miller (1949), McCleary and Lazarus (1949), McGinnies (1949), and Bruner and Postman (1949). McGinnies, for example, exposed tachistoscopically such emotionally toned words as *whore* and *penis* and comparable words neutral in nature. These he presented to his subjects at exposure levels below the report threshold. At each exposure, prior to recognition, the subject's galvanic skin response was recorded and he was asked to report what he had seen. It was found that there was a significantly greater galvanic skin response to the "unrecognized" emotional words than to the "unrecognized" neutral ones. This type of perceptual activity has been called "subception" by McCleary and Lazarus (1949). Bruner and Postman have postulated that there is a hierarchy of response thresholds. They have formulated the concept of "perceptual defense" on the basis of tachistoscopic experiments indicating that anxiety-provoking stimuli may result in the failure to perceive anything. These experiments would appear to present a paradox since they imply that in order to repress or negate a stimulus, the subject must recognize it first for what it is. That is, in order "not to recognize" a stimulus it must first be "recognized." In order to avoid this paradox, Bruner and Postman (1949) postulate a hierarchy of response thresholds in which they assume affective responses may go on at a lower threshold than cognitive ones. This formulation does not, however, explain the type of perception that is observed in our dream experiments. In these it is evident that perception at a cognitive level can go on below the threshold of conscious awareness.

Pötzl's work indicates that there are at least two levels of perception and that stimuli are first perceived preconsciously; only a small part of the percepts taken in are delivered into conscious perception. I think it is justifiable to assume that preconscious perception is an early stage of the perceptual process, ontogenetically speaking, and that with growth of the ego and maturation of the perceptual apparatuses this early, primitive stage of perception becomes inhibited. This early stage of perception is under

the control of the drives and the primary process; later it is replaced by the adult form of reality-oriented perception.

This early form of perception is involved in what Freud (1900)
referred to as the hallucinatory revival of the percept of the need-
gratifying object in his discussion of the meaning of "wish fulfillment." He pointed out that an essential component of the
experience of satisfaction of a need is a particular perception,
the mnemic image of which remains associated thence forward
with the memory trace of the excitation produced by the need.
As a result of this link the next time the need arises, a physical
impulse will at once emerge which will seek to recathect the
mnemic image of the perception and reevoke the original satisfaction. An impulse of this kind is what we call a wish; the reap-
pearance of the perception is the fulfillment of the wish; and the
shortest path to the fulfillment of the wish is a path leading directly from the excitation produced by the need to a complete
cathexis of the perception. Nothing prevents us from assuming
that there was a primitive state of the psychical apparatus in which
this path was actually traversed, that is, in which wishing ended
in hallucinating. The aim of this first psychical activity was to
produce a "perceptual identity"—a repetition of the perception
which was linked with the satisfaction of the need.

In agreement with Linn (1954), preconscious perception may
be thought of as "primary" perception or "primary process"
perception, and is regulated by the pleasure principle, in contrast
to "secondary" or "secondary process" perception, which is under the control of the reality principle. Freud points out that
dreams have preserved for us a sample of the psychical apparatus's primary method of working, a method which was abandoned
as being inefficient, and replaced by the work of the secondary
system whose aim is the "identity of thought," a roundabout path
to wish fulfillment.

Hartmann (1952) states that one characteristic of ego development is the gradual active use by the ego for its own purposes of
primordial forms of dealing with stimuli. Preconscious perception is such a primordial form. With maturation of the perceptual
apparatus, it is gradually inhibited and brought under control of
the ego. Linn (1954) has suggested that there is a discriminating
or scanning function of the ego which exercises a selective action

on the perceptual field. What is accomplished is that there is a delay in the delivery of percepts to consciousness, or an actual suppression of percepts which never reach consciousness, except through a belated hallucinatory revival in dreams or in certain pathological states. Percepts are first delivered preconsciously, scanned and selectively organized by the discriminating function of the ego, and then some of them are permitted to enter consciousness. Preconscious perception would appear to bear a close relationship to the mechanism of repression. Schilder (1953) long ago suggested such a relationship between physiological processes of selectivity and those referred to by the concept *repression*.

The interaction between "primary perception" and the defensive functions of the ego will require extensive investigation, and represents an area in which psychoanalytic ego psychology can find a common meeting ground with experimental and clinical psychological work in the field of personal determinants of perception. Klein (1949), Witkin (1954), and others have been attempting to relate people's characteristic ways of perceiving to their established defensive or coping techniques. Psychoanalysis can make its special contribution through studies of the effect of specific unconscious processes on perception and by establishing the specific adaptational value of a particular mode of perceiving in the total personality economy of each individual.

Much of what has been said above was formulated in different terminology by Pötzl more than 35 years ago. He stated that the primitive perceptual process, which we have called "primary perception," was a normal one, but that it was ordinarily held in check by the work of an "abstraction process." This abstraction process is conceptually equivalent to what Linn (1954) has called a scanning or discriminatory function of the ego. Pötzl asserted that in pathological conditions, such as visual agnosia or alcoholic hallucinosis, there is a centrally conditioned disturbance of this abstraction process and the primitive perceptual process becomes manifest in perceptual distortions and impairments. He stated that only in one condition, the dreams of normal individuals, was the abstraction process inhibited. The release of "primary perception" can be described in terms of a centrally conditioned disturbance of Pötzl's abstraction process, in terms of destruction of higher neural centers with removal of inhibitory forces, or in terms of ego regression with abolition of the scanning or discriminatory function of the ego. The disturbance of a primitive symbolic–perceptual mechanism in organic brain cases showing the syndrome of anosognosia, investigated by Weinstein and Kahn (1950), may be relevant to this discussion.

The results of this investigation can be fitted into Freud's dream theory in the following manner. During the first stage of the dream process the unconscious wish links itself up with the day's residues and effects a "transference" onto them. This stage occurs during the day; the unconscious wish striving to emerge into the preconscious organizes the visual perceptual field associated with the day residue experience. Certain percepts lose their cathexis and are withdrawn from consciousness. This comes about through a discriminating or scanning function of the ego which may be equivalent to what we have in the past called the censorship. These percepts may be subjected to the work of the primary process and undergo distortion at the moment of perception or in close temporal relationship to it. The distorted percepts are stored as memory traces. Unconscious memory images associated with the unconscious wish probably exert a selective action on the visual field and determine which percepts are to be withdrawn from consciousness.

The distortion which begins with perception may continue all during the day as new day residue experiences are drawn into the dream process and additional connections are made with the unconscious wish. During the second stage of the dream process which occurs at night, the unconscious wish is again activated. This is the stage of regression to perception, when the fabric of the dream thoughts is resolved into its raw material. The memory pictures from the past, associated with the dream thoughts, make contact with and are "covered" by the percepts connected with the day residues, some of which have already undergone distortion. Various fusions, condensations, and combinations of memory pictures from the past and visual percepts from the day residues occur; they are aroused to hallucinatory intensity and make up the visual structure of the dream. The third stage of the dream process, secondary elaboration, remains as Freud described it.

In this account it will be noted that no distinction is made between the so-called "progressive" and "regressive" pathways, as described by Freud (1900). I believe that the same "progressive" pathway is followed during the day in the first stage as is followed at night during the movement from the unconscious wish to perception. Only in the first stage is the perceptual field organized by the unconscious wish and primary process, while during the second stage the previously organized percepts are aroused to hallucinatory intensity. This formulation is in accord with Freud's (1925) later ideas about the method in which the perceptual apparatus functions. He originally stated that the pathway from perception to the unconscious was open but that it was impervious in the opposite direction. In his note on the mystic writing pad, he advanced the idea that cathectic innervations are sent out and withdrawn in rapid periodic impulses from within the completely pervious systems Pcpt.-Cs. So long as that system is cathected in this manner, it receives perceptions which are accompanied by consciousness, and passes the excitation on to the unconscious mnemic systems; but as soon as the cathexis is withdrawn, consciousness is extinguished and the functioning of the system comes to a standstill. It is as though the unconscious stretches out feelers, through the medium of the system Pcpt.-Cs., toward the external world and hastily withdraws them as soon as they have sampled the excitations coming from it. In this formulation the unconscious would appear not only to organize the perceptual field by the sampling technique mentioned, but also to control the perceptual system itself and to determine its state of excitability. To this one would have to add that during the state of nonexcitability of the system Pcpt.-Cs., the system Pcpt.-Pcs. may still remain excitable and capable of receiving perceptions.

SUMMARY AND CONCLUSIONS

1. This investigation represents a repetition and extension of Pötzl's classical experiments on dream formation following the tachistoscopic presentation of pictures. In more than 30 experiments Pötzl's chief findings have been confirmed. It was

shown that those portions of the exposed pictures which were excluded from conscious perception went to make up the manifest content of subsequent dreams.

2. It was shown that a remarkable process of preconscious perception is involved in these experiments. This process is characterized both by extreme accuracy of registration and great distortion of the preconsciously perceived percepts.

3. It was shown that some of the preconscious visual percepts retain in the dream the meaning of the object denoted by them, while in other instances the percept is treated as a concrete object divorced from its meaning; these formulations also hold for preconsciously perceived words.

4. The preconscious visual percepts appear not to be available to free association but can be recaptured by confrontation in an experimental situation where control is retained over the visual perceptual field and the dream process itself through the influence of suggestion.

5. The role of suggestion and of transference in these experiments has been discussed. The experimental dreams were shown to be transference dreams and this fact explains why the subjects structure the dream around the tachistoscopically exposed pictures.

6. The preconscious visual process revealed in these experiments was shown to be related to similar perceptual processes found in visual agnosias, eidetic imagery, and alcoholic hallucinosis. The concepts of "primary" and "secondary" perception were discussed. Primary perception is under the influence of the unconscious wish, the drives, and the primary process. It plays an important role in normal dream formation, and becomes manifest in a number of pathological states such as visual agnosia.

7. It was suggested that the process of dream distortion may take place at the moment of and in close temporal relation to perception, and that it may involve the first stage of the dream process, as set forth by Freud, as well as the second stage.

8. The "hierarchy" theory of perception was briefly discussed. The evidence from this investigation supports the theory that perception develops in levels or stages.

9. It was suggested that the dream cannot create a new visual structure any more than it can a new speech. It was shown that memory pictures from the past do not appear in dreams unless "covered" by or "screened" by a recent visual percept and that one of the important functions of day residues is to supply such percepts. Evidence was cited to show that a recent visual impression retains a capacity for hallucinatory revival for several days only.

REFERENCES

Betlheim, S., & Hartmann, H. (1951), On the parapraxes in the Korsakoff psychosis. In: *Organization and Pathology of Thought*, ed. D. Rapaport. New York: Columbia University Press, pp. 288–307.

Blake, R. R., & Ramsey, G. V., Eds. (1949), *Perception: An Approach to Personality*. New York: Ronald Press.

Bruner, J., & Krech, D. (1949), *Perception and Personality*. Durham, NC: Duke University Press.

———— & Postman, L. (1949), Perception, cognition, and behavior. In: *Perception and Personality*, ed. J. Bruner & D. Krech. Durham, NC: Duke University Press.

Fisher, C. (1953a), Studies on the nature of suggestion. Part I: Experimental induction of dreams by direct suggestion. *J. Amer. Psychoanal. Assn.*, 1:222–225.

———— (1953b), Studies on the nature of suggestion. Part II: Experimental induction of dreams by direct suggestion. *J. Amer. Psychoanal. Assn.*, 1:406–437.

Fliess, R. (1953), *The Revival of Interest in the Dream*. New York: International Universities Press.

Freud, S. (1900), The Interpretation of Dreams. *Standard Edition*, 4&5. London: Hogarth Press, 1953.

———— (1915), A metapsychological supplement to the theory of dreams. *Standard Edition*, 14:217–235. London: Hogarth Press, 1957.

———— (1916–1917), Introductory Lectures on Psycho-Analysis. *Standard Edition*, 15&16. London: Hogarth Press, 1961.

———— (1925), A note upon the "mystic" writing pad. *Standard Edition*, 19:225–232. London: Hogarth Press, 1961.

———— (1940), An Outline of Psycho-Analysis. *Standard Edition*, 23:139–207. London: Hogarth Press, 1964.

Hartmann, H. (1952), The mutual influences in the development of ego and id. *The Psychoanalytic Study of the Child*, 7:9–30. New York: International Universities Press.

Hebb, D. O. (1949), *The Organization of Behavior*. New York: John Wiley.

Klein, G. S. (1949), The personal world through perception. In: *Perception and Personality*, ed. R. R. Blake & G. V. Ramsey. New York: Ronald Press, pp. 328–355.

Kluever, H. (Klüver, H.) (1934a), The eidetic type. *Proc. Assn. Res. Nerv. Ment. Dis.*, 14:150–168.

—— (1934b), The eidetic child. In: *Handbook of Child Psychology*, ed. C. Murchison. Worcester, MA: Clark University Press, pp. 699–722.

Kris, E. (1950), On preconscious mental processes. *Psychoanal. Quart.*, 19:540–560.

Linn, L. (1954), The discriminating function of the ego. *Psychoanal. Quart.*, 23:38–47.

Malamud, W. (1934), Dream analysis: Its application in therapy and research in mental diseases. *Arch. Neurol. & Psychiatry*, 31:356–372.

—— Linder, F. E. (1931), Dreams and their relationship to recent impressions. *Arch. Neurol. & Psychiatry*, 25:1081–1099.

McCleary, R. A., & Lazarus, R. S. (1949), Autonomic discrimination without awareness: The interim report. In: *Perception: An Approach to Personality*, ed. R. R. Blake & G. V. Ramsey. New York: Ronald Press, pp. 171–179.

McGinnies, E. (1949), Emotionality and perceptual defense. *Psychol. Rev.*, 56:244–251.

Miller, J. G. (1949), Unconscious processes and perception. In: *Perceptions: An Approach to Personality*, ed. R. R. Blake & G. V. Ramsey. New York: Ronald Press, pp. 258–282.

Narusi, G., & Obonai, T. (1953), Decomposition and fusion of mental images in the drowsy and post-hypnotic hallucinatory state. *J. Clin. & Experiment. Hypnosis*, 1:23–41.

Pötzl, O. (1917), Experimentell erregte Traumbilder in ihren Beziehungen zum indirekten Sehen. *Zeitschr. f. Neurol. & Psychiat.*, 37:278–349.

Rapaport, D. (1951), *Organization and Pathology of Thought*. New York: Columbia University Press.

Rosen, V. (1954), Discussion of paper: The role of preconscious and primitive modes of perception in dream formation, by C. Fisher, read before the New York Psychoanalytic Society, March.

Schilder, P. (1926), Psychoanalyse und Eidetik. *Zeitschr. f. Sexualwiss.*, 13:56–62.

—— (1942), *Mind: Perception and Thought*. New York: Columbia University Press.

—— (1953), *Medical Psychology*. New York: International Universities Press.

Urbantschitsch, V. (1907), *On Subjective Visual Perceptual Images*. Leipzig: Deuticke.

Weinstein, E. A., & Kahn, R. L. (1950), The syndrome of anosognosia. *Archives of Neurology and Psychiatry*, 64:772–791.

Witkin, H. A., Lewis, H. B., Hertzman, M., Machover, K., Meisner, P. B., & Wepner, S. (1954), *Personality through perception: an experimental and clinical study*. NY: Harper (xxvi, 571).

2

DREAMS, IMAGES, AND PERCEPTION: A STUDY OF UNCONSCIOUS–PRECONSCIOUS RELATIONSHIPS (1956)

Charles Fisher

In a recent paper (see chapter 1), I reported the results of a repetition of the classical experiments of Pötzl (1917) on dream production following the tachistoscopic exposure of pictures. These experiments demonstrated that those parts of the tachistoscopically exposed picture which were not consciously perceived appeared extensively in the manifest content of subsequent dreams. I have called the subthreshold process of visual perception involved in these experiments *preconscious perception*. It has been shown that during this process an enormous amount of intricate visual material is taken out of the perceptual field and registered as memory trace in extremely brief time intervals such as $1/100$ or $1/200$ sec.

Based upon Pötzl's original findings, I have shown that in the process of dream formation the preconscious percepts or their memory images undergo the following types of transformations and distortions: (1) translocations or displacements of percepts or parts of percepts; (2) condensations and fusions of percepts

Acknowledgment is made to the Foundations' Fund for Research in Psychiatry for its generous support of this investigation.

with one another; (3) fragmentations such that only certain parts of a percept appear in the manifest dream image; (4) rotational displacements of various kinds, such as mirror reversals or rotations of 90 degrees; (5) changes in size which are analogous to micropsias or macropsias; (6) reduplications and multiplications of the percept analogous to polyopia; (7) ignoring of perspective relations, e.g., a percept in the foreground may be fused with a percept in the background; (8) percepts may appear unchanged and are reproduced in the manifest dream image with photographic fidelity; (9) the preconscious percept may lose the meaning of the object image denoted by it and appear in the dream image with a different meaning attached to it; e.g., a man may be transformed into a cactus plant or a bird may appear as a pillow, etc.; (10) there are changes in shape which are analogous to metamorphopsias.

The above visual mechanisms are utilized by the dream work and some sort of reciprocal relationship exists between them and the unconscious processes which enter into dream formation. I have suggested the possibility that the preconscious visual percepts associated with the day residue experience are worked over by the primary process and the unconscious wish at the moment of tachistoscopic exposure or in close temporal relationship to it. That is, the dream work begins during the day at the moment of perception and the distortion in dreams takes place in much closer relation to the perceptual process than has been generally conceived. There is a widespread opinion that distortion in dreams occurs during the state of sleep, although Freud (1900) hinted that this was not entirely the case. As stated in chapter 1, he pointed out that an unconscious idea is quite incapable of entering into the preconscious and that it can exert its influence only by establishing touch with a harmless idea already belonging to the preconscious, to which it transfers its intensity and by which it allows itself to be *screened*. Freud called this process "transference" and noted that it may leave the idea from the preconscious unaltered or it may force upon this some *modification* derived from the content of the transferred unconscious idea. Freud generally spoke only of unconscious ideas, thoughts, or chains of thought and not of the sensory percepts which might be associated with them. He did not amplify what he meant by "some modification" derived from the content of the transferred idea, or discuss its possible nature or extent. He remarked, however, that the way to distortion was paved by the "transference" of the wish onto recent material.

I have pointed out (chapter 1) that up until the present there is no direct proof that the preconscious visual percepts are subjected to distortion by the dream work at the moment at which the "transference" of the unconscious wish to them takes place. The only evidence is by analogy with Betlheim and Hartmann's findings in their classical paper on Korsakoff's syndrome (1951), and in the work of Pötzl (1917), Schilder (1953), and Kluever (1962) on visual agnosia, eidetic imagery, and hallucinations. In all these investigations there is evidence that preconsciously perceived visual or auditory percepts or their memory traces may undergo the kinds of transformations and distortions listed above in close temporal relationship to the process of perception.

In this paper I would like to present some preliminary results of an investigation on image formation which, I believe, throws new light on the chronological relations of the dream process and on the problem of dream distortion. These results also have implications for the theory of image formation, the thought process, and the relationship between the primary and secondary processes.

METHOD

In 1924, Allers and Teler reported a series of ingenious experiments somewhat related to Pötzl's. They utilized the following technique: They exposed pictures through a tachistoscope to normal subjects at a speed of 1/25 sec. The following day they performed a word association test utilizing as stimulus words the names of objects in the exposed picture which had not been consciously perceived. In addition, and this is the crucial part of the method, they requested their subjects to report and make drawings of any images which developed between the stimulus and response words. They were able to demonstrate in a very striking way that the unnoticed parts of the pictures, that is, the memory images of the preconscious percepts, appeared in the images in an almost photographic way so that some of the subjects were able to attain an almost complete reconstruction of the tachistoscopically exposed picture.

This paper will be largely concerned with a report of a repetition of the experiments of Allers and Teler. The following modifications of their method were made: The exposure time was decreased from 40 to 10 msec, the latter exposure time being that used by Pötzl. In addition to performing the word association test the day after the tachistoscopic exposure of the picture, in some experiments it was begun within a minute or two after such exposure and in other experiments as late as 72 hours after exposure. Following the word association test the stimulus picture was gradually reexposed at increasing time intervals starting at $1/100$ sec and continuing until the parts of the picture which had not been perceived on original exposure were clearly recognized. The stimulus picture was then exposed for an unlimited time during which the subject was asked to find correspondences between the drawings of his images and elements in the picture.

The Allers and Teler experiment was controlled in the following manner: The same word association test was carried out following the exposure of a *blank slide*. The subject was asked to make drawings of his images and these were subsequently compared with the pictures used for exposure in the noncontrol experiments.

Both male and female ward patients from the Department of Psychiatry, Mount Sinai Hospital, were used as subjects. As a whole, this was a very sick group of patients, most of them suffering from serious psychosomatic illnesses, such as asthma, anorexia nervosa, and ulcerative colitis. All of them were psychologically very ill also, either having severe pregenital character-neurotic disturbances or borderline psychotic features. Often the patients were too ill to cooperate in the experiments or dropped out having once started. Because of this, the investigation to be reported leaves much to be desired in the way of experimental design and control. The investigation, therefore, is more in the nature of a pilot study, and any conclusions derived from it are to be considered preliminary and tentative.

The tachistoscope used in these experiments consisted of an SVE projector attached to which was a Rapax camera shutter which permitted exposures varying from 1/200 sec to 1 sec. The tachistoscope was placed about 12 ft from a screen in the center of which was a red fixation dot about ¹/₂ in in diameter. Thirty-five mm Kodachrome slides were projected on the screen. The experiments were carried out in a partially darkened room, the illumination being kept constant.

RESULTS

The following protocols are representative of the results obtained in the Allers and Teler experiment:

EXPERIMENT I. ILLUSTRATING THE APPEARANCE OF PRECONSCIOUS PERCEPTS IN IMAGE FORMATION 72 HOURS AFTER REGISTRATION

A picture (Figure 1.1), the "Three Kings," was exposed for 1/100 sec to a 35-year-old female suffering from epilepsy of about 3 years duration. She was intelligent and had considerable artistic ability.

Response to Exposure
The subject saw three children standing on a seashore as illustrated in Figure 2.1. The three children evidently represent a transformation of the three kings with a reversal of size relationships.

Word Association Test
The word association test was carried out 72 hours after exposure.
The first stimulus word *desert* and the response *sand*. The subject visualized herself riding on horseback across the hot sand. She felt thirsty, dismounted from her horse, and was disappointed at the barren vastness of the desert. She made the drawing shown in Figure 2.2 to illustrate this scene. The horse's head with the flowing mane at the left of the picture, the large cactus at the right of the picture, and the setting sun are especially to be noted.

Figure 2.1. *Experiment I.* The subject's drawing of three children standing on the seashore representing what she saw following tachistoscopic exposure of Figure 1.1.

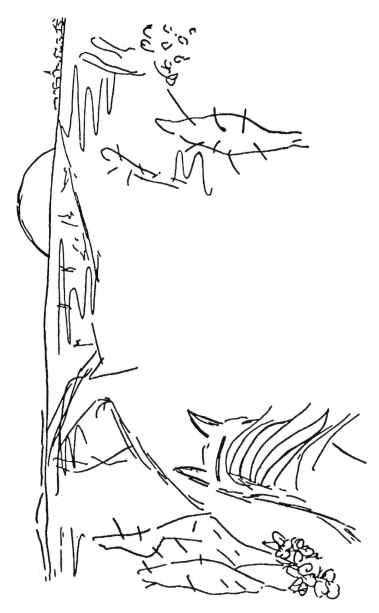

Figure 2.2. *Experiment I.* The subject's drawing of her image of the desert scene. The horse's head with the flowing mane, the large cactus on the right, and the setting sun are especially to be noted. The image in general takes in the lower half of the exposed picture.

Result of Reexposure

When the picture of the three kings was reexposed, the subject noted with great surprise that it contained a concealed and embedded outline of a horse's head in a location corresponding exactly to that in which she had drawn her image of it. Figure 2.3 is an outline drawing of those portions of the exposed picture that were incorporated into the image. She remarked that she had been very much bothered when she drew the horse's head because although she had wanted to draw it in profile she felt compelled to draw it as seen from the rear. Up to this point the subject was still unaware that the picture of the three kings had been exposed when she saw the beach scene with the three children. With great surprise, she recognized that she had transformed the figure of the man on the right into the large cactus plant. She agreed that she had transformed the red fixation point on the screen into the setting sun. She had seen the latter as pinkish red in her imagination and had had the idea of putting in a full sun since she thought of the scene as taking place at high noon. The transformation into a half sun probably took place because at the time of exposure, the fixation dot was bisected by one of the horizontal lines in the exposed picture in such a manner that the lower half was more shadowy than the upper half.

Word Association Test

The stimulus word *sightseers* elicited the response *English tourists*. The subject remembered a group of English tourists disembarking from a boat in Spain. They were dressed in a ludicrous fashion in a variety of brilliant colors. They wore dark glasses and carried cameras and guidebooks. She drew the picture shown in Figure 2.4 (see page 107) to illustrate. This is a quite good and witty caricature showing a small, thin woman on the left carrying a guidebook, a tall skinny man in the middle carrying a camera, and a large fat woman on the right.

Result of Reexposure

The subject spontaneously reported that the English sightseers corresponded to the figures of the three kings. She noted that in drawing them they got progressively larger as she drew them from

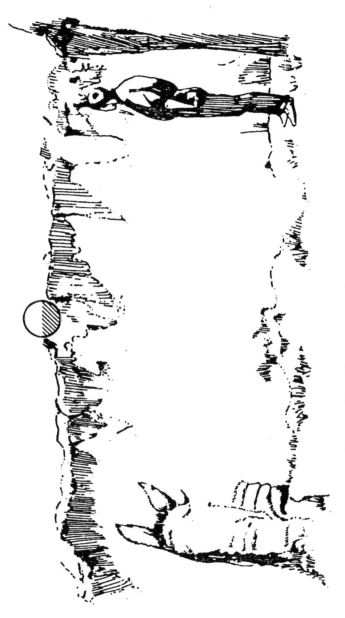

Figure 2.3. *(For legend to Figure 2.3, see page 106.)*

Legend to Figure 2.3

Figure 2.3. *Experiment I.* This is an outline drawing of those portions of Figure 1.1 that were incorporated into the subject's image of the desert scene. Close resemblance between the horse's head and the subject's drawing of her image of it is to be noted. The striations in the rock were transformed into the image of the horse's mane. The resemblance between the large cactus plant and the form of the man on the right is also striking.

left to right. The triangle on the hat of the woman on the right corresponded to the triangular rock on the head of the king on the right. The skirt of this figure corresponded to the shadow on the lower part of this king. The formation of the arm and the bust resemble very closely similar formations on the king. The arm and the hand are especially striking since in the picture of the king the hand seems to be buried as it extends from back to front, and the subject remarked on the similarity of the drawing of the hand and the fact that she had made the hand very small. With respect to the female figure on the left, she pointed to the similarity between the sunglasses and the eye region of the corresponding king. The shape of the hat, the guidebook, the shorts, the forward bending posture, all have correspondences in the exposed picture. At the bottom of the picture there are some perpendicular lines which bear a strong resemblance to the straight skinny legs of the figure. In connection with the middle figure in her drawing, she pointed to the correspondences between the slope of the forehead and the form of the top rock on the middle king. There are also correspondences between the sunglasses, the prominent ear, the chin, the Adam's apple, the body, the legs, and the camera, and similar structures in the exposed picture.

Word Association Test

The fifth stimulus word *mound* elicited the response *anthill.* She imaged an ant struggling with a blade of grass all out of proportion to its own size, and stated that to the ant it was as large as a

Figure 2.4. *Experiment I.* The subject's drawing of the English tourists. These represent transformations of the three kings.

redwood tree would be to a man. The subject made the drawing shown in Figure 2.5 to illustrate this. There are two ants in the picture and between them a strange-looking butterfly. Although the subject spoke about the ant struggling with the blade of grass, she actually drew a curious-looking butterfly.

Result of Reexposure

The subject remarked that the creature in her drawing looked like a Disney butterfly and not a blade of grass. She believed that she had derived this from a shadow that very much resembled it, located above the head of the man on the right as shown in Figure 2.6. She noted that its tail was somewhat darker than the rest of

Figure 2.5. *Experiment I.* The subject's drawing of her image of the anthill. The butterfly represents a transformation of the outline shown above the head of the man on the right in Figure 2.6. Probably the ants are distortions of the figures of the two men.

the creature, corresponding with the way she had made her own drawing. She noted also that the tail extended close to the mouth of the man in the same way as one end of her butterfly touched the mouth of one of the ants. She believed that she had converted the two men into the two ants. This would involve a 90 degree rotation of the butterfly from the vertical to the horizontal and the transposition of the figures of the two men.

Comment
    This experiment illustrates the striking preservation of the memory images of the preconscious percepts which appeared in a photographic way 72 hours after exposure of the picture. In addition to the photographic preservation, a number of striking

Figure 2.6. *Experiment I.* This is an outline drawing of the man and the shadow above his head taken from Figure 1.1 which were transformed into the image of the ant and the butterfly in Figure 2.5.

transformations and distortions are to be noted, e.g., the transformation of the man on the right into the large cactus plant. That is, the figure lost its object meaning of "man" and was given the meaning of "cactus." The transformations of the three kings into English tourists and the 90 degree rotation and other spatial transformations in the image of the ants are of interest.

EXPERIMENT II. ILLUSTRATING THE PROCESS OF CONDENSATION IN IMAGE FORMATION

The subject for this experiment was a 50-year-old woman who was on the ward because of asthma of about 3 years duration. She is a woman of considerable intelligence and character who managed to survive 4 years in Nazi concentration camps, including Auschwitz. She has some artistic ability.

A picture of the Tower of London was tachistoscopically exposed for 1/100 sec (Figure 1.12, p. 63).

Result of Exposure

The subject saw a city street showing a tower on the left, a man and a woman in the right foreground, and a row of houses in the background, as illustrated by her drawing (Figure 2.7). It will be noted that she did not perceive the most striking thing in the picture, namely, the sentry in the red coat. Also she failed to notice the half-concealed figure of the man behind the woman in the right foreground.

Word Association Test

The word association test was begun immediately after the above exposure. The fifth stimulus word *guard* elicited the response word *tower*. The images which developed related to the memory of an Austrian border guard standing near a sentry box. In making her drawing of these images (Figure 2.8), the subject showed considerable confusion. She felt compelled to draw the gun on the back of the guard in spite of the fact that she had in mind something dirty and black such as chimney cleaners carry. She drew a peculiar extension on the back of the cap the guard

Figure 2.7. *Experiment II.* The subject's drawing of what she saw following tachistoscopic exposure. Subject failed to perceive the sentry in the red coat and the half-concealed figure of the man behind the woman in the right foreground.

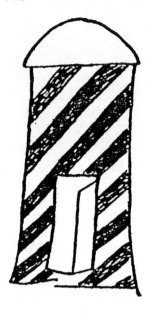

Figure 2.8. *Experiment II.* The subject's drawing of her image of the Austrian border guard and the sentry box. Note the gun on the back of the guard and the peculiar extension on the back of the cap that the guard is wearing.

was wearing, again in an automatic way as though she felt compelled to do so and was puzzled by what she drew.

Result of Reexposure

After the word association experiment was completed and the picture reexposed, the subject compared her drawing with the picture and indicated that it was derived from the parts of the picture which she had not consciously perceived, in the following manner: The sentry box represented a condensation of the main tower in the background with the arched part of the sentry box of the stimulus picture. The sentry was composed of elements taken from the percepts of the man and the woman in the right foreground of the picture, as shown in Figure 2.9.

The subject noticed with great surprise the half-concealed figure of the man. She stated that the barrel of the gun was derived

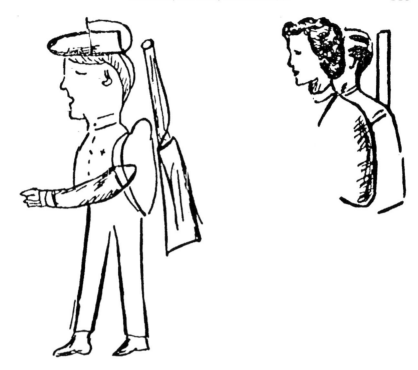

Figure 2.9. *Experiment II.* On the left is the subject's drawing of her image of the guard and on the right the elements from the exposed picture from which it was derived.

from the area behind the man which shows a black shadow. This shadow was fused with the upper arm and elbow of the man to form the gun. The extension on the back of the cap was derived from the back of the man's head. It was as if the two heads were fused together in the formation of the cap. The front part of the cap corresponds to the woman's hair formation. The ear of the man was displaced forward. The jacket may have been derived from the sentry in the picture. Her drawing, therefore, represents a condensation of elements from the woman, the man, and the sentry and reveals a fusion of preconscious percepts derived from the picture with the memory image of the Austrian border guard from the past. It is to be noted that this remarkable process of condensation took place within minutes of the tachistoscopic exposure of the picture.

EXPERIMENT III. ILLUSTRATING IGNORING OF SIZE AND PERSPECTIVE
RELATIONSHIPS RELATED TO THE PRECONSCIOUS PERCEPTS APPEARING
IN IMAGE FORMATION

The picture of the Tower of London (Figure 1.1) was exposed
for 1/100 sec to an intelligent woman of 39, a professional por-
trait painter of considerable talent. The subject was on the ward
because of a gall bladder syndrome associated with intense pain
of many years duration. On the day of this experiment the subject
was experiencing great pain and was not very cooperative. Following exposure of the picture she reported that she did not see
anything. In spite of this, the word association test was carried out.

Word Association Test
The second stimulus word *gun* elicited the response *bird*. The
subject imaged two dead birds, pheasants or grouse, hanging by
their legs from a nail. They had been shot and she described
them in these words: "The way hunters bring them home and
hang them." The subject made a sketch showing the two hanging
birds as illustrated by the figure on the left in Figure 2.10.

Result of Reexposure
The subject indicated that she had composed the hanging birds
out of certain percepts taken from the exposed picture, as illustrated by the figures on the right in Figure 2.10. The birds' legs and
the lower parts of their bodies corresponded to the overlapping
towers in the background of the picture. The main part of the bodies was taken from certain shadows and lines on the gray stone
buildings while the heads and necks of the birds were derived from
certain structures in the fence in the foreground. In composing the
pheasants, both size and perspective relationships were ignored.

Comment
Although at the time of the exposure, the subject saw nothing
and it was unclear whether she had paid any attention to the
picture, there appears to have been extensive preconscious registration of percepts. It is of interest that four subjects, including
this one, have produced dreams or images in response to exposure of the picture of the Tower of London that have to do with

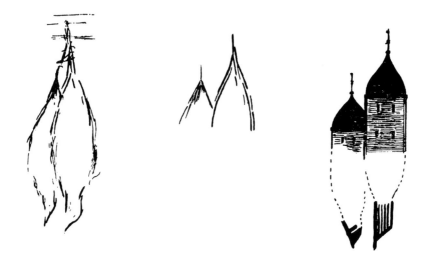

Figure 2.10. *Experiment III.* The hanging birds on the left were derived from the overlapping towers in the background and the structures in the fence in the foreground of Figure 1.12.

hangings and executions. None of them recognized the picture as the Tower of London at the time of exposure but all of them knew of it as a place where hangings and executions had taken place at one time. It must be assumed that this associative connection was made preconsciously and the percepts transformed in accordance with it during the dream or image work.

EXPERIMENT IV. ILLUSTRATING THE COMPULSIVE EMERGENCE OF A PRECONSCIOUS PERCEPT DURING IMAGE FORMATION

In this experiment a structurally much simpler picture was utilized (Figure 2.11) because the experiments described above may be justifiably criticized on the grounds that they involve the exposure of very complex pictures in which any sort of percept may be found. This picture shows two gentle cats and a parakeet. It will be noted that the parakeet faces to the right and that its beak is turned toward, and is in close approximation to, the face of

Figure 2.11. The picture of the two cats and the parakeet which was used for tachistoscopic exposures in experiments IV and V.

the cat on the right. A colored version of this picture was exposed for 1/100 sec to the subject used in experiment II. In the colored picture the parakeet has a blue body and wings speckled with black and gray. The cats are white and gray with black spots.

Result of Exposure

The subject stated that she saw two white and black animals which resembled dogs or pigs. She did not see the parakeet. In

Figure 2.12. *Experiment IV.* The subject's drawing of the mammal–bird creature seen following tachistoscopic exposure.

her drawing of what she had seen (Figure 2.12) there are two curious looking animals. They appear to be fusions of the cats and the bird. The bodies are mammal-like but the heads and tails are birdlike. The subject had great difficulty in making this drawing and compulsively drew it in ways that she did not intend.

Word Association Test

The fourth stimulus word *cat* elicited the response *mouse.* The drawing of her images showed a cat and a mouse (Figure 2.13). While drawing the cat the subject became confused and remarked that the cat was more like a hawk pursuing a bird. She drew a curious birdlike mammal which has a bird's head, tail feathers, and four legs with catlike claws.

In the above experiment it can be seen that there was a compulsive emergence of the bird into consciousness, an image which fused with that of the cat, resulting in the subject's inability to draw a cat. Instead, an image that condensed the features of both bird and cat was produced. The next experiment illustrates this process in an even more clear-cut manner.

The second stimulus word *dog* elicited the response *house.* The subject reported that she imagined a watchdog standing in front

Figure 2.13. *Experiment IV*. The subject's drawing of the cat on the left and the mouse on the right. Note the inclusion of birdlike features in the drawing of the cat.

Figure 2.14. *Experiment IV*. The subject's drawing of the watchdog standing in front of the house. Note the resemblance of the dog to a bird
and to the parakeet.

of a house (Figure 2.14). She attempted to draw the dog but in
spite of all her efforts she found herself drawing a bird. The
animal she drew had a bird's head, body, long tail feathers, and
closely resembled the body and general configuration of the parakeet in the exposed picture. The subject became very confused,
wanted to know what was wrong, could not understand why she
continued to draw a bird, stating that she knew very well how to
draw a dog and had done so many times. In this experiment the
compulsive emergence of the image of the bird was much more
complete and there were fewer features of a mammal in the drawing than in the *cat–mouse* experiment.

Result of Reexposure

When the subject was permitted to compare her drawing with the picture of the two cats she suddenly noticed the resemblance between her drawing of the bird-dog and the parakeet. It is of interest that she initially referred to the parakeet as a pigeon. She recalled that her father kept pigeons and that though he was a misanthrope he loved animals. Sometimes he used to kill the pigeons to eat. She manifested the greatest surprise and said it was fantastic since she never had any idea that the bird she drew had been derived from the originally exposed picture. The house she drew corresponded very closely to her father's pigeon house which she remembered from her childhood, although at the time she drew the house she did not connect it with the memory of the pigeon house.

The subject recalled that her father kept a vicious, wild wolf dog that acted as a watchdog. This animal once bit her and at various times had bitten every member of the family. She also recalled that her father kept a cat that frequently slept in the pigeon house and that he would chase it out to prevent it from harming the pigeons. The birdlike dog which the subject drew seems, therefore, to represent a condensation of the memory images of the watchdog and the pigeons with the parakeet in the exposed picture.

When the picture of the two cats was reexposed at gradually increasing time periods, the parakeet was not fully identified until the exposure period had reached 2 sec. This exposure period represents one of the more prolonged ones obtained for the recognition of the percept of the bird among quite a series of subjects. This result may be an indication of perceptual blocking or defense, but at the present time the statistical data at hand are too confusing to enable one to maintain this position with confidence. The recognition time for the parakeet of 2 sec indicates that the original exposure time of 1/100 sec was approximately 200 times below recognition threshold.

I can summarize only briefly the extremely interesting psychological material which emerged during this experiment. The seemingly innocent and idyllic picture of the two cats and the parakeet has reactivated in all the subjects to whom it was exposed very deep-seated oral–sadistic material based on the idea that cats prey on birds. In this particular experiment, the picture reacti-vated very painful memories of the subject's concentration camp experiences and the terrible hunger and starvation associated with them. There was a compulsive emergence, in spite of the subject's conscious intentions, of an aggressively oral bird–mam-mal creature. There were many fusions and condensations of the cats with the bird, evidently related to unconscious conflicts hav-ing to do with eating and being eaten and showing confusion between the eater and the eaten, the biter and the bitten, the aggressor and the one aggressed against. All of this was associated with the emergence of certain childhood material as revealed, for instance, in the drawing of the bird-watchdog and the pigeon house which related to the subject's sadistic, misanthropic father and the memories of his killing birds. The material brought out clearly the identification with the aggressor noted by many ob-servers in the prisoners of Nazi concentration camps. There were indications that the cruel Nazi guards were unconsciously associ-ated in her mind with memories of her sadistic father.

EXPERIMENT V. ILLUSTRATING THE DUPLICATION OR MULTIPLICATION OF PRECONSCIOUSLY PERCEIVED PERCEPTS IN IMAGE FORMATION

The same picture of the two cats and the parakeet was exposed for 1/100 sec to the same subject used in experiment III.

Result of Exposure
The subject recognized the two cats but did not see the para-keet. She made the drawing shown in Figure 2.15 which is almost a photographic reproduction of the two cats.

Word Association Test
A word association test was given immediately after the expo-sure of the picture. The second stimulus word *feathers* elicited the response word *pillow*. It is to be noted that this response was obtained no later than 5 minutes after the exposure of the pic-ture. Her image was of a pillow open at one end with the feathers pouring out. She drew the picture shown in Figure 2.16 to illus-trate this.

Figure 2.15. *Experiment V.* The subject's drawing of what she saw following tachistoscopic exposure of Figure 2.11.

Figure 2.16. *Experiment V.* The subject's drawing of the pillow and feathers. Note that the pillow has the form of a bird and the outline of the feathers resembles a cat. A second bird can be seen below the body of the first.

It was noted that the subject had quite unconsciously drawn the pillow in the shape of a bird which resembled and faced in the same direction as the parakeet in the exposed picture. A second and smaller bird can be seen under the body of the first one. The subject stated that the area representing the feathers resembled the body and face of the cat. These illustrations were made by the subject herself and it was she who pointed out these resemblances. At the time she made the original drawings she had no idea that she was incorporating into them the features of the bird and the cat; her intention was to draw the pillow and feathers.

This experiment demonstrates the very interesting phenomenon of reduplication or multiplication of a preconscious percept. The subject unconsciously reduplicated birds and cats all through her drawings. The birds were noted to resemble the parakeet and all of them were facing to the right. In certain drawings as many as a half dozen or more birds can be found. The tenth stimulus word *robin redbreast* elicited the response *nest*. The subject made the drawing shown in Figure 2.17 to illustrate her images. The

Figure 2.17. *Experiment V.* The subject's drawing of the nest resting on a branch. Note the concealed birds in the branch.

picture shows two birds concealed in the branch on which a nest is resting.

The ninth stimulus word *sick* elicited the response *patient.* She made the drawing shown in Figure 2.18 to illustrate her image.

Figure 2.18. *Experiment V.* The subject's drawing of the sick patient in bed. Note the concealed birds in the folds of the blanket.

Again, several concealed birds may be seen in the folds of the blanket around the child's neck. The subject also stated that the

shape of the pillow resembled the outline of the body of one of
the cats.

Result of Reexposure

During the reexposure period the percept of the parakeet began to reemerge but was not clearly identified until 1 sec. At
1/10 sec the subject saw the area occupied by the parakeet as a
spot of spilled milk between the two cats. She made the drawing

Figure 2.19. *Experiment V.* The subject's drawing of what she saw during
the reexposure period at 1/10 sec. Note the concealed bird in the
representation of the spilled milk.

shown in Figure 2.19 to illustrate what she had seen. Although
she was completely unaware of it, she had drawn several concealed birds in her representation of the spilled milk.

The drawings of the images in relation to the exposed picture and the subject's comments and behavior during the experiment permit one to interpret the images which intruded themselves into consciousness in much the same way as one interprets dreams. It is possible to arrive at the latent unconscious meaning behind these images. In the various drawings the subject made there were several repetitions of the theme of a bird or a child's head against the body of the cat. There seemed to be reversals between the bird and cat, that is, between child and mother. In the *pillow–feathers* image the bird may be thought of as nursing on the cat's body and the white feathers may represent milk. During the reexposure period the bird itself was seen as a spot of milk since concealed birds could be found in the drawing of the spilled milk. In this instance, the cat appears to be eating the bird which becomes the milk. The associative material and the drawings suggest that the subject was struggling with intense oral strivings, that there was confusion in her mind between activity and passivity, between mother and child, between male and female. During the reexposure period as the oral material became more apparent, the subject began showing increasing anxiety accompanied by a marked deterioration in the quality of her drawings.

It is worthy of note that this patient's symptoms were referrable to her gastrointestinal tract, that there was a history of manic–depressive insanity in the family, one brother having committed suicide, and that the patient had very early been forced into a mothering role within the family both because of her mother's incompetence and her father's open incestuous attachment to her.

COMBINED PÖTZL AND ALLERS EXPERIMENT

Five experiments have been performed which combine the Pötzl and Allers techniques in the following manner: A picture was exposed followed by the immediate carrying out of the word association test and the recording of drawings of the images produced. After the completion of the word association test, a suggestion to dream was given. The next day, the subject was requested to make drawings of the manifest dream images. These drawings were then compared with those of the images which had developed during the word association test and both were then compared with the tachistoscopically exposed picture. Although these preliminary experiments are not yet conclusive, in several instances it has been possible to demonstrate that some of the images which developed during the word association test appeared in identical form in the manifest images of the dream of the following night.

Summary of Results

The Allers and Teler experiment was performed 18 times using 12 subjects. The experiments discussed above are representative of the kind of positive results obtained in 11 instances. Negative results were obtained in seven experiments. In these instances it could not be demonstrated that memory images of the percepts taken from the exposed picture appeared in the images which developed during the word association test. This failure may have been due to the following factors: (1) The subject was either anxious, hostile, or uncooperative and therefore unable to engage in fantasy. In these instances, the response times during the word association test were rapid but the associations tended to be superficial and impersonal. Further observation of these negative results may help throw some light on the factors blocking free fantasy. (2) The subjects' drawing ability was so poor that they were unable to make accurate representations of their images. Therefore, comparison with elements in the exposed picture was impossible. (3) Because of unknown factors the memory images of the percepts from the exposed picture did not emerge from the preconscious into consciousness.

In six control experiments in which a blank slide was used, no correspondences of a convincing nature were noted by the subjects between the drawings of their images and elements in the pictures that were used for exposure in the noncontrol experiments.

Discussion

The results of these experiments show in a very striking way that the preconscious memory images of percepts from the tachistoscopically exposed picture appear in the images that develop during the word association test. The proof of this lies in the close similarity in form and structure between the images that the subject draws and elements from the exposed picture, e.g., the horse's head in experiment I. Additional proof is furnished by the fact that very often the subject locates the drawings of his image on the page in a position which corresponds very closely to the location of the percept in the exposed picture from which it was taken. Even in those cases where displacements and rotations take place, a certain spatial similarity can be demonstrated, as in the instance of the butterfly which was located close to both the head of the man and the ant.

A few observations in connection with the results of the word association experiments are of interest. At least three types of behavior were observed in the subjects while they made the drawings of their images: (1) The subject may unconsciously draw the memory image of the preconscious percept while he is attempting to draw something else. For example, the subject who demonstrated the multiplication of the memory image of the birds included a number of concealed birds in her drawings. (2) In making the drawings various degrees of automaticity or compulsiveness develop in different subjects. The subject, for example, may intend to draw a horse's head in profile and finds that the pencil draws a back view of the horse's head. (3) A more extreme degree of compulsiveness may develop as in the example of the subject who found herself drawing a bird in spite of all her efforts to draw a dog. These drawing disturbances are associated with varying degrees of confusion, wonder, and astonishment. These observations may be relevant to some remarks that Kris (1950, 1952) has made about doodling. He pointed out that doodling comes extraordinarily close to "preconscious fantasy thinking" from which it differs insofar as only visual images are involved. Some observations of Urbantschitsch (1918) on unconscious visual impressions and their appearance in eidetic images are of interest in this connection. He waved a card with a five-digit number before the eyes of a subject so rapidly that nothing was seen. Within minutes suitable subjects were able to obtain the number in their eidetic images. In several instances, one digit of a six-digit number failed to appear eidetically in spite of all the subject's efforts. Subsequently, the subject noted a disturbance in the writing of the missed digit which she compulsively formed in the same manner as it had appeared in the number used in the eidetic experiment, although at the time she had no idea that there was any relationship to the experiment. This compulsive writing of the digit in a certain form resembles closely observations made on the subject who compulsively drew the bird instead of the dog.

In the above discussion I have laid emphasis on the transformations and distortions undergone by the preconscious percepts or their memory images during the process of dream or image formation. Just as striking, however, is the photographic preservation of many of the percepts. For example, in the experiment involving the horse's head, the memory image of this percept was perceived in great detail and appeared in the subject's imagery three days after the original tachistoscopic exposure. I have evidence that such delayed appearance of the memory image of the preconscious percept in dreams or imagery can be as long as 5 or 6 days. These findings suggest that Freud's (1900) contention that a day residue cannot be older than 24 hours is probably not correct.

I would now like to discuss the implications of the results of this investigation as they relate to the process of dream formation and distortion and especially to the chronological relations of the dream process. In this discussion it is important to make a sharp distinction between perception and memory, between percept and memory image. In connection with the Pötzl experiment, I have previously stated (chapter 1) that the various transformations and distortions observed may take place during the process of perception or in close temporal relationship to it. This statement needs to be clarified. That a subthreshold process of preconscious perception takes place has been amply demonstrated. It has not been proven, however, that the transformations and distortions noted take place during the perceptual act itself. Three possibilities exist: (1) Transformations may take place during the perceptual act itself; that is, during the 1/100 sec period of tachistoscopic exposure. (2) Transformations may occur in the memory images resulting from the registration of the preconscious percepts. Or (3) transformations may take place both in the percept and the memory image. It should be emphasized that one cannot speak of perception in the absence of a stimulus object. The perceptual aspect of these experiments is involved only in the 1/100 sec during which the subject is confronted with the stimulus object. Subsequent to this any changes that take place must occur in the memory image. Although the decision as to the occurrence of transformations in the percept or the memory image cannot be made on the basis of these experiments, the older workers in this field, such as Pötzl, Schilder, and Kluever, appear to have assumed that they may take place during the perceptual act itself. They have based this conclusion on the fact that they observed the same kinds of transformations and distortions in patients with visual impairments due to occipital lobe lesions (visual agnosia), as Pötzl reported in his dream experiments. These transformations and distortions could be demonstrated to take place during the process of perception. More recent work by Bender and Teuber (1947, 1948), on visual impairments following occipital lobe injuries, had demonstrated such changes as fusions of disparate lines, displacements, and changes in size, shape, and perspective similar to those found in the dream and imagery experiments. The older workers also made analogies with the transformations that occur in eidetic imagery. In this instance, however, one cannot speak of transformations during perception since eidetic images are observed following the removal of the stimulus object and therefore involve changes in the memory images. The investigation of Narusi and Obonai (1953) on the decomposition and fusion of mental images also involves transformations of memory images rather than percepts.

The most significant result of the Allers experiment is the clear demonstration that at least some of our conscious mental images go through a process of development which appears to be identical to that of the pictorial images of dreams. I have previously presented evidence that the manifest dream images are formed by condensation of recent memory images of preconscious percepts derived from a tachistoscopically exposed picture with past memory images associated with the unconscious wish. It would appear that the images which emerge into consciousness during the word association test are formed in precisely the same manner. Furthermore, it has been shown, contrary to Allers's contention, that the preconscious percepts or their memory images involved in the formation of these conscious images undergo the same types of distortion and transformation as those that enter into the formation of the manifest dream images. I have suggested that the dream work and dream distortion begin during the day in close temporal relationship to the perceptual process associated with the day residue experience. The process of preconscious perception and the working over of the percepts or their memory images by the unconscious wish and the primary process may take place in an extremely brief time interval. The Allers experiments tend to confirm this formulation since they show that the preconscious percepts or their memory images may appear in consciousness transformed and distorted by all the mechanisms noted *within minutes* after tachistoscopic exposure.

Preliminary results indicate that identical images may appear during the combined Allers–Pötzl experiment, e.g., during the word association test, and in subsequent dreams the same images may emerge. This would tend to demonstrate that the process of dream distortion begins with the transformation of the percept or its memory image in close temporal relationship to the registration of the memory trace. During the night, in what Freud (1900) called the "regression to perception," these latent images are aroused to hallucinatory intensity and enter into the manifest visual structure of the dream. I do not wish to imply that manifest dream images are derived solely from the reactivation of these latent preconscious memory images, but only that these may play a significant role in dream formation. Transformations and distortions which begin in the percept or its memory trace may continue all during the day and night as new day residue experiences and the sensory percepts associated with them are drawn into the dream process and additional connections made with the unconscious wish.

I have previously (chapter 1) proposed certain modifications of Freud's dream theory. In the light of the above discussion these modifications need additional clarification. During the first stage of the dream process the unconscious wish links itself up with the day's residues and effects a "transference" onto them. This stage may occur during the day. The unconscious wish striving to emerge into the preconscious makes contact with the visual percepts, conscious and preconscious (or their memory traces), which are associated with the day residue experience. Certain percepts lose their cathexis, are withdrawn from consciousness, and become preconscious. This may take place through the agency of a discriminating or scanning function of the ego or may occur because of perceptual field factors. That is, the stimulus conditions may be such that a percept is not able to attain consciousness because the task is beyond the perceptual capacities of the subject. The latter alternative has been amply demonstrated in the dream and imagery experiments. For example, no subject was able consciously to perceive the parakeet in 1/100 sec. All subjects needed 1/10 sec and generally much longer. It has not yet been conclusively demonstrated that there exists a central, selective, organizing principle that causes percepts to be withheld from consciousness and that acts either through the ego or from the side of the unconscious wish. The preconscious percepts or their memory traces appear to be subjected to the work of the primary process in close temporal relationship to the day residue experience.

To continue with a modification of Freud's dream theory, the distortions and transformations which begin in the percept or its memory trace may continue on during the day as new day residue experiences are drawn into the dream process and additional connections are made with the unconscious wish. During the second stage of the dream process which occurs at night, the unconscious wish is again activated. This is the stage of "regression to perception" when, as Freud (1900) put it, "the fabric of the dream thoughts is resolved into its raw material." The memory pictures from the past associated with the dream thoughts make contact with and are "covered" by the recent memory images of the percepts connected with the day residue, some of which have already undergone distortion. Various fusions, condensations, and combinations with memory pictures from the past and memory images of visual percepts from the day residues occur; they are aroused to hallucinatory intensity and make up the visual structure of the dream.

Through the combined Pötzl–Allers experiment, we are able to obtain a glimpse into the psychic apparatus and follow the course of development of the dream from the perceptual act associated with the day residue experience through the memory trace of the percept, to note the transformations and distortions that take place in the percept or the memory image, and finally to relate the manifest dream image to the preconscious percept and its memory trace.

The results of this investigation confirm the findings of Allers and Teler that between the stimulus and response words of the association test images arise which are derived from the preconsciously perceived parts of the tachistoscopically exposed picture. Contrary to their contention, I have found that these images appear to be derived from the same kinds of transformations of the preconscious percepts or their memory traces as are involved in the formation of dream images. These transformations therefore may fall under the influence of the unconscious wish, the primary process, and the drives. Indeed, these conscious images do not appear to differ from dream images except that they occur in the waking state and do not attain hallucinatory intensity. Some of them may even have the fantastic quality of dream images. In the context of the experimental situation, the associations and behavior of the subject while making his drawings, and from the content of the drawings themselves, these conscious memory images may frequently be interpreted in the same manner as dreams. These findings suggest that the unconscious wish and the primary process may invade and mold some aspects of our conscious imagery and point to the kind of transition between the primary and secondary process which has been stressed by Schilder (1953) and Rapaport (1951).[1]

---

[1]In discussing this matter, Rapaport (1951) stated, "Schilder, impressed by the continuous transition of primary and secondary processes (the former predominant in unconscious, the latter in conscious thought) sought to unite the two by considering them simply different stages of the evaluation of thoughts as they evolve from the "sphere." Thus he considered all thoughts as conscious, differing from each other only in the degree of evolution. What he could not so subsume he considered "not psychological," i.e., physiological.—In final analysis this appears to be a purely terminological difference, once the continuous transition between primary- and secondary-process thought—to express which Schilder developed his terminology—is accepted as a fact of observation. It is at present so accepted, and expressible in the usual concepts of psychoanalysis" (p. 502).

Freud (1915) did not set up as sharp a dichotomy between the systems Ucs. and Pcs. as is generally supposed. In his paper on "The Unconscious" he discussed the communications between the two systems and pointed out that the Ucs. is continued into its so-called derivatives, is accessible to the influence of life, perpetually acts upon the Pcs., and even is, on its part, capable of influence by the latter system. He stated that, "The content of the system Pcs. or (Cs.) is derived partly from the instinctual life (through the medium of the Ucs.), and partly from perception" (p. 194). This formulation fits in with the idea that the conscious images under discussion are derived from the fusion of recent memory images of preconscious percepts with past memory images associated with the unconscious wish.

Rapaport (1951) has pointed out that wishful thoughts, superstitions, biases, and other autisms that slip into our everyday thought are usually not recognized as autistic. He states, "Our theoretical understanding of autism within 'the normal range' is extremely limited. Part of our ignorance is due to our inadequate knowledge of preconscious processes" (p. 416). I believe that the mechanisms described in the formation of some of our conscious imagery provide a theoretical basis for the understanding of autism (primary process thinking) within "the normal range" and throws additional light on the relationship of unconscious to preconscious processes. I would suggest that the process of imagery formation reported occurs normally and may be regarded as autism within the normal range.[2]

I do not believe that the emergence of these images into consciousness, images which have a dreamlike, primary process quality, are merely artifacts of the experimental situation. There is no reason to believe that this imagery process cannot occur normally. We need only consider that the perceptual apparatus is constantly bombarded by subthreshold stimuli and that some of these stimuli are preconsciously registered and may subsequently be involved in image formation, if experiences occur analogous to the

---

[2]In discussing the cardinal differentiating characteristic of the primary and secondary process Rapaport (1951) states, "The claim is often made that ordered thinking (secondary process) is distinguished from the primary thought process by unity of structure and absence of contradiction. This claim sounds sufficiently plausible and convincing yet exact definitions for "unity" and "lack of contradiction" are lacking. If everyday conversation is to be considered a sample of ordered thought processes, it has yet to be shown in what sense it fulfills these two criteria" (p. 178).

word association test; that is, one may normally hear a word which will reactivate the preconscious memory trace and produce an image. Imagery experiments which confirm this have been reported by Narusi and Obonai (1953).

The results of the dream and imagery experiments have important implications for the theory of perception. In discussing these implications it is necessary to make a distinction between the empirically proven fact of subthreshold preconscious perception, and the various transformations and distortions which have been described. Although it is very possible that the latter may occur during the perceptual act itself, this has not been decisively demonstrated for perception but only for the memory image. Basing his conclusions largely on Pötzl's findings and on observations made on patients with occipital lobe injuries, Schilder (1953), however, was of the opinion that percepts go through a phasic development involving the transformations and distortions mentioned before the final viridical percept is delivered into consciousness. He pointed out that the patient with visual agnosia registers individual parts of percepts but is unable to make a whole of them. These unintegrated parts undergo spatial displacements and condensations. The process by which the unintegrated parts are integrated, that is, the synthetic function of perception, is not demonstrable in consciousness. Schilder considered it to be somatic, believed that it had several stages, and was not to be considered unconscious in the dynamic psychological sense. As Rapaport (1951) has pointed out, Schilder wrestled with the issue generally bypassed in the psychoanalytic literature that not all of what is not conscious is unconscious in the dynamic sense; some of it is organic to begin with and some of it is structuralized and as such is not amenable to psychological analysis. This implies that, if the transformations and distortions which have been described are considered, with Schilder, to take place during the act of perception, they are not to be thought of as being produced by dynamic psychological forces but as somatic physiological processes inherent in the visual apparatus itself. This is what Schilder meant when he stated that though affects and drives play a most significant role in perception, there are aspects of perception which are totally independent of any drive. Kluever

(1942) came to similar conclusions. He emphasized that the perceptual transformations and distortions under consideration are not brought about by emotional or unconscious factors but exist independently as basic mechanisms of the visual system. He pointed out that it is one thing to admit that objects perceived as reduplicated or multiplied may have emotional significance; it is an entirely different thing to assert that polyopia is created by emotional factors. If visuospatial factors lead to the condensation of several persons into one, the condensation, Kluever asserted, is not necessarily created by an affective factor, although once created it may serve as a vehicle for affective needs.

The interrelationship between the primary process and the transformations and distortions which take place in the perceptual and memory apparatuses needs further investigation. We are confronted with the apparent paradox that these ego apparatuses function in their primitive and preliminary stages in a primary process-like manner and in their more mature reality-oriented phases in a secondary process manner. This seeming paradox is heightened by the fact that the primary process is generally considered to belong to the id. Insofar, however, as the perceptual and memory mechanisms under consideration, interacting with the drives, seem to belong to the primary process or may actually be the primary process itself, it would make more sense to consider the latter to be the thought process of the primitive or archaic ego. Glover (1949) has pointed out that, strictly speaking, organized elements of the mind such as percepts and memory images should not be considered as belonging to the id. This formulation stresses the thought aspect of the primary process rather than the energic aspect. Primitive phases of the operation of the ego apparatuses of perception and memory can be thought of as permitting the freer discharge of drive energies and of entering into drive-organized image and dream formation.

The sharp differentiation which Kluever makes between the action of the drives and the visuospatial factors that he considers to be basic and independent mechanisms inherent in the visual system, is probably not tenable, since in the living organism these mechanisms are continuously interacting with the drives. However, it seems useful to stress the possibility that in the physiological maturation of the ego apparatuses of perception and memory

there are early phases during which they are capable of functioning only in certain ways, e.g., with condensations and displacements. These early mechanisms do not disappear with further
development of the organism but are simply overlaid by more
mature, reality-oriented perceptual and memory processes. Furthermore, these early phases persist in the organism and constitute preliminary stages in the development of reality-oriented
percepts and memories. Kluever's formulation for the perceptual
system is lent support by the investigation of Narusi and Obonai
(1953) on the memory system. Their results indicated that primary process-like decompositions and fusions of mental images
occur within the memory trace as normal physiological processes
of decay.

Although Freud (1912) stated that unconsciousness is a regular
and inevitable phase in the processes constituting our mental
activity he excluded perception from this generalization. He
stated that:

> Every mental act begins as an unconscious one, and it may either
> remain so or go on developing into consciousness, according as it
> meets with resistance or not. . . . A rough but not inadequate anal-
> ogy to the supposed relation of conscious to unconscious activity
> might be drawn from the field of ordinary photography. The first
> stage of the photograph is the "negative"; every photographic
> picture has to pass through the "negative process," and some of
> these negatives which have held good in examination are admitted
> to the "positive process" ending in the picture [264].

The results of the dream and imagery experiments suggest that
perception, like any other mental activity, first goes through an
unconscious phase before the percept appears in consciousness.
Both Frink (1918) and Dalbiez (1941) a good many years ago
noted that Freud had been inconsistent in his formulations
about perception.

The relationship of the transformations described as taking
place in the preconsciously perceived percept or its memory image to similar changes that have been reported in eidetic imagery
experiments needs further investigation. Both Urbantschitsch
(1918) and Kluever (1942) have reported that in eidetic experiments stimulus objects that are not consciously perceived may

appear in subsequent eidetic images. Kluever has shown that in these so-called "fragmentary" eidetic images the memory image of the stimulus object undergoes the same kind of transformations as are found in Pötzl's dream experiments. It is possible that in these imagery experiments we are dealing with the residual eidetic capacity latent in all of us.

In connection with the conception of preconscious perception, the so-called functionalist school of psychologists has produced some striking evidence that discriminatory perceptual activity can take place below the threshold for conscious recognition. Such evidence has been reported by Miller (1949), McCleary and Lazarus (1949), McGinnies (1949), and Bruner and Postman (1949). As described in chapter 1 McGinnies exposed a number of tabooed words such as *whore* and *penis* through a tachistoscope, and comparable words neutral in nature, at exposure levels below the report threshold. At each exposure, prior to recognition, the subject's galvanic skin response was recorded and he was asked to report what he had seen. It was found that there was a significantly greater galvanic skin response to the "unrecognized" tabooed words than to the "unrecognized" neutral ones. McCleary and Lazarus (1949) repeated this experiment utilizing nonsense syllables in place of meaningful words. For some of these an unpleasant disturbing affect was established by accompanying a brief exposure of the syllable with an electric shock. It was found that galvanic skin responses were greater for the previously shocked syllables than they were for those that had not been accompanied earlier by shock. Even though the exposure was too brief to permit a correct perception, the word elicited the autonomic response which had been conditioned to it. The authors concluded that at tachistoscopic exposure speeds too rapid for conscious discrimination the subject is still capable of responding in a discriminatory way. They designated this type of subthreshold perceptual activity, "subception." In a recent critical review of current theories of perception, Allport (1955) stated that if the findings of McCleary and Lazarus are further confirmed they might take place as an important and theoretical challenging phenomenon. Allport goes on to state:

> The results of this remarkable study seem to show that there is a very rapid and unconscious, but nevertheless "veridical," level of

perception that goes on at the same time as the slower and less accurate process of consciously perceiving, and that with exposures below the ordinary threshold of visual perception this rapid unconscious activity gives us, in quite appropriate emotional terms, the significance of an object which, though it stimulates us through our eyes, we do not visually perceive. Such a possibility does violence to our settled habit of conceiving the organism as a being that is stimulated, then perceives or recognizes, and then reacts. Could it be that meaning from past experience is a deep-lying physiological process or ensemble of events geared in with bodily activities, and that *conscious* perception is only a superficial part or manifestation of this meaning-ensemble? This interpretation, in any case, would enable us to get away from the anthropomorphic notion of some inner perceiving agent that first "cognizes" and then sends out the appropriate signals for response [p. 319].

The concept of subception has been related by the psychologists to the conception of "perceptual defense." That is, the idea that verbal stimuli that are emotionally disturbing or threatening tend to require a longer recognition time than neutral words, to be so misperceived as radically to alter their form or meaning, and to arouse their characteristic emotional reactions even before they are recognized. The work in this area has presented the dilemma that in order to suppress or negate a stimulus the subject must recognize it first for what it is. That is, in order "not to recognize" a stimulus it must first be "recognized." Allport states that the theory of perceptual defense results in the weirdest kinds of nonsense. If the defending agent is something inside the individual that controls perceptual activity we have a manikin theory or a homunculus situation. Allport deplores the specter of a "subconscious pre-perceiving perceiver" and has made ironic comments in such terms as "the inference here is that the subject represses, delays, or distorts his perception of something that he has not yet seen so that he will not see it." Or, "it was as though they had recognized the words in exposure times too short for them to be recognized." Bruner and Postman (1949) have made similar comments; for example, "the experiments suggest to the guileless investigator the image of a super-ego peering through a Judas eye scanning incoming percepts in order to decide which shall be permitted into consciousness" (p. 25).

The above quotations from Allport indicate the kind of dilemma the academic psychologists have fallen into in face of growing evidence that some kind of subthreshold perception takes place. The results of the dream and imagery experiments demonstrate clearly that perception on a *cognitive* level can go on preconsciously. The confusion of the psychologists is due to the failure to accept the psychoanalytic concepts of the Ucs. and the Pcs. The integration of these concepts into their thinking would do away with the necessity for a manikin theory. The evidence suggests that the perceptual process goes through a complex development involving a preliminary phase which takes place below the threshold of consciousness. Perception and consciousness are not equivalent, and the question raised by Allport in the above quotation, as to whether *conscious* perception is only a superficial part or manifestation of a deep-lying physiological meaning-ensemble, may have to be answered in the affirmative. Instead of thinking in terms of an organism as a being that is stimulated, then perceives or recognizes, and then reacts, the evidence suggests that it would be preferable to think in terms of an organism that is stimulated, then reacts, and finally part of the reaction appears as conscious perception. Consciousness and response are not identical and not all response involves consciousness. Adaptive response can involve preconscious and unconscious processes also. The concept of preconscious perception does not imply an anthropomorphic notion of a "subconscious pre-perceiving perceiver." It merely assumes that much of the psychic response of the organism, including perceptual response, takes place outside of awareness and that conscious perception represents the final synthesis of a complex perceptual act, as Schilder (1953) pointed out many years ago.

I will not here enter into a discussion of the concept of perceptual defense. I agree with Allport that if the defense is considered to be carried out by the perceptual process itself we would have to believe that a physiological process operates in such a way as to prevent itself from operating. Allport believes that the evidence for this proposition is not convincing. However, the concept of subception or preconscious perception on a *cognitive* level will have to find its place in perceptual theory. Without resorting to a manikin theory this concept may provide for a mediating mechanism whereby values, needs, and inner directive states may influence what is delivered into conscious perception, either by acceleration or delay, and provide a basis for "perceptual defense," or "perceptual vigilance" respectively.

Summary

1. This investigation confirms the findings of Allers and Teler that the memory images of preconsciously perceived parts of tachistoscopically exposed pictures subsequently appear in conscious images.
2. The results show that the preconscious percepts or the memory images or both are subject to the same kinds of transformations and distortions as has been previously reported in Pötzl's dream experiments.
3. It has been shown that the memory images of the preconscious percepts may appear in conscious imagery within minutes after tachistoscopic exposure or as long as 72 hours afterward.
4. Preliminary experiments indicate that the images which may arise in consciousness during the Allers and Teler word association experiment may be identical to the images which subsequently occur in the manifest content of the dream.
5. The results throw light on the process of dream distortion and the chronological relations of dream formation. They indicate the process of dream distortion (working over by the unconscious wish and the primary process) commences in close temporal relationship to the laying down of the memory trace of the preconscious percept associated with the day residue experience.
6. The implications of this investigation for: (a) the psychology of the dream process; (b) image formation; (c) the thought process; (d) the relation of the primary to the secondary process; and (e) perceptual theory were discussed.

References

Allers, R., & Teler, J. (1924), Uber die Verwertung unbemerkter Eindrucke bei Assoziationen. *Zeitschr. f. Neurol. & Psychiat.*, 89:492–513.

Allport, F. H. (1955), *Theories of Perception and the Concept of Structure*. New York: John Wiley.

Bender, M. B., & Teuber, H. L. (1947), Spatial organization of visual perception following injury to the brain. Part I. *Arch. Neurol. & Psychiat.*, 58:721–739.

——— ——— (1948), Spatial organization of visual perception following injury to the brain. Part II. *Arch. Neurol. & Psychiat.*, 59:39–62.

Betlheim, S., & Hartmann, H. (1951), On Parapraxes in the Korsakowschen Psychose. In: *Organization and Pathology of Thought*, ed. D. Rapaport. New York: Columbia University Press.

——— Postman, L. (1949), Perception, cognition and behavior. In: *Perception and Personality*, ed. J. Bruner & D. Krech. Durham, NC: Duke University Press, pp. 14–31.

Dalbiez, R. (1941), *Psychoanalytic Method and the Doctrine of Freud*. London: Longmans, Green.

Freud, S. (1900), The Interpretation of Dreams. *Standard Edition*, 4&5. London: Hogarth Press, 1953.

——— (1912), A note on the unconscious in psycho-analysis. *Standard Edition*, 12:255–266. London: Hogarth Press, 1958.

——— (1915), The unconscious. *Standard Edition*, 14:159–204. London: Hogarth Press, 1957.

Frink, H. (1918), *Morbid Fears and Compulsions: Their Psychology and Psychoanalytic Treatment*. New York: Moffat, Yard.

Glover, E. (1949), *Psycho-Analysis*. London, New York: Staples Press.

Kluever, H. (1962), Mechanisms of hallucination. In: *Studies in Personality*. New York: McGraw-Hill, pp. 175–207.

Kris, E. (1950), On preconscious mental processes. *Psychoanal. Quart.*, 19:540–560.

——— (1952), *Psychoanalytic Explorations in Art*. New York: International Universities Press.

McCleary, R. A., & Lazarus, R. S. (1949), Autonomic discrimination without awareness: The interim report. In: *Perception: An Approach to Personality*, ed. R. R. Blake & G. V. Ramsey. New York: Ronald Press, pp. 171–179.

McGinnies, E. (1949), Emotionality and perceptual defense. *Psychol. Rev.*, 56:244–251.

Miller, J. G. (1949), Unconscious processes and perception. In: *Perception: An Approach to Personality*, ed. R. R. Blake & G. V. Ramsey. New York: Ronald Press, pp. 258–282.

Narusi, G., & Obonai, T. (1953), Decomposition and fusion of mental images in the drowsy and post-hypnotic hallucinatory state. *J. Clin. & Experiment. Hypnosis*, 1:23–41.

Pötzl, O. (1917), Experimentell erregte Traumbilder in ihren Beziehungen zum indirekten Sehen. *Zeitschr. f. Neurol. & Psychiat.*, 37:278–349.

——— Allers, R., & Teler, J. (1960), Preconscious Stimulation in Dreams. Associations and Images. *Psychological Issues*, Monogr. 7. New York: International Universities Press.

Rapaport, D., Ed. (1951), *Organization and Pathology of Thought*. New York: Columbia University Press.

Schilder, P. (1953), *Medical Psychology*, tr. & ed. D. Rapaport. New York: International Universities Press.

Urbantschitsch, V. (1918), Uber unbewusste Gesichtseindrücke und deren Auftreten im subjektiven optischen Anschauungsbilde. *Zeitschr. f. Neurol. & Psychiat.*, 41:170–182.

3

A STUDY OF THE PRELIMINARY STAGES OF THE CONSTRUCTION OF DREAMS AND IMAGES (1957)

Charles Fisher

In this paper, I will present the results of some combined dream-imagery experiments utilizing certain methodological refinements of both the Pötzl and Allers techniques. The experiments to be reported involve both the study of image formation and the relationship of the latter to the construction of manifest dream images.

Method

The process of image formation was investigated by a modification of the method utilized by Allers and Teler (1924). These investigators exposed pictures through a tachistoscope to normal subjects. The following day they performed a word association test utilizing as stimulus words the names of objects in the exposed picture that had not been consciously perceived. In addition, and this is the crucial part of the method, they requested

This research has been aided by a grant from the Foundations' Fund for Research in Psychiatry.

their subjects to report and make drawings of any images which developed between the stimulus and response words. They were able to demonstrate in a very striking way that the unnoticed parts of the pictures, that is, the memory images of the preconscious percepts, appear in subsequent conscious imagery in an almost photographic way so that some of the subjects were able to attain a nearly complete reconstruction of the tachistoscopically exposed picture.

There are certain methodological objections to the above procedure. In the first place, it can be maintained that the images that develop are responses to the stimulus word of the association test and bear no relationship to the hypothesized registration of a preconscious percept. Furthermore, one cannot be sure that he is selecting the proper words for the association test. The second objection is that the pictures used for exposure, both by Allers and Teler and by myself in my preliminary experiments, were so complex that a multiplicity of percepts may be found in them. To obviate these objections, the following modifications in the method were introduced. The word association test following tachistoscopic exposure was abandoned altogether. Instead, subjects were simply asked to close their eyes and to describe and to make drawings of any images that developed.[1] It can be seen that

---

[1] A more detailed description of the actual experimental procedure utilized follows. Prior to the actual experimentation, an attempt was made with all subjects to establish a good rapport. With patient subjects, for example, this was done by discussing their illness, progress of therapy in the hospital, etc. The establishment of a good rapport is important because the relationship between the subject and experimenter is an important variable influencing the kind of results obtained. The experiments were carried out in a partially darkened room. The rom was $15^1/2 \times 9 \times 12$ ft. The only illumination was that emanating from the SVE projector used as the tachistoscope. This projector contains a 300w, 120v General Electric bulb. The projector was located on a table 11 ft from a white, beaded wall screen 38 x 28 in; 35 mm slides were used and the projected image of these slides just about covered the screen. The tachistoscope used was the same simple apparatus previously described, e.g., a SVE projector with an attached Rapax camera shutter, permitting exposures of 1 sec, 1/2 sec, 1/5, 1/10, 1/25, 1/50, 1/100 and 1/200 sec. In all experiments to be reported an exposure time of 1/100 sec was utilized with the exception of experiment II. In this latter experiment, a different tachistoscope, which I will not describe at this time, was utilized, permitting an exposure time of 1/500 sec but with a much more intense illumination.

During the experiment the subject sat behind the tachistoscope, placing him about 15 ft from the screen.

As to the nature of the experiments, the subjects were told only that they had to do with producing images and making drawings of them. Following tachistoscopic exposure and the report of what was seen, the subject was instructed as follows: "I would like you to relax, close your eyes, and let any images that will come into your mind. Try not to be critical and tell me the first thing that comes to your mind." After giving his description

this constitutes a process of "free imagery" analogous to "free association." The free imagery was begun *within minutes* after tachistoscopic exposure in most of the experiments to be reported and was continued for a period of 30 to 60 min. In addition, much simpler pictures were utilized for tachistoscopic exposure, such as geometrical forms (triangle, star), four-digit numbers, or words. In all experiments, exposure conditions were so arranged, by utilizing very lightly drawn figures, that only a flash of light was seen.

Following the period of free imagery, the stimulus picture was gradually reexposed at increasing time intervals starting at 1/100 sec, the usual time of tachistoscopic exposure, and continuing until the picture, which had not been perceived on original exposure, was clearly recognized. This provided a comparison between the duration of the tachistoscopic exposure and the recognition time for the picture under the conditions of the experiment. From these figures, it is possible to get a rough estimate of how far below threshold the original exposure took place. For example, if the original exposure was at 1/100 sec, and the threshold of recognition at 1/2 sec, then the original exposure time was estimated at 50 times below threshold. Following the reexposure period, the subject was requested to make comparisons between the drawings of his images and the number, words, or picture now exposed upon the screen.

Ward patients from the Department of Psychiatry, Mt. Sinai Hospital, members of the hospital personnel, some of the staff doctors, two 9-year-old children, and several personal friends were used as subjects.

With a few subjects, two types of control experiments were done: (1) A blank slide was exposed followed by a period of free imagery; (2) free images were obtained without any stimulus whatever, even that of a blank slide. This was done in order to compare the types of imagery which developed under these conditions with that resulting from the exposure of a figure or picture.

---

of the image, the subject was asked to make a drawing of it. These instructions were not rigidly followed and many of the subjects were given a great deal of encouragement and reassurance.

These experiments are of a preliminary, exploratory nature and should properly be considered a pilot study. A carefully designed and controlled experiment permitting the quantifying of results and a sounder validation is now under way.

RESULTS

To date, 18 free imagery experiments have been carried out. The following protocols will illustrate the types of positive results obtained in 15 instances.

EXPERIMENT I

The number 6481 was tachistoscopically exposed for 1/100 sec to a female ward patient and the subject saw only a flash of light.

During the free imagery period, immediately following tachistoscopic exposure, the subject produced 21 images and made drawings of them. The first drawing that the subject made was of a double row of pearls (Figure 3.1). This, the subject indicated later, during the reexposure period, resembled a row of 8's. The second drawing was of a spiral, described as looking very much like a 6 lying on its side. The third drawing (Figure 3.2) shows a similar spiral crossed by four diagonal lines. During the reexposure period, the subject stated that the spiral represented a 6 rotated 180 degrees, that the four straight lines were either reduplications of the number 1 or a primitive representation of the number 4. By the ninth drawing (Figure 3.2), the subject began to make a series of squares that overlapped at one corner. In this drawing, eight such overlapping squares can be seen. At the points of overlap of the squares, the lines form concealed 4's. The subject made numerous drawings of this sort and by the sixteenth drawing, two clearly drawn 4's broke away from the general mass of overlapping squares and were drawn in isolation.

While she was making these drawings, the subject had no idea that they resembled numbers. Instead, she thought of the double row of pearls as typewriter keys and of the spiral 6-like figures as

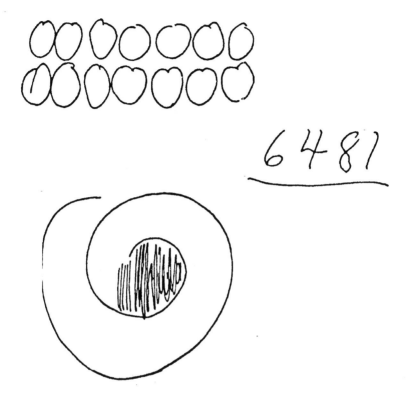

Figure 3.1. *Experiment I*. Double row of pearls representing multiple 8's, above. Spiral, representing a 6 lying on its side, below.

snails. Only after it was pointed out to her during the reexposure period did she notice that they resembled numbers. It would appear that the four numbers, not consciously perceived at the time of tachistoscopic exposure, appeared in her images transformed into geometrical forms which, although they clearly resembled numbers, were assigned quite different meanings by the subject. All the 21 images seem to bear some relationship to the exposed numbers in their formal properties. Certain characteristics of these images are worth noting. First, the tendency toward multiplication of the images is very striking. Not a single 8 appears, but a whole row of them. The same is true of the 4 which was continuously reduplicated in the overlapping squares. Second, there appears to be a tendency toward a more primitive representation of number so that the 4 is represented by four straight

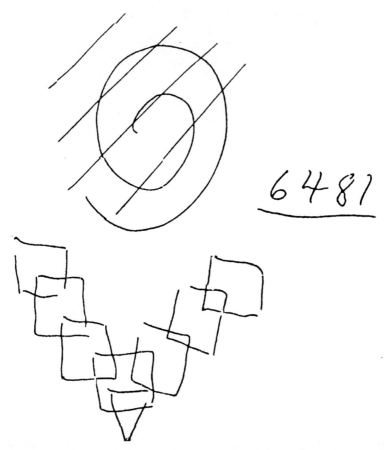

Figure 3.2. *Experiment I.* Spiral on the top representing a reversed 6 crossed by four lines representing the number 4, above. Series of over-lapping squares showing concealed 4's below.

lines much in the way that children count on their fingers. Also, it is possible that the 4 is represented as a multiple of the squares themselves. Third, there is a tendency toward the reversal of figures so that the 6 appeared upside down rotated 180 degrees. The 4's too were drawn in mirror image, i.e., reversed. Fourth, the intricacy of the means of representing the numbers is very striking. The many drawings composed of multiple overlapping squares are a good example of this. It is of great interest that this sort of geometrical pattern is highly suitable for the representation of concealed 4's. I might add that at least one other subject utilized a similar method of representation of the number 4.

EXPERIMENT II

The same number, 6481 was tachistoscopically exposed for 1/500 sec to one of the hospital personnel who reported that he saw nothing. During the period of free imagery, he produced

Figure 3.3. *Experiment II.* Fencelike structure showing three concealed 4's.

and drew seven images. The first image (Figure 3.3) was of some white boards, a sort of fencelike structure. The subject drew four boards in such a manner that the top of the fence contained three clear-cut concealed 4's. The second image was represented

Figure 3.4. *Experiment II.* The Indian goddess Siva. The six arms represent the number 6; the right upper arm the number 1; the two left upper arms a reversed 4; the body and head the number 8.

by a drawing of the Indian goddess Siva (Figure 3.4). This extremely interesting drawing shows a squatting figure with six arms. During the reexposure period, the subject stated that the six arms stood for the number 6 and the head and trunk of the squatting figure for the number 8. The two upper arms on the left were crossed in such a way as to produce a reversed 4. The uppermost straight arm on the right, the subject stated, stood for the number 1. In this manner, all four digits of the number 6481 had been represented in the drawing. Again, in this experiment we see some of the same mechanisms at work as were described in the first experiment; namely, the multiplication of images, the concealed 4's, the lack of awareness that numbers were being drawn, the reversal of images, the representation of the number 6 in a primitive form, that is, by six lines, and the images appearing with meanings attached to them independent of the concept of number. It is to be noted that the concealed 4's were contained in overlapping V-shaped forms.

EXPERIMENT III

The same number, 6481, was exposed to another subject, one of the staff physicians who saw only a faint vertical line. During the period of free imagery, immediately following exposure, the subject produced 23 images; and the following day, in a second period of free imagery, he produced 13 more. Most of his images consisted of variations of an angular pattern that appeared to be connected with the angle of the number 4. The eighth image consisted of two overlapping acute angles forming a clear-cut 4 at their point of intersection, shown in the top left picture in

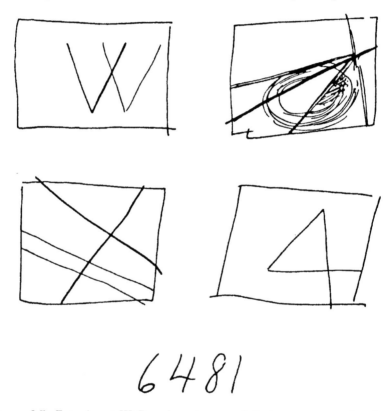

Figure 3.5. *Experiment III.* Drawing at upper left shows two overlapping acute angles containing concealed 4's; at upper right a rotated 4; at lower left a 4, reversed 4's and a primitive representation of the number in the four lines; at lower right a clear-cut number 4.

Figure 3.5. It can be seen that this representation of the 4 is identical with that utilized by the subject in experiment II. All the subject's images were drawn inside of a rectangle and in many of them the sides of the rectangle were utilized in some variation of the number 4. For instance, in the right-hand picture at the top of Figure 3.5, a very good 4 rotated 90 degrees can be made out. The drawing on the lower left also contains a 4, probably several reversed 4's, and the four lines themselves can be looked upon as a primitive representation of the number 4. The twenty-seventh image (Figure 3.5, lower right) is a clear-cut number 4, although the subject when he drew it was not aware of this. As noted, all the images seem to relate to the preconscious registration of the number 4, but there was an interesting indication that the other numbers, namely, 1, 6, and 8, had been registered. At the end of the imagery period, the subject numbered the small rectangles containing his drawings and when he was through, he absent-mindedly retraced the numbers 16 and 18, and only these.

EXPERIMENT IV

An interesting result was obtained with another subject to whom the number 6481 was exposed. During the imagery period she had an image of an envelope with her address on it. In writing her address, she unintentionally inserted a vertical line in the number 3 in such a manner that a concealed 4 was composed, as shown in Figure 3.6.

EXPERIMENT V

A slide with the words *Exit, Star, Mink,* and the number 246 was exposed (Figure 3.7) to the subject used in experiment III; he reported he saw only a flash of light. During the free imagery period he produced and drew 12 images. This subject has considerable artistic ability, was once a professional artist, and made his drawings with a free use of color.

Many of the images which this subject produced related to the idea of a destructive weapon or instrument "going away" from him. For example, the sixth image (Figure 3.8) was of a meteor or comet tail "going away into the distance." This was the first in a series of images having to do with heavenly bodies. During

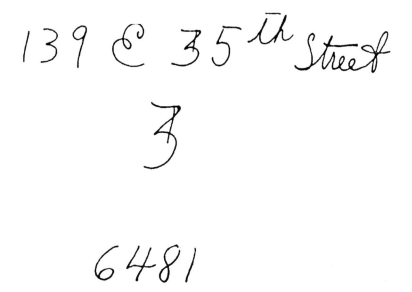

Figure 3.6. *Experiment IV.* Showing the concealed 4 in the number 3.

the reexposure period, the subject stated that the curved meteor tail was derived from the number 6 and the entire image represented a reversed number 2. The seventh image was of an interplanetary projectile, "going away," with trailing lines representing energy (Figure 3.9). Around the projectile he drew eight yellow stars, later indicating that they were derived from the stimulus word *Star.* The tenth image (Figure 3.10) the subject described as the letter *N* smeared over by violence and broken up. The diagonal brown smear represented violence and the background sky or space.

The subject manifested great surprise when he saw the exposed number and words. He stated that all his images depended on the word content. He thought that the "going away" concept was derived from the word *Exit* and that his images of meteors, comets, stars, and heavenly bodies were derived from the word *Star.* The image of the letter *N* was of special interest. The subject stated that it was a reproduction of the *N* in the word *Mink.* He pointed out the elongated right vertical bar in this letter and the irregular lines at the junction of this bar with the oblique. The similarity between the *N* in the drawing and the *N* in the exposed

Figure 3.7. *Experiment V.* Showing the actual slide used for tachistoscopic exposure. Note especially the formation of the letter *N* in the word *Mink*.

word is shown in Figure 3.11. The irregular lines corresponded to the brown smudge of violence in his image; he called them "lines of destruction."

Comment

It is evident that a good part of the exposed slide filtered into the subject's images. The image of the letter N from the word *Mink* emerged in the most striking photographic manner. The subject felt correctly that he had unconsciously apperceived the meaning of at least two of the words, namely *Exit* and *Star,* and that these determined his "going away" images and the images of the heavenly bodies. The numbers and letters intrude themselves in the various ways indicated. At least 6 of the 12 images connected with the idea of destruction, and four of these with

Figure 3.8. *Experiment V.* The meteor or comet tail "going away into the distance."

the concept of "going away." The subject himself had the general feeling that the images were largely concerned with weapons of destruction. At the time of the experiment he was in a very depressed and hostile mood. Apparently the words and numbers and some of the geometrical forms derived from them were unconsciously elaborated into images of violence. The predominant theme, in accord with certain unconscious trends in this subject, related to a struggle between violence turned outward or against himself. This is best illustrated by the meteor image that both comes toward him and then goes away. Most of the images of

Figure 3.9. *Experiment V.* The interplanetary projectile. Note the eight black dots representing stars.

Figure 3.10. *Experiment V.* Letter *N* smeared over by violence and broken up.

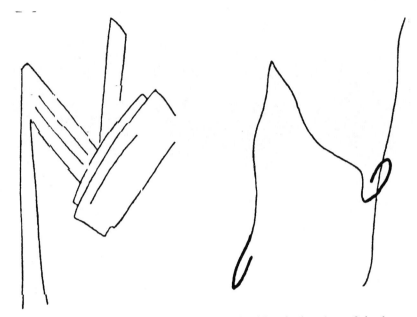

Figure 3.11. *Experiment V.* Comparison of subject's drawing of the letter *N* shown on the left, with the *N* in the word *Mink,* on the right.

violence were directed outward in the "going away" direction, and this concept was derived from the word *Exit.*

Experiment VI. Combined Dream-Imagery Experiment

This experiment was begun by having the subject, a female member of the hospital personnel, produce spontaneous images without the presentation of any stimulus.[2] The images that arose in the subject's mind were associatively connected to events of the evening before when the subject had gone to the Metropolitan Opera. Her images and drawings consisted largely of elaborate human figures, as indicated by the drawing in Figure 3.12, representing the image of an opera singer.

Following the free imagery control period a six-pointed star was exposed. The subject saw only a flash of white light. She

[2]The production of spontaneous images in a preliminary control period was carried out with only a few subjects, but such controls will form an important aspect of the design of new experiments now under way.

Figure 3.12. *Experiment VI.* Illustration of the type of elaborate human figure appearing in subject's spontaneous images.

produced and drew 13 images. A striking phenomenon could now be observed. Whereas during the control imagery period, the subject drew elaborate human figures, most of the human forms that appeared in her 13 images were drawn as stick figures; altogether 36 such stick figures were drawn (Figure 3.13). They

Figure 3.13. *Experiment VI.* Typical stick figures appearing in subject's images following tachistoscopic exposure.

were composed in the following manner (Figure 3.14): a circle was drawn for the head and a straight vertical line attached to it; at the lower end of the vertical line, a V-shaped structure was drawn to indicate the legs. The vertical body line was crossed obliquely by a second line to indicate the arms. Figure 3.14 shows one of the subject's stick figures on the left. The picture on the right indicates the manner in which the stick figure was contained within the geometrical form of the six-pointed star.

Following the imagery experiment, the subject was given a suggestion to dream. The next morning she reported the following dream: "I was younger. I had an impression of a museum or a gallery. Just my mother and myself. We were standing in front of the museum."

The subject drew a large building (Figure 3.15) to represent the Museum of Natural History. She began to draw her mother and herself standing in front of the building, but she erased what she had drawn because she had placed the figures too low. She

Figure 3.14. *Experiment VI.* Typical stick figure on the left. Heavy black lines in drawing on right show the derivation of the stick figure from the star.

stated, "I like to draw stick figures." She nevertheless drew herself and her mother in the manner indicated in the illustration. She was then asked to draw the forms as stick figures since she had had an impulse to do so. She drew the two stick figures in the same manner as I described above, but this time she added a triangular outline to represent the dresses worn by her mother and herself (Figure 3.16).

During the reexposure period, following the reporting of the dream, the subject noticed the correspondence between these stick figures and the geometrical form of the six-pointed star. It can be seen that if the inverted V forming the legs is imagined to be rotated upwards 180 degrees, as indicated by the broken lines, the complete form of the six-pointed star is reconstituted. I wish to stress the observation that similar geometrical forms derived from the six-pointed star, e.g., the stick figures, appeared both in the drawings of the images and of the dream which followed.

Figure 3.15. *Experiment VI.* Subject's drawing of her manifest dream image.

Figure 3.16. *Experiment VI.* Stick figure version of mother and child shown in Figure 3.15, on left; on right showing derivation of stick figures from star.

EXPERIMENT VII. COMBINED DREAM-IMAGERY EXPERIMENT

The six-pointed star was exposed to a physician who had been analyzed and had ready access to unconscious material. The experiment was carried out by my secretary, who also acts as my assistant. The circumstances of the experiment are important, because, as will become clear later, the subject interpreted the situation as placing himself in an inferior and submissive role in relation to a dominant woman.

During exposure the subject saw nothing but a flash of light. During the free imagery period the subject produced 29 images and made drawings of them. A great majority of these images resulted from fragmentation of the exposed six-pointed star. A star of this sort can be thought of as composed of different kinds of geometrical forms (Figure 3.17). For example, (1) it is composed of six points, e.g., acute angles attached to one another in a circular pattern; (2) it is composed of six overlapping X's arranged in a circular form; (3) it is composed of three capital M's, whose middle bars overlap, or of six ordinary capital M's overlapping and arranged in a circular pattern. Of the 29 images, 10 were based on the acute angles forming the points of the star, 5 were based on X figures and 5 were based on the M or the M with the crossed middle bar.

Figure 3.17 illustrates three of the images which were derived from the acute angles of the points of the star. Image No. 3 was of the corner of a rug in the subject's childhood home when he was 6 or 7 years of age and relates to memories of his reading comics while lying on the living room rug. It was associated with later images relating to certain comic strip characters, such as Disney's Goofy, the dog.

Image No. 14 represents two spread thighs with a vague hermaphroditic genital. This image was derived from one of the points of the exposed star that had a missing tip, referred to in Figure 3.17 as "point missing." It happens that the exposed star was rather crudely drawn and the tip of one point of the star was actually missing. The image is one of many that were produced having voyeuristic content and relating to childhood memories of watching someone urinating. The particular image under discussion was associated with a childhood memory when at the age

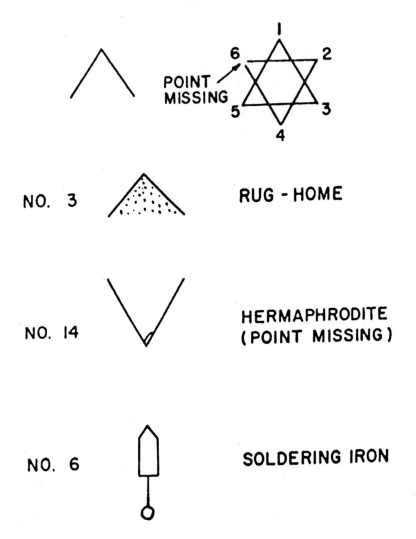

Figure 3.17. *Experiment VII.* Images derived from point fragments of the star.

of 3 the subject watched a little girl spread her thighs and urinate. The idea of "hermaphrodite" and "point missing" is connected with the subject's observation of the missing penis in the little girl.

Image No. 6 was a soldering iron associated with both recent and childhood memories. Although a whole soldering iron was drawn, what actually appeared in the image was the point of the iron in a shape corresponding to the point of the star.

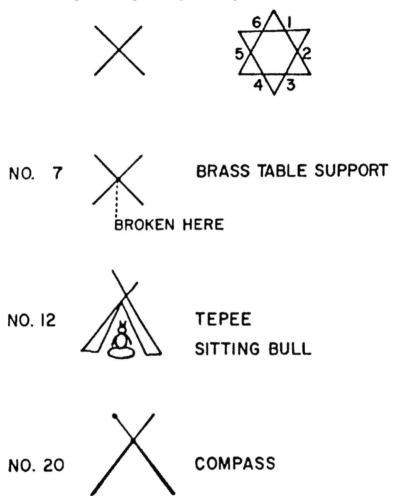

Figure 3.18. *Experiment VII.* Images derived from X fragments of the star.

Figure 3.18 illustrates three of the images which were derived from the X forms contained in the six-pointed star. Image No. 7 represents a crossed support of a brass table that had recently been broken at the point indicated and had been taken to a repair man for soldering.

Figure 3.19. The drawing on the left shows the image of the tepee produced by the subject in experiment VII. The drawing on the right shows the tepee in the image of the 9-year-old boy.

Image No. 12 was of a tepee with Sitting Bull squatting in the opening. This image contains both an X figure and an angular point. This was another urinary image, the word *tepee* containing a pun on the word *pee* and Sitting Bull having an associative connection with a recent memory of a toilet joke about Sitting Bull.[3]

Image No. 20 was another X figure in the shape of a compass apparently without associative content.

Figure 3.20 contains some examples of images derived from the M figures contained in the six-pointed star. Early in the period of free imagery the subject wrote down in the manner indicated the word *mother*. He then wrote "something blocking me." Up to this point, the subject had felt blocked and produced images with great difficulty. From here on there appeared to be some release of inhibition and the subject produced a veritable flood of urinary images, 14 such images appearing in rapid succession. Either at the time the subject wrote the word *mother* or some

[3]In a recent free imagery experiment carried out with a 9-year-old boy, an almost identical image of a tepee developed following the tachistoscopic exposure of the same six-pointed star (Figure 3.19). This image too, was derived from the joining of the X and angle figures.

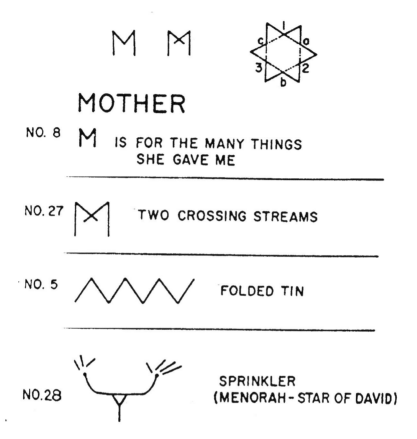

Figure 3.20. *Experiment VII.* Images derived from M fragment of the star.

hours afterwards, the song about mother which begins "M is for
the many things she gave me" began to run through his mind in
a perseverating manner.

Image No. 27 was seen as two people facing one another urinating in such a way that the streams of urine crossed. It is striking
that the subject did not draw human figures but represented them
in the shape of the letter *M*, the crossing middle bars indicating
the streams of urine.

Image No. 5 is of a folded piece of tin after it had been run
through a tin-folding apparatus. This image can be seen to contain M-like figures or may have been derived from the star points.

Image No. 28 was of a lawn sprinkler owned by the subject. As
the subject drew it, he became aware that his drawing was not a

very good representation of the actual sprinkler but much more closely resembled a menorah, a candelabrum used by Jews for ceremonial purposes. This image is probably as close as the subject came to recapturing the six-pointed star. This type of six-pointed star is a Jewish symbol and is called the Star of David. The menorah generally has on it such a star in some decorative pattern.

As I have indicated, 20 of the 29 images were derived from the fragmentation of the six-pointed star. Some of the remaining images represented transformations of two preconscious percepts taken in from the environment of the experimental situation. Several images were derived from the scope part of a second projector that was in the room but not noticed by the subject at the time of the experiment. Several other images represented transformations of the facial profile of my secretary.

Figure 3.21 shows two images that were derived from the scope part of the projector. Image No. 10 is the long snout of the Disney dog, Goofy. This was another urinary image; the subject thought of the snout as phallic in shape and wet on the end.
Image No. 11 was of a urinal modeled after Goofy's nose and the projector. On the left in Figure 3.22 is a drawing of the front part of the projector; on the right is a drawing of Goofy. The general resemblance between the two is rather impressive.

If the 29 images are thought of as a totality, certain general trends can be noted in their order of development. Although they were produced as a discontinuous series, the subject opening his eyes after each image to draw it, they nevertheless show certain patterns of meaning. The first 13 images contained many phallic representations and appear to relate to fears of castration, the broken brass table support that had to be soldered being an example of this. During the period that the first 13 images were produced, the subject appeared blocked. At the end of this period he wrote down the word *mother* and indicated that something was inhibiting him. Following this, he produced in rapid succession 14 images essentially relating to the act of urination. There developed first the image of a toilet and memories of being in the bathroom watching his mother urinate, followed by images and memories of watching horses urinate. The images seem to refer to the idea of a strong, dominating, phallic mother figure who

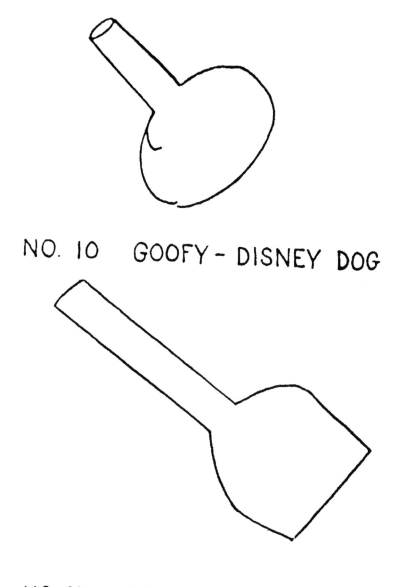

NO. 10   GOOFY - DISNEY DOG

NO. 11   URINAL

Figure 3.21. *Experiment VII.* Images derived from scope part of projector.

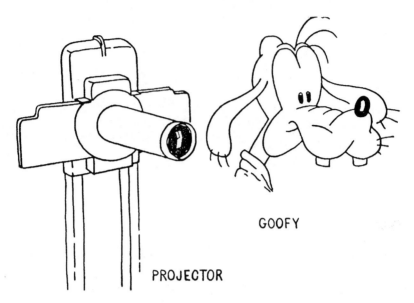

GOOFY

PROJECTOR

Figure 3.22. *Experiment VII.* Drawing of scope part of projector, on left; Goofy, the dog on the right.

was able to produce a large stream of urine rapidly. The images also contained displacements of phallus to nose, as in the image of Goofy, the dog. At least one percept derived from my secretary's profile was converted into an image showing displacements to the nose of both breast and phallus. A striking feature is the large amount of voyeuristic material that emerged during the imagery period.

At the end of the imagery experiment, the subject was given a suggestion to have a dream that night. The next morning the subject reported the following dream:

> The dream took place in a library. I was looking to see what manuscript *he* had. I do not know to whom the "he" refers. I was looking through some sort of opening in a large glass window at the librarian who was sitting in a chair in front of a desk upon which lay the manuscript. The librarian said, sarcastically, "Is this the one you want?" I said, "Yes." I looked at it and it was not the right one. It had printed on it the word *diabetes.* I had expected something else to be written there. I had the feeling that I had seen a

second manuscript that also had something written on it and I
believed that this was the one that I wanted.

The subject made a drawing of his dream showing the librarian
sitting on a chair at a desk (Figure 3.23). On the desk he made

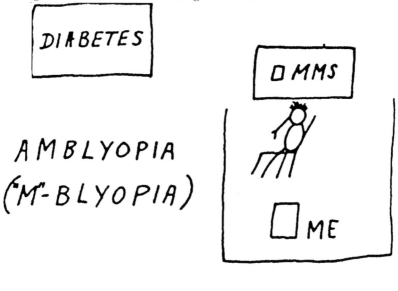

DREAM

Figure 3.23. *Experiment VII*. Subject's drawing of his manifest dream
image.

a square indicating the manuscript and put next to it the letters
MMS. Note that he wrote the abbreviation for "manuscript" in-
correctly, that is, MMS instead of MS. To the left he drew a second
square indicating the manuscript and wrote on it the word *diabetes*. The drawing of the librarian sitting on the chair is of great
interest. The legs of the librarian and the legs of the chair are
drawn in such a confused way that it is difficult to tell which is
which. The figure was drawn without arms or features but a long,
protruding, bifurcating snout was attached to the head. Below
the figure of the librarian he drew a structure representing the

window through which he was looking at the librarian and indicated his own position by the word *me*. When he had finished this he had an impulse to write the word *amblyopia*, as indicated in the illustration. This seemed to come to his mind out of nowhere.

Associations to Dream

The librarian in the dream brought to the subject's mind two women whom he had known years before, both of them librarians. Both of these women were like his mother and my secretary, very small in stature. All three of the women stood for his mother. Both the librarians and the secretary he thought of as small, efficient, and fast moving. It was significant that one of the librarians was married to an overt homosexual of an extremely effeminate type. The subject had at one time been intimate with the second librarian and had sustained serious disappointments at her hands. Although his mother and all the substitutes mentioned were small, the subject viewed them from the point of view of a small child. He conceived of them as large, dominating, efficient, and aggressive. The idea of their moving about fast was related to the fantasy of a fast urinating, phallic woman. At one point, my secretary had asked the subject if he wanted her "to leave the room." Unconsciously, this triggered off the fantasy of her "leaving the room" to urinate.

The subject pointed out certain very interesting features of his drawing of his dream. First, he thought of the curved line emerging from the librarian's body not as a leg but as a stream of urine. Second, he pointed out the peculiar protruberance that he had attached to the head and stated that it represented a phallus with a bifurcating stream of urine. Third, he stated that he thought of diabetes as a urinary disease, related to the fact that as a child he had a constriction of the meatus of his penis that produced a urinary defect. It brought about both a blocking of the urinary stream and a bifurcation or spraying of the stream of urine. This constriction was surgically corrected when he was 7. He related this to the many sprinkler and spraying images that he had produced and contrasted the urinary blocking with the idea of the large, fast, urinary stream produced by the fantasy phallic mother. Fourth, he pointed out his error in the abbreviation of "manuscript" and stated that the way he had written it made him think simply of M's. He thought that the M's had the same meaning as the M figures that appeared in his imagery. That is, they were symbols for a urinating penis and also representations of the urinating penis of the phallic mother. Fifth, he stated that the word *amblyopia* was a play on words and really meant to him *M-blyopia*, meaning a dimness of vision for M's. This referred to all the voyeuristic aspects of both the images and the dream. The dream itself is a voyeuristic one and begins with the idea, "I was *looking* to see what manuscript he had." In the dream, the subject is looking through a window at the librarian and his drawing indicates that he was watching her urinate. The "he" in the sentence quoted is obscure but perhaps relates to the confusion in gender. The reference to amblyopia probably also relates to the idea of tachistoscopic exposure and to the visual confusion of a child in reference to the female genital. Sixth, the subject pointed out that he had indicated his own position in the dream by the word *me*. This again contains another M.

It is evident that the manifest dream images incorporate the same preconscious visual percepts that had arisen during the imagery experiment. The M figure of the six-pointed star played a special role and was elaborated in the ways indicated. In addition, the displacement of phallus to nose took place in both the dream and the imagery and was derived from preconscious visual percepts of the facial profile of my secretary and the scope part of the projector.

Interpretation of Dream

Both the imagery and the dream were stimulated by certain unconscious fantasies aroused in the subject by the fact of his placing himself in the role of a subject in relation to a woman. This reactivated childhood fantasies of a small, submissive, castrated boy in relation to a dominating phallic mother. It aroused all the subject's infantile conflicts centering around his childhood urinary difficulty. It revived intense voyeuristic wishes directed toward the fantasy of the phallic mother.[4] Above all, the

---

[4]The intensely voyeuristic nature of this dream was undoubtedly related to the tachistoscopic nature of the experiment, as I have pointed out earlier (chapter 1). The fleeting nature of the visual stimulus in the experiment can in itself be an important factor in activating voyeuristic impulses. The subject was asked to look at something that he could

dream expresses the wish to obtain the *right* manuscript from the mother, that is, the *right* penis rather than the defective one. Behind this was an accusation against the mother that she had given him the wrong, defective organ. The song about mother and M standing "for the many things she gave me" is an ironic comment on his mother's deficiencies in giving. The dream revives the infantile trauma. He had expected something else to be written on the manuscript but instead he was given the one labeled *diabetes,* symbolically representing the organ with the "urinary disease." All this was expressed by the transformation of the M fragment of the star into a phallic symbol.

The morning following the dream the star was gradually reexposed at increasing time intervals. The recognition time for the star was 1 sec, indicating that the original exposure had taken place approximately 100 times below threshold.

Comment

It would appear that a good part of the manifest dream pictures was adumbrated by the images that had developed earlier during the imagery experiment. The most striking was the appearance of the M fragment of the star in both the images and the manifest dream. Almost the entire manifest dream can be traced to preconscious visual residues of the day before. The librarian sitting at the desk was derived from the memory of the secretary sitting at the desk during the experiment. The secretary was transformed into a librarian by virtue of the fact that she was thought of as someone who "prepares manuscripts." The M fragment was utilized in the symbolic transformation of the manuscript because of the latter's associative connection to the conceptual series, secretary-librarian-mother. The window through which the dreamer was looking at the librarian was probably derived from a one-way viewing screen on the wall of the experimental room. The word *amblyopia* had preoccupied the dreamer the day before. It appears that this consciously perceived and remembered word was fused in some manner with the preconsciously perceived M fragment. The role of consciously perceived and remembered

---

not see. In this particular experiment, this reactivated memories of looking at the "absent" female genital.

visual percepts in the formation of the manifest dream still presents some puzzling features. I now have considerable evidence that such percepts may be fused with preconsciously perceived visual percepts and thus drawn into the dream. The snoutlike structure on the face of the librarian was derived from the scope part of the projector. It is an interesting feature of these experiments that some of the latent content of the dream emerges and becomes evident through the process of drawing the dream. It is very likely that this content would not become evident if the dreams were reported only verbally and not drawn. One could, for example, easily overlook the significance of the M's if one depended solely on the verbalization of the word *manuscript*. The snout on the face of the librarian was not visualized and the face itself was vague in memory. Only while drawing the figure was the snout quite unconsciously attached to the face. There is no doubt that because dreams are largely visual in structure the usual purely verbal analysis results in the overlooking of significant latent content. This fact was known to Freud (1900) who, many years ago, commented on the work of Marcinowski (1912) on the drawn dream. He noted the appearance of concealed latent content in the drawings.[5]

The raw material for the dream appears to be already present in the images that develop shortly after tachistoscopic exposure. It is not only the visual material that is present but a good part of the latent ideational content of the subsequent dream can already be detected. For example, the vast amount of urinary material in the images was connected with the subsequently developing manifest dream images of the bifurcating snout, the word *diabetes*, and the curved line suggesting the urinating librarian. The idea of the mother who gives something also showed up in the images and in the latent content of the dream. A striking feature is that the images that developed during the imagery experiment appeared to be less disguised and closer to the unconscious content than the manifest dream images derived from

---

[5]So far as I know this interesting work of Marcinowski on the drawn dream has never been repeated. He was able to demonstrate that in the drawings of landscapes, for example, parts of the human body, especially the genitals, would emerge.

In the 1912 edition of *The Interpretation of Dreams*, Freud, in referring to Marcinowski's use of dream drawings, observes that "These drawings bring out very clearly the distinction between a dream's manifest and latent meaning. Whereas to the innocent eye they

them. When the manifest dream was reported the entire phallic, urinary content of the dream and the latent wish expressed by it remained completely concealed. At night during the dream work the raw material of the dream revealed in the imagery experiment was subject to further distortion, censorship, and compromise formation, that is, to defensive processes on the part of the ego. Additional memorial content was drawn into the dream work during the night. In contrast to the evident unconscious sexual content of the images, the manifest dream was subjected to secondary revision, and appeared to deal with an innocent problem of obtaining a manuscript from a librarian. Although the images of the imagery experiment appear to constitute the raw material of the dream, they are by no means equivalent to the dream in their formal characteristics.

DISCUSSION

The results of these experiments show in a very striking way that the memory images of the preconscious percepts derived from the tachistoscopically exposed picture appear in the images that develop during the period of free imagery.[6] It is my tentative impression that the free imagery technique is superior to the Allers and Teler word association test in that it provides a better demonstration for the connection between the exposed picture and the subsequently developing images. The proof of this connection lies in the close similarity in form and structure between the images that the subject draws and elements from the exposed picture. This kind of proof carries the maximum conviction when simple material is used for exposure, such as numbers or geometrical figures. When the number 4 appears in a clear-cut fashion its emergence can hardly be ascribed to accident. However, when the percepts or the memory images are subjected to various types

appear as plans, maps, and so on, closer inspection shows that they represent the human body, the genitals, etc., and only then do the dreams become intelligible" (1900, p. 356).

[6] A rather extensive recent literature demonstrating the reality of the phenomenon of subthreshold or preconscious perception is rapidly accumulating. I refer especially to the work of Klein, Spence, Holt, and Gourevitch (1958), Smith and Henriksson (1955), Nixon (1956), Luborsky and Shevrin (1956), and Kragh (1955).

of distortion the demonstration becomes less convincing. Nevertheless, the development of similar methods of representation in different subjects, for example, utilization of overlapping squares which contain concealed 4's, strongly suggests that we are not dealing here with accidental phenomena. The results of this investigation have many implications, some of which I will now discuss.

CHARACTERISTICS OF THE IMAGES

Their relationship to both recent and remote memory content presents some interesting features. Some of the images that develop in the imagery period appear simply as photographic or distorted representations of the preconscious percepts resulting from the tachistoscopic exposure of the number or figure; for example, the number 4 in experiment III is without any seeming connection with other memory content. Other images appear to represent a condensation of a recent memory image with the memory image of the percept from the exposed picture, as in the case of the brass table support in experiment VII. Still other images, such as that of the corner of the rug in experiment VII, represent a condensation of a percept from the exposed picture with a childhood memory image and the unconscious wishes associated with it. These latter images are constructed in precisely the same manner as the manifest images of dreams. In fact, the manifest dream images may be, in part at least, simple reactivations of this kind of image. Images associated with repressed unconscious childhood memory content do not appear in all subjects but only in those who are freer, less inhibited, and less resistant. The degree of defensive activity on the part of the ego during the imagery experiment varies a great deal from subject to subject. In some subjects it is so great and the imagery process so blocked that percepts from the exposed picture cannot be demonstrated in the imagery produced. In others, such as the subject in experiment III, geometrical patterns derived from the exposed picture appear devoid of any psychological content. In still others, as in the subject in experiment VII, recent and childhood unconscious content may emerge very freely and in a less disguised form, as has been pointed out, than in the subsequent dream.

I have previously shown that manifest dream images represent condensations of preconscious sensory percepts with sensory memory images from the past associated with the unconscious wish. Freud (1900) described a dream as a substitute for an infantile scene modified by being transferred onto a recent experience. The infantile scene, he stated, is unable to bring about its own revival and has to be content with returning as a dream. He did not, however, take into sufficient account the role played by preconscious visual percepts in the construction of manifest dream images but appeared to ascribe the manifest dream to the reactivation of visual memory traces associated with the infantile scene. I have suggested that Freud's contention that an unconscious wish cannot emerge into consciousness unless it is "covered" by a recent day residue to which it transfers its intensity needs to be expanded to include the idea that the visual scenes associated with the unconscious wish cannot enter consciousness unless they become fused with preconscious visual percepts associated with the day residue. Experiment VII shows in a striking way how the recent preconscious percept determines and molds the form in which the infantile visual memory appears in consciousness. For example, there was not a reactivation of the memory of the entire rug from the infantile scene but only an angular corner of it emerged in consciousness. The angular corner conformed in its visual pattern to the point of the star. Thus, the infantile memory scene does not necessarily emerge in the manifest dream images in a photographic manner, but it is frequently distorted in the process of condensation with the recent preconscious percept.[7]

Second, it is a remarkable fact that the imagery produced during the free imagery experiments may be derived almost exclusively from the exposed picture. It is as though the preconscious percepts from the exposed picture hold the imagery process in a vise and mold the form in which recent or remote memory scenes are incorporated into the imagery. The preconscious percepts are worked over by the imagery process in a highly complex manner, the same perceptual content being utilized over and

---

[7]Findings such as these have a bearing on the problem of the form of recovery of childhood memories and confirm conclusions recently arrived at by Kris (1956).

over again in different images. However, in certain experiments, in a manner identical to that which I have reported for dreams, it was found that preconscious percepts derived from the environment surrounding the experimental situation were also drawn into the imagery process. A good example of this is the transformation of the projector into the image of Goofy.

Third, it is interesting to observe how in experiments such as the one utilizing the exposure of the star, perfectly neutral and seemingly innocuous percepts can be utilized in the molding of images with a highly charged unconscious content. It does not seem to matter how bland the perceptual content is, it can be utilized by emerging unconscious impulses for purposes of representation and the perceptual content will be subsequently delivered into conscious imagery, distorted, and symbolically transformed. The degree of unity attained by the images is very striking, as is the extent to which they center around a single unconscious tendency dominant at the moment of the experiment and activated by the transference relationship between the subject and the experimenter.

Fourth, several distinct processes appear to go on during the act of preconscious registration. Some of the words, numbers, or figures are not only preconsciously perceived but are also apperceived; that is, their meaning is unconsciously cognized and this meaning may determine the content of the subsequent images. Thus, the exposure of the word *star* eventuated in an image in which stars appeared. Other words may be preconsciously registered but are not apperceived as such, although some of the letters may be utilized in the images; for example, the interesting emergence of the letter N which was apperceived as the letter N. Some of the perceptual forms, whether derived from pictures, words, or letters, may be preconsciously registered, not apperceived and used predominantly as geometrical forms with new meanings attached to them. The fragmentation of the star in the complex manner indicated is an interesting example of this.

Relationship of Preconscious Registrations to Unconscious Processes
In an earlier paper, I have suggested that in the Pötzl experiment, the transference relationship is the chief motivating force

for the dream and that the experimental situation, the experimental procedure, and the content of the experimental instructions activate significant unconscious wishes in the subject that are expressed in the dream. It was shown that these unconscious wishes make special use of the preconscious registrations taking place during the actual experimentation. These findings have implications for any and all experimental work which involves the giving of instructions to human subjects. The unconscious meaning to the subject of the experimental situation and his relationship to the experimenter constitute important variables which are generally ignored.

Recently, George Klein (1956a,b) has elaborated upon this problem in a significant and penetrating way. He points out that in an experimental situation involving visual discrimination we may speak of a periphery and a center in the visual field, that is, in the psychological sense, not to be confused with the anatomical fovea and the periphery of the retina. Adequate appraisal of an experimental situation must recognize the activity of object qualities outside the reaches of an executive intention. By executive intention Klein refers to the conscious motivation in the subject to execute the experimental instructions. In addition to the executive intention in any experimental situation, there is an aura of fringe motives, such as the unconscious wishes that I have dealt with, that are also activated during the course of the experiment. It is these fringe motives that appear to make use of what Klein calls the "peripheral properties of things" and what I have referred to as "preconscious percepts." These assumptions carry the implication that the actual range of perceptual registrations that occur in an experiment is much broader than is required to meet the explicit requirements of instruction. Klein remarks that the perceptual system works as if it picks up a great deal, concerns itself with a little, and acts upon still less. He goes on to state that if more is perceptually registered than is actually seen or intentionally relevant, it is not justified to assume that the qualities of conscious experience and the distal invariants involved exhaust the totality of what is registered. Further, whatever is registered, even though "irrelevant" to conscious intention, may nevertheless *persist* and attain independent status. In an experiment, registration is much more inclusive than an adaptive discriminative selection requires. Such peripheral registrations provide a source of discharge for active, even though not dominant motives, and further coordinations with fringe motives is what gives permanence or persistence to these peripheral registrations, i.e., creates memory residues. It is these latter memory residues that are utilized in dreams and images.

Klein (1956a,b) states that the possibility of peripheral registrations, of thing qualities attaining perceptual status independently of immediate relevance to an executive intention, has received relatively little attention in perceptual theories. And yet a legitimate question for perceptual theory is involved here. He raises the question as to which of the infinity of impingements upon the sensory surfaces become memories:

> Do they all? We walk along a road and an array of impingements varying with every step we take collide with our sensory surfaces. Many acquire some retinal reality, reach some stage of partial formation; they register. But can we speak of them as acquiring thereby the structural status of memories? Indeed, have we any right to assume that they are preconsciously registered or perceived at all? That they persist? If so, if some are and some are not, what are the rules of elimination? While such a wide range of registration is amply attested to by the Poetzl and Fisher studies and by clinical observation, the conditions of such registration and their persistence are not yet well understood [1956a, p. 176].

The questions raised by Klein cannot be given a complete answer at the present time. We do not know whether all peripheral impingements persist, nor the rules of elimination. It is certain, however, that extensive peripheral registration far below conscious recognition threshold takes place, that such registrations may acquire memory status and may be utilized on a major scale not only in dreams but also in our background conscious imagery, and quite probably in reverie states, daydreams, and hypnagogic hallucinations. In connection with the problem of the conditions for the persistence of a peripheral registration, the linking up of such a registration with an unconscious wish is at least one factor in making for survival.

Klein has stated:

The problem has been recognized in connection with the participation of day residues in dreams. Thus, such "peripheral" registrations resonating with significant motives and wishes may initiate the process that flowers later as a dream. But why certain day residues and not others? What does the preconscious percept acquire in cathectic charge that gives it permanence and persistence? Some preconscious percepts do apparently acquire such status, but under what terms and conditions? Freud pointed out that certain preconscious perceptions are at an advantage in this respect: they are recent and hence unencumbered by associations; they are also briefly given (that is, they are not hypercathected and therefore do not have the *single* concrete meaning of an adaptive, hypercathected percept). If we add the property of fluidity and that of the interchangeability of medial forms, then we can see the possibility that peripheral forms have a unique value in the discharge of latent wishes [1956a, pp. 180–181].

Klein discusses the relationship of peripheral registration to repression. He states that:

If we assume that many more registrations occur than enter consciousness and if such registrations persist, obviously there are bases other than "repression" (in the psychoanalytic sense) that eliminate them from awareness. But what is their relation to *repression* in the usual sense? Do such peripheral formations—the outcomes simply of the way our visual apparatus works rather than "repression"—have a value in the discharge of latent wishes? Analytic theory has not exploited the importance of the peripheral formations implied in the distinction between center and periphery. It has dealt with repressed contents only [1956a, p. 181].

The experiments that I have described give a partial answer to some of the questions raised by Klein. In these experiments, the repression of peripheral registrations or preconscious percepts is not at issue. Under the conditions of the experiments, the percepts are registered at approximately 50 to 200 times below conscious recognition threshold. They could not have been repressed from consciousness because they were not capable of entering consciousness in the first place. It seems probable that peripheral registration brought about by *visual factors alone* have a unique value for the discharge of latent unconscious wishes in dreams and images. This problem has been discussed at length in an earlier paper (chapter 2). Whether another type of influence on peripheral registration can go on, that is, an influence that is related to the selective elimination of percepts from consciousness *during the perceptual act itself* by a process analogous to repression, has not been decisively proved in spite of extensive work on perceptual defense (see Allport, 1955).

IMPLICATIONS FOR THE THEORY OF PERCEPTION: THE PROBLEM OF THE LOCUS OF TRANSFORMATION AND DISTORTION OF PERIPHERAL REGISTRATIONS

If one assumes that preconscious perception, subception, peripheral registration, or impingement, or whatever name one chooses to apply, is a reality, this phenomenon would have important implications for the theory of perception. It would necessitate the abandonment of the prevalent view that perception and consciousness are equivalent, that a percept is initially registered consciously and then becomes preconscious or unconscious as a memory trace. Recent evidence supports the idea that perception is a process extended in time, however instantaneous it may appear to be, and that all percepts have an initial preconscious registration. Even those that appear to enter consciousness instantaneously must make contact with a preexisting memory schema in order for meaning and recognition to occur. The preconscious registrations under discussion, however, do not attain consciousness in this instantaneous way. Some of them may never reach consciousness at all but remain in a preconscious state. The dream and imagery experiments suggest that other preconscious registrations develop into memory images and are delivered into consciousness in a delayed manner, as Pötzl indicated long ago, in the form of manifest dream images or other types of imagery. As Klein has suggested, these half-developed percepts have a unique value in the formation of dreams and other autistic processes. Under the influence of the unconscious wish and the primary process the half-formed percepts that initially are unable to attain consciousness can do so in a delayed manner.

The following tentative formulation may be suggested. The events leading to the process of conscious perception may be broken down into three phases: (1) the registration of the percept; (2) contact with a preexisting similar memory schema in relation to which the percept is incorporated as a new memory schema; and (3) the emergence into consciousness of the percept. The evidence indicates that both the phases of registration and contact with a preexisting memory schema take place unconsciously (preconsciously).

In describing the perceptual process under discussion I have alternately utilized the terms "preconscious perception" or "preconscious registration." It would be more consistent to utilize the term "preconscious registration." What is ordinarily called conscious perception takes place in the presence of a stimulus object and involves all three of the phases mentioned. When the perceptual process is slowed down by the utilization of the tachistoscope, only the first and probably the second phases take place in the presence of the stimulus object, while the third phase, the emergence of the percept into consciousness, occurs in a delayed manner when the stimulus object is no longer present. It therefore involves the emergence of memory images rather than percepts in the strict sense.

In previous papers (see chapters 1, 2) I have discussed at length the problem of the locus, from a temporal point of view, of the regularly occurring mechanisms which play a role in the development of dreams and images. I refer to the mechanisms of fragmentation, reversal, rotation, condensation, displacement, etc. These distorting mechanisms are at work at some point in the three phases of the perceptual process that I have outlined, but it is difficult to ascertain in which. It is possible that the percept in the process of preconscious registration (first phase) does not undergo distortion and that such distortion, when it develops, does so at some point in time between the registration and the emergence of the percept into consciousness. That is, it may take place during the phase of contact with the preexisting memory schema or during the phase of emergence into consciousness. Evidence derived from the imagery experiments suggests that total registration of the stimulus object may take place in a highly photographic manner but that the total percept may not appear in consciousness. For example, the six-pointed star in experiment VII appeared to attain total registration but never appeared as such in the subsequent imagery. It emerged in the imagery rather as separate fragments which, if combined together, would reconstitute the total percept of the star. The fragmentation of the star may therefore have occurred, from the point of view of temporal sequence, after the registration of the percept. If this were so, such fragmentation would occur either within the memory schema or the memory schema could be thought of as disintegrating into fragments as the latter emerge into consciousness. The weak, subthreshold registrations involved in these experiments may form highly unstable memory schema that readily fragment and undergo the various types of distortion and transformation mentioned.

The evidence from these experiments suggests that the first two phases of the perceptual process, namely, registration and contact with a memory trace, take place unconsciously.[8] This idea meets with great resistance among most investigators in the perceptual field because it is erroneously interpreted as implying the existence of double perception, a preperceiver or a manikin theory. Recently, Wallach (1949) presented the idea that a primary perceptual process must make contact with a memory trace before recognition and meaning can arise. He stated that the phase of contact with the memory trace represents a process of recall not experienced by the perceiver. A process of recall not experienced by the perceiver is, therefore, one that takes place outside of consciousness, although Wallach does not appear to recognize this implication.

Klein (1956a,b) has pointed out that Gestalt theory has overlooked the possible significance of peripheral registrations. It has failed to recognize the possibility that perception in its actual occurrence is a temporally extended event in which the outcome in experience is seemingly immediate but is not actually so. Klein

---

[8]Colby (1955) has recently proposed a new, ingenious model of the psychic apparatus and has come to some conclusions about the perceptual system quite similar to those proposed here. He suggests that percept formation is an entirely unconscious process and that registration of the percept takes place in systems which lack the quality of consciousness. Consciousness arises, he states, when contents are permitted to enter another system which has the quality of consciousness.

suggests that there are intermediate events *leading up to* the final conscious perception that may be separately registered and achieve independent status perceptually.

That the perceptual process contains a preliminary unconscious phase was recognized by the French philosopher Dalbiez (1941). In his interesting critique on psychoanalysis he stated, "It might also be pointed out that in his two schemata of the psychic apparatus Freud speaks of external sensation as though it were always conscious. If he had been a true realist,[9] how could he have failed to recognize the vitally important fact that external sensation is intrinsically unconscious, and only becomes conscious through a supplementary act? (p. 42)[10]

Many years ago, Frink (1918) pointed out, in discussing Freud's model of the psychic apparatus, that it would be logical to recognize that external sensation begins with an unconscious phase.

It is of historical interest that in a letter to Fliess, dated June 12, 1896, Freud (1954) first set forth the theory that memory is present not once but several times over and that it is registered in various species of "signs." At this time Freud believed that there were at last three such registrations. The first of these he labeled Pcpt.-s (signs) and stated that it is the first registration of the perceptions, that it is quite incapable of being conscious and that it is arranged according to associations of simultaneity. The second and third registrations Freud labeled Uc. and Pc. It is not altogether clear what Freud meant by Pcpt.-s, but it appears to have been a concept of unconscious perception. In his later model of the psychic apparatus Freud (1900) dropped this first registration and never mentioned it again in his subsequent work.

---

[9]In this discussion, Dalbiez uses the terms *realist* and *idealist* in their philosophical sense.

[10]"Many writers (and among them some who claim to be realists) admit that all psychic phenomena are endowed with spontaneous consciousness. They hold that in an extraceptive sensation, such as the sight of a tree, we are aware of the material object and of our own sight of it *at the same moment*. They call this concomitant or direct consciousness, a concept which we categorically deny. It is quite logical for idealists to accept it, but we cannot understand how realists can come to defend it. The sensory operation whereby we see a tree is not a mode or property of the tree, so that it is strictly impossible for us to apprehend both the tree and our own sight of it by one and the same act. In knowing the tree, we do not by *any means* know our own sight of it; we apprehend the latter afterward, by a second act. The consciousness of extraceptive sensation is therefore a reflected consciousness, an act of cognition which implies another prior to itself. This prior act (the extraceptive sensation) is intrinsically unconscious. . . . [Dalbiez, 1941, p. 19].

Freud presented the following diagram to illustrate the different transcriptions.

I   II   III

PCPT - PCPT-S - UCS - PCS - CONSC.

If this diagram is rearranged so that Pcpt. is put at the end of the series next to Consc. to represent conscious perception, as in Freud's later model, the diagram would correspond more closely to the theory advanced here.

I   II   III

PCPT-S. - UCS - PCS - CONSC - PCPT.

IMPLICATIONS FOR THE PSYCHOLOGY OF THE DREAM PROCESS

I would like to discuss the recent experimental work on perception and especially the increasing evidence that there is a preconscious or unconscious phase to the perceptual process in relation

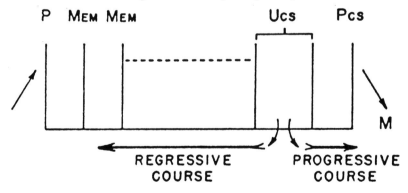

Figure 3.24.

to Freud's first model of the psychic apparatus. Figure 3.24 shows the model. This diagram has stood for more than 50 years as an explanatory model of the dream process. It will be remembered, however, that Freud presented it rather apologetically, noted that

it was only an analogy intended to assist his attempt to make
the implications of mental functioning intelligible, and warned
against mistaking the scaffolding for the building. The model as
set up combined two ideas: the first, an analogy with a combined
microscope or telescope, and the second, the reflex arc, with the
current flowing from the perceptual to the motor end of the
apparatus. One of Freud's chief motives for constructing this
model was an attempt to explain the visual character of dreams.
He formulated his explanation in terms of a "hypothetical regression" within the psychic apparatus. He was interested in explaining the empirically established fact that the logical relations
belonging to the dream thoughts disappear during dream activity. In the hallucinatory dream, the excitation moves in a backward or regressive direction. During the regression the logical
relations of the dream thoughts lose any means of expression
except in perceptual images. In regression the fabric of the dream
thoughts is resolved into its raw material, that is, into perceptual
images. As noted in the model, Freud locates the impetus to the
construction of dreams in the system Ucs. The dream instigator
makes an effort to advance into the preconscious in the progressive direction and from there to attain access to consciousness.
But this pathway is barred by the censorship barrier existing between the unconscious and the preconscious. The progressive
course is thereupon abandoned, and the dream assumes a backward, regressive course through the unconscious memory systems
to the Perception–Conscious system where it is aroused to hallucinatory intensity.

The model enabled Freud to explain many of the aspects of
dream formation and to stress especially the regression to a primitive, preverbal type of thinking, namely, in terms of visual images
or "regard for representability in plastic images." Freud noted
that three kinds of regression take place in the dream, namely,
topographical, temporal, and *formal,* stating that at bottom they are
one and the same thing, since what is older in time is more primitive in form and in psychical topography lies nearer to the perceptual end. Both Brenner (1955) and Jacobson (1953) have recently
raised critical objections to the telescopic model on various
grounds. Brenner prefers an explanation of the dream in terms
of Freud's later structural hypotheses. In place of a topographical

regression he states that there occurs in sleep a suspension of many of our ego functions. There is regression from secondary-to primary-process thinking that is preverbal and consists largely of sensory images, primarily visual ones. Although what Freud called temporal and formal regression may be retained, it is questionable whether the notion of a topographical regression to perception is any longer a useful, explanatory concept.

The telescopic model allows an explanation of regression to perceptual images; yet there are a number of important aspects of dream formation which cannot be fitted into it. The first omission is that the model does not incorporate the role of the day residue. If the dream impulse, that is, the unconscious wish, is turned away at the frontier of the censorship, at the border of the preconscious, and does not pass through it, it cannot make contact with the preconscious day residue. Furthermore, if the dream impulse does not pass through the preconscious, or what today in structural terms we would call the ego, those modifications which Freud called dream distortion cannot take place. Freud (1900) himself was aware of this and in a long footnote commented on some of the gaps that he had left in his treatment of the dream. He stated, "Nor have I entered into the obvious problem of why the dream thoughts are subjected to distortion by the censorship even in cases *where they have abandoned the progressive path toward consciousness and have chosen the regressive one*" (p. 541; emphasis added). The implication here is that in the regressive course the dream impulse does not pass through the psychic agency which imposes the distortion, that is, the preconscious system or the ego. The third difficulty of the telscopic model is that Freud equated perception with consciousness. Although he spoke of all other mental processes as beginning in an unconscious phase and developing into consciousness he excluded perception from this generalization.

As Smith and Henriksson (1955) have stated, though the Freudian system of perception, contrary to contemporary models, is part of the self-regulating dynamic system of the whole organism, for Freud, as for the structural psychologists of his time, a percept is either instantaneously present in consciousness or does not exist at all.

Simply as a model expressed in terms of a progressive and regressive course the diagram contains logical inconsistencies. Freud stated (1900, p. 541) that if we attempt to proceed further with this schematic picture we should have to reckon with the fact that the system next beyond the preconscious (on the right side of the model) is the one to which consciousness must be ascribed; in other words, perception is equivalent to consciousness. In addition to this, if we insert on the left side of the model the system Pcs. between the Ucs.-Mem. systems and Pcpt., a step which is necessary if we are to include the role of the day residue and the agency making for dream distortion, we are left with a model which, beginning from the system Ucs., contains the same agencies or systems, whether we move to the right in the progressive direction or to the left in the regressive one. That is, the linear model is changed into a circular one, and the distinction between progressive and regressive courses becomes obliterated, as shown in Figure 3.25.

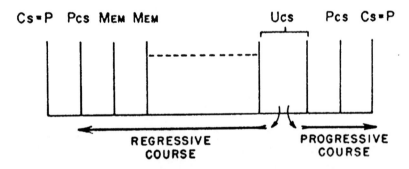

Figure 3.25

In the light of Pötzl's investigation and recent confirmations of his findings, the role of the perceptual process in dream formation now appears to be more complex than indicated in Freud's formulation. A place needs to be found for the empirically proven facts of preconscious registration. I would like at this time to present a diagram (Figure 3.26) which attempts to show the relationship of the phases of the perceptual process to dream formation and to the systems Cs., Pcs., and Ucs. This is not intended to be a substitute model of the psychic apparatus and does not incorporate Freud's later structural concepts.

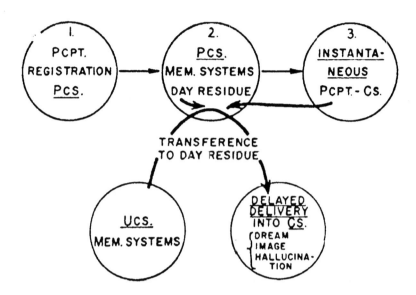

Figure 3.26. Relation of perception to dream process and systems C.s, Pc.s, and Ucs.

The three circles at the top of the diagram indicate the three phases of the perceptual process outlined earlier, namely, (1) preconscious registration of the percept; (2) preconscious contact with the preexisting memory schema and the conversion of the percept into a new memory schema; and (3) the phase of instantaneous emergence into consciousness. The temporal course of the dream process is indicated by the heavy arrow and its extensions, beginning in the system Ucs. in the lower left circle. The diagram is intended to demonstrate the role of the percepts, preconscious and conscious, associated with the day residue, in the formation of the manifest dream images; e.g., to explain the regression of the dream thoughts to sensory images, mostly visual, for which purpose Freud set up his model. The diagram permits an explanation of the dream process whether the dream is thought of as being instigated by the unconscious wish or as stimulated by the day residue. I will use the latter instance as an example. Some of the percepts associated with the day residue experience attain registration, move through the upper three circles, and arrive in consciousness instantaneously. Another large group of percepts, subthreshold in their intensity, move only as

far as the middle circle and become preconscious memory images. These events take place during the day *in close temporal
association with the day residue experience.* Simultaneously with
them, the unconscious wish transfers its intensity onto these memory traces that now undergo distortions of a primary-process-like
nature. At this stage we do not have a dream but only the preliminary stage of the dream in the form of the kinds of images which
develop in the imagery experiment. These memory images are
formed in the same way and by the same mechanisms as some of
the manifest dream images. They can be shown to be associated
with the same unconscious content as the latter and to be composed of a fusion of the memory images of the preconscious
registrations and old memory pictures associated with the unconscious wish. We can assume that further elaboration of these images may continue all through the day and into the night. *The
dream itself arises when there is a second activation* of the unconscious wish during sleep, transference onto the preconscious day
residue, and an arousal of some of the same memory images laid
down during the day. These, in a sense, form the raw material of
the sensory structure of the dream. But on this occasion, the
memory images of the preconscious registrations are delivered
into consciousness in a delayed manner, aroused to hallucinatory
intensity, and make up the manifest pictures of the dream. These
pictures, too, are composed essentially of the memory images of
the preconscious registrations fused with infantile memory images associated with the unconscious wish. In addition, some of
the percepts which attain instantaneous consciousness fall back
into the preconscious state, when attention cathexis is withdrawn
from them, undergo the various transformations and distortions
described, and are drawn into the dream process. From this description, it can be seen that it has not been necessary to make
a distinction between a progressive and regressive course, in the
topographical sense.

   It might appear from the above formulation that I am using the
term "day residue" in an unusual sense. My intention, however, is
to stress the perceptual events that are associated with the day
residue. If we take the experiment involving the dream about
the manuscript, the day residue in the ordinary sense can be
considered to be the individual's experience of being a subject

for an experiment. Ordinarily, one would only stress the preconscious trains of thought, as Freud did, associated with such an experience. The concept of the day residue needs to be expanded to include the total experience of the subject while undergoing it, not only his preconscious thoughts and feelings at the moment, but, most importantly, the sensory events that surround it, and, for purposes of dream formation, especially the subthreshold percepts that are registered during it. It is the sensory material, both preconscious and conscious, that is registered as memory trace, that becomes the raw material for the dream, and is utilized in the process of the translation of the dream thoughts into plastic visual or other sensory images. This raw material appears to be already present in the images which develop shortly after tachistoscopic exposure. Not only is the visual material present but a good part of the latent ideational content of the subsequent dream is already adumbrated, as was previously noted in the discussion of experiment VII.

IMPLICATIONS FOR THE THEORY OF SYMBOL FORMATION

The numerous symbolic transformations which have shown up in these experiments may throw some light on the genesis of symbol formation. A case in point is the symbolic transformation of geometrical forms derived from the star in such a manner that the angle, X, and M forms were all translated into phallic symbols. It would appear that preconscious visual percepts registered simultaneously with the activation of an unconscious process may be symbolically transformed in relationship to the nature and meaning of that process. If the geometrical form of the preconscious percept resembles the organ to be unconsciously symbolized, it will undergo symbolic transformation. It is known from Freud's work that elongated objects are readily transformed into phallic symbols. In experiment VII the star points and the M fragments were symbolically transformed into the urinating phallus. It is also of interest to observe how the star point with the missing tip took on the symbolic meaning of the female genital.

STATES OF CONSCIOUSNESS AND COGNITIVE ORGANIZATIONS

Rapaport (1951) has pointed out that cognitive organizations and the varieties of consciousness accompanying them have rarely, if ever, been systematically studied, and that they may well be crucial for a coordinated theory of personality and cognition. He presented observations that lent support to the following theses: (1) Consciousness can be usefully treated as an organization subserving cognition; (2) consciousness is not a singular phenomenon but one which has a whole range of varieties each corresponding to a different cognitive organization. In his very interesting self-observations on thought experiences, ranging from dreams through intermediate forms like hypnagogic hallucinations, reveries, and daydreams to ordered waking thoughts, Rapaport was able to show that the same cognitive motifs were treated with different cognitive means at different levels of consciousness. He pointed out that thoughts, daydreams, dreams, reverie states and other forms of cognition can be distinguished from each other by objective criteria. The criteria he found were: use of visual imagery, use of verbalization, awareness of awareness (implying the ability to turn round upon the content or state of consciousness), explicitness vs. implicitness, differentiation, recruiting connative enrichment by means of the mechanisms of condensation, displacement, etc. He also stated that the motivations involved in the various forms of cognition range from high level derivative motivations to basic drives. The various cognitive organizations are accompanied by varieties of awareness, i.e., consciousness, that appear to be specific to them. Varieties of consciousness are themselves organized means of cognition.

In the experiments reported in this paper two varieties of consciousness or cognitive organization, that of the dream and that present during the free imagery experiment, were studied. In these experiments, especially those combining imagery and dreams, Rapaport's contention that the same cognitive content can be treated with different cognitive means at different levels of awareness has been confirmed. It was shown that the cognitive content which appeared during the imagery experiment is also present in the subsequent dream. It is difficult to describe the state of consciousness present during the imagery experiment since in some ways it is an artificial one. It would seem to lie somewhere between the state of reverie and daydream, but it lacks the spontaneous qualities of these states since the subject makes a conscious effort to observe his images. It shares with the daydream the use of visual imagery, awareness of awareness, and explicitness as against implicitness. It is, however, a discontinuous state since at intervals the subject opens his eyes to make drawings of his images. The closing of the eyes cuts off external stimulus input and produces a narrowing of consciousness. Although the subject appears wide awake, there are certain similarities to the reverie or daydream state. It should also be noted that in the word association experiment, when the eyes are not closed, similar types of imagery may appear, although I have the impression that this does not happen with as great ease as when the eyes are closed. It is probable that much of this imagery would remain at preconscious levels if special effort were not made to turn the hypercathexis of attention upon it. Nevertheless, I believe it reasonable to suppose that the kinds of images that develop in states of reverie, daydream, and hypnagogic hallucinations, are similar in their origin and structure to those that develop in the free imagery experiments. Furthermore, it has been shown that they may be identical in form and origin to those that develop in nocturnal dreams. The images that develop during the imagery experiment, although discrete and discontinuous, are not just random but have some organization and they tend to circle within a narrow range around the same cognitive content. In their totality they can be interpreted, in some instances, in much the same manner as dreams and the latent unconscious wish behind them elucidated.

Theory of Contact of Percept with a Memory Trace Mechanism

I would like to formulate the phase of contact of the percept with a preexisting memory trace system in terms of Hebb's (1949) theory of cell assemblies and phase sequences.[11] According to

---

[11]See Allport (1955) for a summary of Hebb's theory as well as for a brilliant and detailed critique of modern theories of perception.

Hebb, aside from the primitive unity of figure and ground, perception is a learned process. In the perception of identity the percept is not given at the start as an immediately organized whole; it has to be gradually acquired. The work of Senden (1932) and Riesen (1947) has shown that newly seeing human beings (after congenital cataract removal) and chimpanzees reared in darkness are amazingly poor in the perception of figures or objects. They have great difficulty in recognizing figures and in having, with regard to them, the experience of identity. A course of patient learning is required to bring out the potentialities of the way things look. Normal human infants go through a similar process. The immediate correctness and apparent simplicity of adult perceptions of objects and forms may be entirely misleading as to the genesis and physiological basis of these perceptions. The process of perceptual learning, according to Hebb, involves piecemeal, repetitive, and summative processes, demanding eye movements and many separate visual fixations; so that as adults we are able to perceive a square at a glance only by virtue of this earlier complex learning. Perception is an additive serial reconstruction (rapid and unconscious for the normal adult), and the perception of identity depends upon a series of excitations from the parts of the stimulus figure.

Since learning, that is, past experience, must be provided for in the perceptual process, Hebb postulates a memory trace mechanism.[12] This trace mechanism Hebb calls the "cell assembly." This consists of a group of cortical neurones functionally associated and involving sensory to sensory as well as sensory to motor connections. The cortical organization of a cell assembly is considered to occur not merely in the visual area of the cortex but also in the adjacent and more topographically random associative regions. The cell assembly is conceived as a three-dimensional latticework and it is defined as the unit of perception. It represents the physiological basis of the most simple percept. The next stage in the organization is an assembly of these unitary assemblies. This process is the basis of the perception of a *complex* and it involves what Hebb calls the "phase sequence." Perception

---

[12]By drawing on Hebbian theory, Fisher anticipated the important role this theory would play in contemporary cognitive neuroscience in which it is a mainstay in explaining memory formation [Ed.].

of identity involves the firing of such cell assemblies and phase sequences. The joining of the aggregate of neurones may take time and repeated excitations of the elements may be needed throughout the early years of life or even later. If the aggregating occurs at a later period it takes an appreciable time and many trials; we recognize it as "learning." If it occurs very quickly under conditions in which its repetitive or trial-and-error aspects cannot be observed, we call it perception.

According to Hebb's theory then, there is a multiple laying down of traces in the cell assemblies in the process of perceptual learning, e.g., a multiple laying down of the angles of a triangle. The process is piecemeal, repetitive, and involves eye movements and many separate visual fixations. Subsequently, during the act of perceiving a triangle, the already laid down cell assemblies and phase sequences are fired. The new percept comes in and organizes existing assemblies into new assemblies and results in an alteration in the earlier trace structures. Rapaport (personal communication) has suggested that further modification may take place by endogenous changes in the cell assemblies and phase sequences, or during memorial reconstruction there may be an active selection of certain aspects of the phase sequence.

Although it is not stressed by Hebb, the integration of a new percept into a preexisting cell assembly must take place unconsciously. In the ordinary perception of identity we may consider that the cell assemblies and phase sequences are fired and the percept attains consciousness. In the dream and imagery experiments where a weak subthreshold stimulus is used it may be that the preexisting cell assemblies and phase sequences related to the trace of a six-pointed star, for example, are likewise fired, but with a lessened intensity that does not permit the attainment of consciousness. Instead, there is a delayed delivery of the activated phase sequence into consciousness in subsequent dreams or images. In the process of this delayed delivery, either due to endogenous changes within the cell assemblies and phase sequences or to something that takes place at the moment of emergence into consciousness, the phase sequence may decompose into fragments or undergo the other kinds of transformations and distortions that have been described. There may be some relationship between the process of multiplication that appears over and over again in the dream and imagery experiments and Hebb's idea that there is a multiplication of the percept in the cell assembly during the process of perceptual learning. In other words, there may be a regressive reactivation of the multiple cell assemblies and phase sequences that were originally involved in the process of learning to identify the percept. It is not at all clear, however, how this comes about. The manner in which the percept undergoes fragmentation may be similar to the piecemeal way it was originally laid down in the cell assembly.

SUMMARY

1. New experimental results extending earlier work on dreams and imagery were reported. These experiments involve the utilization of a new method for studying imagery. The method consists of the eliciting of free images in a process analogous to free association immediately following the tachistoscopic exposure of pictures.
2. A series of imagery experiments utilizing numbers or simple geometrical forms during tachistoscopic exposure was presented. It was shown that preconsciously registered percepts from these figures appeared in subsequent imagery within minutes after tachistoscopic exposure.
3. The mode of formation of the images and their characteristics were described in detail; for example, their relationship to recent and remote memory content, their relationship to meaning content, implications for the theory of symbol formation, relationship to states of consciousness, etc.
4. Several combined dream-imagery experiments were reported. It was shown that the images which develop during the imagery experiment may appear in an identical or related form in the subsequent dream and provide some of the raw material of the manifest content of the dream.
5. The relationship of preconscious registrations to unconscious processes was discussed, and it was indicated that the former

may have a unique value for the discharge of latent unconscious wishes. The importance of fringe motives and peripheral perceptual impingements in an experimental situation was stressed.

6. A diagram showing the relation of perception to the dream process and to the systems Cs., Pcs., and Ucs. was presented. It was proposed that perception is a process extended in time which can be broken down into three phases: (a) the registration of the percept; (b) contact of the percept with a preexisting memory schema; and (c) the emergence into consciousness of the percept. It was suggested that the first two phases take place outside of consciousness.

7. The problem of the locus of transformation and distortion of peripheral registrations was discussed. It was suggested that distortions and transformations of the percepts take place subsequent to registration during the phase of contact of the percept with a preexisting memory trace or during the phase of emergence into consciousness. This problem was formulated in terms of Hebb's theory of cell assemblies and phase sequences.

REFERENCES

Allers, R., & Teller, J. (1924), Uber die Verwertung unbemerkter Eindrucke bei Associationen. *Zeitschr. Neurol. f. & Psychiat.*, 89:492–513.
Allport, F. H. (1955), *Theories of Perception and the Concept of Structure.* New York: John Wiley.
Brenner, C. (1955), *An Elementary Textbook of Psychoanalysis.* New York: International Universities Press.
Colby, K. M. (1955), *Energy and Structure in Psychoanalysis.* New York: Ronald Press.
Dalbiez, R. (1941), *Psychoanalytic Method and the Doctrine of Freud*, Vol. 2, tr. T. F. Lindsay. London: Longmans, Green.
Freud, S. (1900), The Interpretation of Dreams. *Standard Edition*, 4&5. London: Hogarth Press, 1953.
——— (1954), *The Origins of Psychoanalysis. Letters to Wilhelm Fliess, Drafts and Notes: 1887–1902.* New York: Basic Books.
Frink, H. (1918), *Morbid Fears and Compulsions: Their Psychology and Psychoanalytic Treatment.* New York: Moffat, Yard.
Hebb, D. O. (1949), *The Organization of Behavior.* New York: John Wiley.
Jacobson, E. (1953), The affects and their pleasure-unpleasure qualities in relation to the psychic discharge processes. In: *Drives, Affect, Behavior*, ed. R. M. Loewenstein. New York: International Universities Press, pp. 38–66.

Klein, G. S. (1956a), Perception, motives and personality: A clinical perspective. In: *Psychology of Personality*, ed. J. L. McCary. New York: Logos Press, pp. 121–196.

———— (1956b), Motives and the perception of objects. In: *Psychology of Personality*, ed. J. L. McCary. New York: Logos Press, pp. 37–115.

———— Spence, D. P., Holt, R. R., & Gourevitch, S. R. (1958), Preconscious influences upon conscious cognitive behavior. *J. Abnorm. & Soc. Psychol.*, 57:255–266.

Kragh, U. (1955), *The Actual-Genetic Model of Perception-Personality*. Lund: Gleerup.

Kris, E. (1956), The recovery of childhood memories in psychoanalysis. *The Psychoanalytic Study of the Child*, 11:54–88. New York: International Universities Press.

Luborsky, L., & Shevrin, H. (1956), Dreams and day residues: A study of the Poetzl observations. *Bull. Menninger Clin.*, 20:135–148.

Marcinowski, J. (1912), Gezeichnete Traume. *Zentralbl. Psychoanal.*, 2:490.

Nixon, N. F. (1956), Symbolic associations following subliminal stimulation. *Internat. J. Psycho-Anal.*, 37:159–170.

Pötzl, O. (1917), Experimentall erregte Traumbilder in ihren Bezichungen zum indirekten Sehen. *Zeitschr. f. Neurol. & Psychiat.*, 37:278–349.

Rapaport, D. (1951), Consciousness: A psychopathological and psychodynamic view. In: *Problems of Consciousness*. New York: Josiah Macy, Jr., Foundation, pp. 18–57.

Riesen, A. (1947), Development of visual perception in man and chimpanzee. *Science*, 106:107–108.

Senden, M. (1932), *Raumund Gestaltauffassung bei operierten Blindgeborenen vor und nach der Operation*. Leipzig: Barth.

Smith, G. & Henriksson, M. (1955), The effect on an established percept of a perceptual process beyond awareness. *Nordisk Psykologi*, 7:170–179.

Wallach, H. (1949), Some considerations concerning the relation between perception and cognition. *J. Personal.*, 18:6–13.

4

FURTHER OBSERVATIONS ON THE PÖTZL PHENOMENON: THE EFFECTS OF SUBLIMINAL VISUAL STIMULATION ON DREAMS, IMAGES, AND HALLUCINATIONS (1959)

Charles Fisher

Editor's Statement

In publishing Dr. Charles Fisher's article, which originally appeared in its complete version only in the French journal *L'Évolution Psychiatrique,* some 25 years ago, we not only wish to honor our distinguished colleague, but also to affirm the contemporary relevance of his seminal contributions to the subliminal field of research. Cognitive psychologists and neuroscientists are currently studying mental activities occurring outside conscious awareness, viewed as the initial phase in the processing of information.

This is the original English version of the paper presented to the Groupe de l'Évolution Psychiatrique, July 1958, Paris, France. It was published, translated into French by Dr. I. F. Foncin, in *L'Évolution Psychiatrique,* 1959, 4:541–566.

A more objective method for evaluating the emergence of subliminal registrations into dreams and images is described in chapter 5.

The introductory section of this chapter has been omitted because it summarizes the research reported in the previous three chapters.

Though these contemporary researchers, with few exceptions, avoid reference to the Freudian model, their work converges on many points with earlier, psychoanalytic concepts and previous research findings in the psychoanalytic domain. In his brief but lucid historical overview (to be found at the end of the present article as Addendum II), Dr. Fisher touches on some of the parallels between the disciplines.

Leo Goldberger

DIFFERENTIAL UTILIZATION OF SUBLIMINAL AND SUPRALIMINAL REGISTRATIONS IN DREAMS

It was Pötzl's idea that only the unnoticed or subliminally registered elements of a tachistoscopically exposed picture were utilized in dreams or hallucinations. While there is no doubt that subliminally registered elements play an extensive role in dream formation, it has been our experience that consciously perceived elements are also incorporated into dreams, a fact that every analyst knows from daily experience with tracking down day residues during dream analysis. The following experiment was designed to investigate the role of consciously perceived stimuli in dream and image formation and their interaction with subliminally registered elements.

When a picture such as the one shown in Figure 4.1 is tachistoscopically exposed for 1/100 sec, the vase with the swastika on it is readily perceived and discriminated, while the snake cannot be perceived at all. On average, the recognition threshold for the snake is 1/2 sec, representing an exposure time 50 times longer than 1/100 sec.

The night following the exposure to this stimulus, one subject had the following dream: He dreamed that his cat had died and that its corpse was brought to a synagogue. He drove there with his wife for the burial. A young Jewish woman appeared, who was to take charge of the disposal of the cat's body. She was disposing of the cat's corpse by eating its kidneys "like an Eskimo might," taking a chunk in her mouth and cutting it off with a knife and

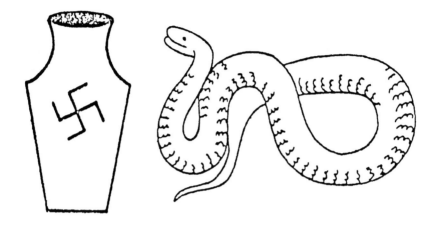

Figure 4.1

eating it. The subject observed that a long piece of fat was attached to the kidneys.

He was asked to make a drawing of the kidneys with the piece of fat; the drawing is shown in Figure 4.2. It can be seen that this drawing bears a quite striking resemblance to the snake's head and the upper part of its body. It should be borne in mind that the subject had not consciously perceived the snake, but the assumption is that it was subliminally registered and appeared in his dream. Further, it can be observed that the two kidneys and the attached piece of fat are a fairly good representation of the testicles and penis.

I cannot go into the details of the interpretation of this dream but will discuss briefly the utilization of both the consciously perceived vase with swastika and the subliminally registered snake in the formation of the dream. The subject for this experiment is a Gentile who happens to have only one testicle and is sterile. There has been a great deal of conflict between him and his wife over the fact that he is not able to give her a baby. The dream occurred on the night of the day that the subject had gone with his wife to visit her sister, who had just given birth to twins. This manifestation of excessive fertility had reactivated in the subject and his wife the conflict over their childlessness. The dream has to do with both the subject's wishes to give his wife a baby and his fantasies of her as a hostile, destructive female who wishes to

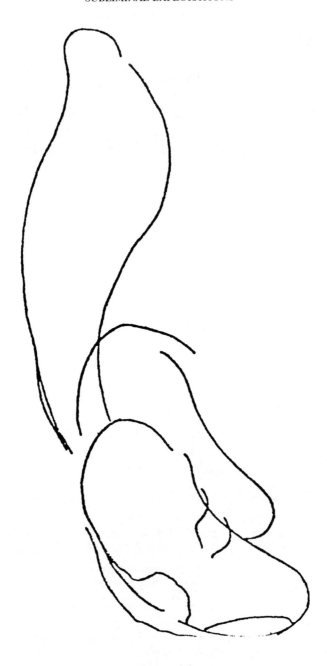

Figure 4.2

castrate him, all of this expressed in oral terms. The subject's associations indicated that he was identified with the dead cat and that the Jewish woman who was eating the cat's kidneys represented his wife. The appearance of the Jewish woman in the dream was stimulated by the consciously perceived swastika on the vase, which aroused in the subject memories of the Nazis and of their accusations against the Jews. Specifically, he connected the eating of the kidneys with the "ancient accusation against the Jews contained in the Protocols of the Elders of Zion that at Easter Jews eat Gentile babies, especially their foreskins." It can be seen, therefore, that both the consciously perceived swastika and the subliminally registered snake served as day residues.

Incidentally, we chose the vase and the snake to investigate symbol formation. The results suggest that some rather complex processes enter into the utilization of the percept of the snake as a phallic symbol. The snake's head and proximal part of the body were transformed into the kidneys with the attached piece of fat. Only when the drawing was made of these by the subject did he observe that it resembled the actual male genitals, and that the kidneys were testicle-shaped. This was a displacement from testicles to kidneys, probably representing a wish fulfillment—although the subject has only one testicle, he has two kidneys.

The day before the dream experiment, an imagery experiment was done with this subject: Following tachistoscopic exposure of the same stimulus of the vase and the snake, he was asked to close his eyes, produce images, and make drawings of them. A number of these images showed some interesting condensations of the supraliminal vase and the subliminal snake (Figure 4.3). This figure represents a drawing of one of the subject's images, described as a mummy case, old, rich, and antique, with a sheen on it. The decorative markings were described as black, and it was said to have a mummy inside, wrapped with *coils* of linen. Later on, during the reexposure period, the subject noted the resemblance between the decorative markings and the markings on the snake. He spontaneously pointed out that the mummy case had the shape of the vase and that the outer case resembled the *coils* of the snake in its decorative markings, its coloring, and the fact that it had a sheen on it like a snake. At the time that he had the image and drew it, however, the subject was totally unaware that

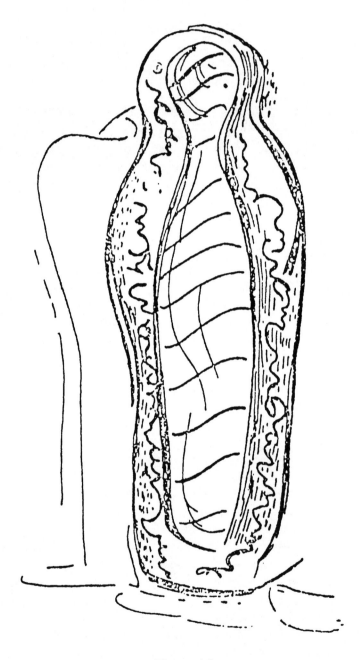

Figure 4.3

the shape of the mummy case resembled that of the vase. It seems likely, therefore, that the image represents a condensation of the consciously perceived but forgotten vase and the subliminally registered snake. The subject stated that the mummy case represented a dead womb, and it is possible that the designation "mummy case" was a play on words. The notion of a dead womb and the mummy case probably has some associative connection with the sterility theme, which subsequently reappeared in the dream of the next night. The mummy case contained a body, and the linen wrappings designated as *coils* probably represent another transformation of the coils of the snake. Because the tachistoscopic stimulus consisted of two striking and universal sexual symbols, it is important to notice that the dreams, images, and associative material all centered around sexual intercourse and ultimately involved the subject's problem with his wife.

With a second subject, the same stimulus was utilized in an imagery experiment. This experiment illustrates a progressive and striking emergence of the subliminally registered stimulus of the snake into consciousness. It shows, in addition, interesting condensations of the supraliminal vase with the subliminal snake.

Figure 4.4 represents an image of one of the 40 thieves of Ali Baba hiding in a jug. Later, the subject felt that the circular cover of the jar was taken from the central loop of the snake and the *coils* of the man's turban were transformations of the coils of the snake.

The second image (Figure 4.5) represents an amphora, derived from the vase, the emerging smoke becoming transformed into a genie. Note the sinuous snakelike structure of the smoke.

The genie reminded the subject of a mermaid he used to draw (Figure 4.6). He noted particularly the mermaid's scales, and then went on to state that when he was a child he was very much interested in reptiles and collected them, that the mermaid scales made him think of snakes.

The subject then had an image of an actual snake (Figure 4.7) that reminded him of an anti-Nazi cartoon. The snake is shown crawling through a vase, representing Europe, and bursting through its base. Upon the snake's head is a swastika. The cartoon represents the rape of Europe by the Nazis.

Figure 4.4

In this experiment, we see the gradual emergence of the percept of the snake beginning with the "coils" of the turban in the first image, the sinuous snakelike formation of the snake in the second, the mermaid's scaly tail in the third, and finally, the almost photographic emergence of the snake in the last image. In addition, in three of the images there was a condensation with the vase. In the last image, the swastika was detached from the vase and placed on the snake's head. Also, the symbolic sexual meaning of the vase and the snake must have been unconsciously understood. The actual image became a metaphorical representation of the "rape of Europe."

A few days prior to this imagery experiment the stimulus of the vase and the snake was utilized in a dream experiment with the same subject. The important part of the dream dealt with the

Figure 4.5

Figure 4.6

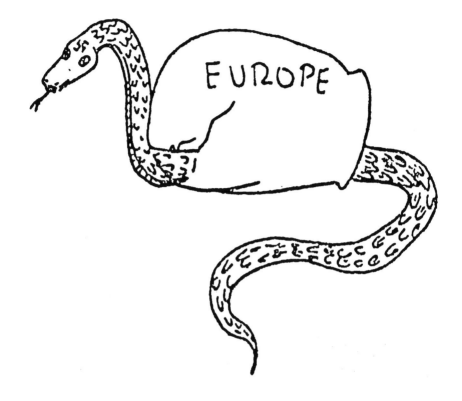

Figure 4.7

subject's unconscious homosexual feelings about the experimenter. In the dream, a doctor approaches the subject from the
rear and puts his arms around the subject's chest. The subject
could not see the doctor, only the arms in front of him. He drew
the picture shown in Figure 4.8, representing the arms of the
doctor embracing him. Later on, during the reexposure, the subject pointed out that the shape of the fingers and thumb of the
right hand were transformations of the head of the snake. It was
as though the doctor *coiled* his arms around him like a boa con-
strictor.

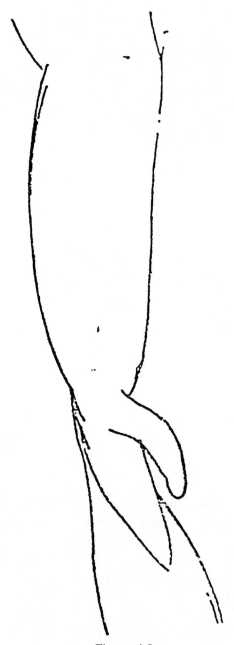

Figure 4.8

Throughout the subject's images and dreams, there was striking evidence that the symbolic phallic significance of the snake was unconsciously apperceived. However, aside from the breakthrough of the percept of the snake in the image of the rape of Europe, the snake never appeared as such in the images and dreams. It was displaced in a distorted and disguised way to the extremities, either the arms or legs. This is shown clearly, for example, in the snakelike arms of the doctor who embraced him, the scaly mermaid's tail, and the sinuous structure of the smoke that represented the lower half of the genie's body.

The experiments that I have described, utilizing the stimulus of the vase and the snake, demonstrate not only the important role subliminally registered percepts play in the manifest pictorial structure of dreams and images, but also that the consciously perceived elements, namely the vase and the swastika, act as significant day residues. In the dreams of the first subject, the most affectively charged element in the dream, namely, the kidneys with the piece of fat, were clearly derived from the subliminally registered snake. The same is true of the dream of the second subject; I refer to the snakelike embracing arms of the doctor. In the dreams of both subjects, the consciously perceived vase and swastika served as day residues activating significant preconscious dream thoughts relating to the Nazis and the subjects' feelings of anti-Semitism.

The two experiments just described, as well as data from five additional subjects who were exposed to the same stimulus, suggest that the dream work deals with a subliminal stimulus in a different manner than it does a supraliminal, consciously perceived one. The subliminal registration appears in the dream in image form as an indirect representation, disguised and distorted in relation to the wish-fulfilling drive aspect of the dream. The supraliminal stimulus, on the other hand, has a tendency to appear as a direct derivative of the stimulus and to activate preconscious trains of thought which appear in secondary process terms. For example, the kidneys with the piece of fat are what I refer to as an indirect derivative of the subliminal snake—the transformed image of a kind that would not ordinarily occur to anyone in the conscious waking state. The supraliminal swastika activated associations having to do with Jews, Nazis, anti-Semitism, and so forth of the same kind that one might have in the waking state, and these are what I call direct derivatives.

These experiments confirm our earlier impressions, as well as Shevrin and Luborsky's (1958) work, demonstrating that, although Pötzl (1915) was correct about the role of subliminal registrations in dream formation, he was incorrect in assuming that the noticed, supraliminal, conscious parts of tachistoscopically exposed pictures played no role in dream formation. These experiments have important implications for the theory of thinking and the relationship of the primary to the secondary process. They suggest that very complex and intricate processes go on within the ego apparatuses of perception and memory. They indicate, for example, that one and the same memory image can be utilized simultaneously for both primary and secondary process thinking. I refer specifically to the complex vicissitudes of a supraliminal and consciously remembered percept. After a tachistoscopic exposure, the subject can remember the next day or a week later that he perceived and discriminated the vase with the swastika. In the interval, however, the memory image of the percept may fall into the preconscious state, undergo the same kinds of condensations, displacements, and other primary-process-like transformations as registrations that were subliminal to begin with, and be utilized in dreams, images, and hallucinations. Furthermore, they may undergo complex condensations with subliminally registered percepts. These observations give some idea of how intricate the relationship between primary and secondary process must be.

THE UTILIZATION OF SUBLIMINAL REGISTRATIONS IN HALLUCINATIONS

The second problem that I wish to take up is the influence of altered states of consciousness on the Pötzl phenomenon. Specifically, I will discuss briefly some experiments with a hallucinating subject who was studied by the method of subliminal visual stimulation using the tachistoscope. In addition, stimuli were made subliminal by utilizing the masking technique described by Urbantschitsch (1907). A stimulus may be made subliminal by decreasing the exposure time, by decreasing illumination, or by placing the object at a distance too far for the subject to discriminate. A fourth possible method was described many years ago by Urbantschitsch in his book on eidetic imagery: the use of parts of pictures that had been covered up by thin sheets of paper to the point where nothing could be discriminated. The assumption was that there had been subliminal registration of percepts through the sheets of paper. This extremely interesting finding of Urbantschitsch (1907) has, to my knowledge, never been reinvestigated.

Pötzl was led to undertake his dream experiments as a result of certain observations he made while working with patients with visual agnosias. He observed that these patients registered visual percepts outside of awareness which subsequently, and in a delayed manner, were delivered into consciousness and projected outward in hallucinatory form. He then proceeded to perform some tachistoscopic experiments on patients who had visual hallucinations (Pötzl, 1915). He reported a study of a patient with alcoholic hallucinosis and cerebral hemianopsia who was hallucinating. He found that prolonged exposure of objects and pictures provoked no hallucinations, but that hallucinations were produced regularly when pictures were exposed tachistoscopically. These hallucinations appeared in a discontinuous series, those parts of the exposed picture that had remained unnoticed appearing in the subsequent hallucinations. The hallucinations resembled dream pictures in that they showed condensations, displacements, mirror images, and reversals. Following these experiments, Pötzl decided to repeat the procedure in the normal hallucination, namely, that of the dream, and again he was able to demonstrate the same finding.

Although Pötzl's dream experiments have been repeated by myself and a number of other investigators, and his essential results confirmed, there has never been a report of a repetition of the 1915 experiments on hallucinations.

METHOD

The experiments were carried out in the following manner: A number of pictures were exposed tachistoscopically at speeds of either 1/50 or 1/100 sec. The subject was asked to describe and draw what he had seen during exposure. He was then asked to close his eyes and let pictures come into his mind or to look at the wall or screen to see if any hallucinatory images developed. He was asked to describe and draw any images or hallucinations that developed immediately after exposure or after a lapse of one or several days. Some weeks later, after completion of the series of experiments, all the subliminal stimuli were reexposed for prolonged periods and the subject was asked to compare his drawings with the pictures.

Several experiments utilizing the masking technique of Urbantschitsch were carried out in the following manner: Colored pictures, depicting rather dramatic scenes, were covered with thin sheets of translucent paper, to the point where nothing could be discriminated. With the two pictures used, four or five sheets were required for this purpose. The picture was mounted on cardboard, covered with the sheets of translucent paper. The subject was instructed simply to fix his eyes on the seemingly blank page and to stare at it. He was then asked to report and draw anything that he saw.

Threshold determinations were made after the completion of the experiments by removing the sheets of paper one by one until the picture was identified.

Case I

A 13-year-old black youth, Bobby, who was hallucinating vividly in both the auditory and visual fields, was the subject.[1] The patient was diagnosed as having a schizoaffective psychosis. The diagnosis was complicated by the fact that 7 years earlier, the patient had been treated for a juvenile paresis, and, as a matter of fact, he behaved more like a paretic than a schizophrenic. At the time I saw him, he was having visual hallucinations of monsters who tear people up and take out their bones, and of devils, angels, and the Lord. In spite of his hallucinatory condition, he was an excellent subject, extremely cooperative and able to verbalize and describe his hallucinations in great detail, capable of relating himself to

---

[1] The patient was hospitalized in the psychiatric ward of Bellevue Hospital, New York, where these experiments were conducted.

the experimenter, and, in addition, he happened to be an excellent artist who enjoyed making drawings of his hallucinations and imagery.

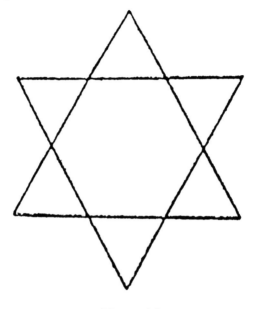

Figure 4.9

Experiment I. A six-pointed star (Figure 4.9) was exposed to the subject for 1/50 sec. On exposure, Bobby saw nothing but a flash of light. About an hour after the exposure of the picture, the patient had a hallucination (Figure 4.10). He saw a male friend of his swallowing something that was red hot. The drawing that the subject made is a sagittal section of the head showing the red-hot object going down the boy's throat. Notice its star-shaped form. The presumption is that the star was subliminally registered and appeared transformed into the red-hot object in the hallucination.

Experiment II. The next experiment carried out with Bobby involved the exposure of a picture showing two cats and a parakeet (Figure 2.11). During exposure, the subject saw a house and a farm but neither the cats nor the bird.

The subject was then asked to look at the door on which the picture had been projected. He immediately stated that he saw a bird with a cracked eye (Figure 4.11). "It looks like an ordinary

Figure 4.10

person but it can fly and stand up. It is part bird and part man and it has a long horn on its nose." This is the first time the subject ever hallucinated a bird. It is possible that the crest on the bird's head is a displacement from the cat ears and the horn on the beak a displacement from a cat's tail. At any rate, it is reasonable to suppose that the bird was derived from the subliminal registration of the parakeet. When, some time later, Bobby's conscious recognition threshold for the parakeet and star were determined, they were found to be markedly elevated and accompanied by serious perceptual distortions. He saw the two cats on

Figure 4.11

top of one another and the star as having 10 points, at exposure times far longer than normal subjects need for full and accurate discrimination.

Experiment III. The picture of a double profile (Figure 4.12), such as is used by the Gestalt school to illustrate alternating figure–ground relationships, was exposed to the subject for 1/50 sec. On exposure, he saw nothing but a flash of light. One of the images that he had was described as half-snake, half-rhinoceros

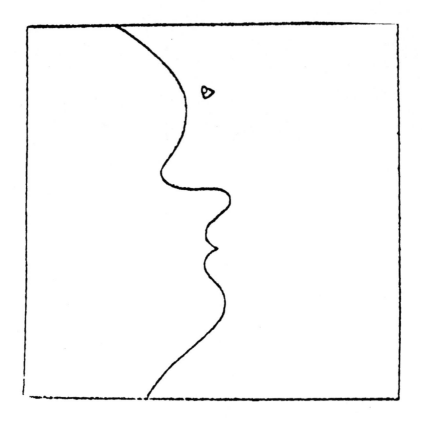

Figure 4.12

(Figure 4.13). It can be seen that this drawing is composed of a wavy double line and probably represents a distortion of the double-profile picture. Note how much the left side of the drawing resembles the profile line in the exposed picture.

Experiment IV. A colored picture showing a Minoan bull fight was covered up with five sheets of translucent paper so that, on looking at it, one appeared to see only a blank sheet of paper (Figure 4.14). This picture shows a national sport of ancient Crete, a dangerous diversion in which male and female acrobats leaped and somersaulted over the backs of charging bulls. The drawing depicts a woman doing a handspring on the back of the bull. I wish to point out just two elements in the picture, namely, the long hanging strands of hair and the shape and formation of the left breast.

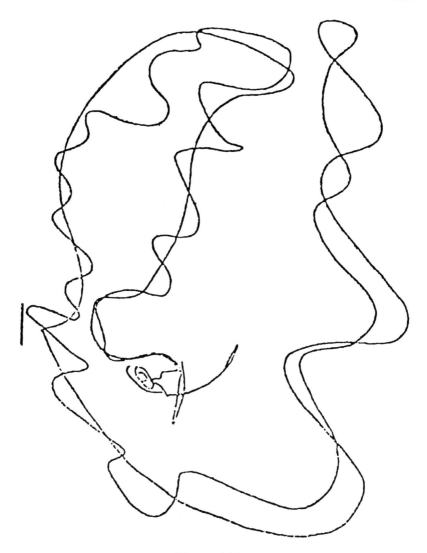

Figure 4.13

The patient was asked to look at the covered-up picture for a minute. During exposure, he saw nothing. He was then asked to close his eyes and to produce images. The first image that he produced he described as a man (Figure 4.15). He drew a man's head and then said that it was an octopus; he proceeded to draw the octopus shown in the figure, described as having "12 foots."

Figure 4.14

It seems probable, and this was confirmed by the subject, that the octopus represents a condensation of the long strands of hair hanging from the girl and the breast, the breast having been transformed into the eye of the octopus.

Case II

Several tachistoscopic experiments were carried out with a 45-year-old woman (Mrs. H) who was thought to have a hysterical

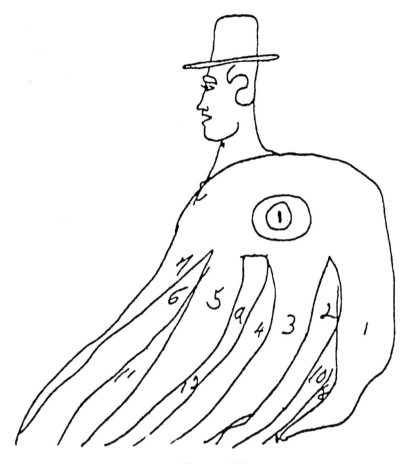

Figure 4.15

blindness but later turned out to have a chromophobe adenoma of the pituitary with pressure on the optic chiasm, producing an almost total organic blindness. Before the pituitary blindness was discovered, when it was believed that the patient had a hysterical blindness, we thought it would be interesting to attempt some tachistoscopic experiments on her, both for diagnostic purposes and to see if the Pötzl phenomenon could be elicited. It was believed that if the patient were in fact suffering from hysterical blindness, tachistoscopically exposed stimuli would be registered and might appear in subsequent dreams. It should be noted that in addition to being blind, this subject had almost continuous vivid visual hallucinations, many of them of a highly unpleasant nature. For example, she would see black worms all over her body or gray balloons floating in front of her. That there was some residual vision present is suggested by the fact that at times there was a dim perception of the walls of the room or vague perceptions of movement.

Experimental Method. I told the subject that I was going to do some experiments to test her vision. I placed her in front of the screen and flashed the light of the projector on and off a number of times, asking her to tell me whether it was light or dark. She seemed unable to distinguish when it was on or off. After doing this a few times I exposed a picture for 1/100 sec without letting her know that I had done so. I then asked her to describe her hallucinations and followed their course of development over a period of days.

Experiment I. The double-profile stimulus was exposed for 1/100 sec, immediately after which the subject was asked to describe and draw what she was hallucinating. She drew a series of figures that she said looked like heads in profile facing to the right. In spite of the fact that the subject was apparently blind she was able to draw by feel.

Six hours after exposure some additional descriptions and drawings were obtained of the subject's hallucinations, which represented images of a little white soldier. She made a drawing of a Januslike figure with a profile on the right and one on the left. She made many drawings of this sort and a series of additional profile drawings of the soldiers. She evidently began to hallucinate the little soldiers early in the afternoon after the exposure of the picture. She stated that she saw their heads, the heads were covered as though made of soap or wax, they were all white, and there was no motion. She continued to hallucinate these soldiers off and on for 4 days. She believed that I brought these soldiers into her hallucinations through some kind of suggestion or hypnosis, that I held something in my hand and put it into her head.

It seems probable that the little white soldiers were transformations of the tachistoscopically exposed reversible profiles. This is suggested by the Januslike appearance of the heads, by the fact that these were hallucinations never experienced before, which appeared shortly after tachistoscopic exposure, and by the subjective feeling of the patient that is some mysterious manner I caused her to hallucinate.

Experiment II. The picture of the Tower of London (Figure 1.12) was exposed for 1/100 sec in the same manner as previously described, that is, without the subject apparently being aware of the exposure. The night of the day of the experiment the subject had a long dream. Briefly, in this dream the subject was inside a building, looking out through a window from which she could see people passing by in the street. The building and the setting were described as very old, such as one might have seen several hundred years ago. The principal incident in the dream had to do with the subject walking down a corridor, at the end of which was a closet. She opened the closet and found a dead man there. The man had been murdered. The patient drew a picture of the dead man in the closet, stating that all she could see was the jacket part of the man, so she had drawn him without arms or legs. She described the closet as being dark.

The following considerations suggest that the pictorial content of this dream was derived from subliminally registered elements of the tachistoscopically exposed picture: The building and the setting, described as several hundred years old, could have been derived from the antiquity of the Tower of London. The dream also involves a street scene and people walking by. Most importantly, this particular picture has elicited dreams, images, or hallucinations of death, murder, and executions in practically all subjects to whom it has been shown. The black sentry box lends itself to associations about death and coffins, and the Tower of London seems to evoke ideas about executions or murder. The drawing of the murdered man in the closet shows several interesting features that have frequently shown up in experiments with other subjects. For example, because the sentry box is so black, the dark trousers of the sentry merge into the blackness and are hardly distinguishable. Therefore, an image is produced of half a man, without legs and sometimes without arms. In this instance, the subject specifically noted the absence of arms and legs and said there was "just the jacket part of the man." It is also to be noted that the head was drawn as very large with some shading. Because of the guard's huge bearskin, this picture very frequently elicits images of very large heads.

The results that I have reported confirm Pötzl's 1915 observations on hallucinating patients. They tend to show that subliminal registrations emerge in hallucinations within minutes of tachistoscopic exposure and may continue to appear in subsequent hallucinations over a period of at least several days. The manner in which the subliminal registrations are utilized in hallucinations seems to be identical to that of normal dreams and images.

The memory images of the subliminally registered percepts undergo a number of significant transformations. These recent memory images of percepts that have not attained consciousness appear to be extremely plastic and to undergo fragmentations, condensations, displacements, rotations, and other transformations. The memory image of the percept may appear in the hallucination in its original form, for example, the parakeet in a picture that showed up in the hallucination as an actual bird. On the other hand, and this appeared to occur with great frequency in Bobby's hallucinations, the memory image of the percept may lose its original meaning and emerge with a new meaning attached to it. Thus, the star showed up in the hallucination as a red-hot object which is being swallowed, but retained the form of a star. It is because the memory images of these subliminal registrations are so plastic, and because they lose their reality-oriented meaning, that they are suitable for the representation of egocentric, autistic expressions such as occur in dreams and hallucinations. If percepts can come to mean *anything*, they are especially suitable for the expression of unconscious wishes and drives, and the demands of reality need not be considered. They provide the perceptual clay out of which the dream visions are molded. Thus, strands of hair may become the arms of an octopus, a profile line may become a snake, and so on.

It was Pötzl's idea that the subliminal process of registration of visual percepts goes on continually but that these percepts are prevented from attaining consciousness by some central inhibiting mechanism. During sleep, in the presence of brain damage, or in a psychosis, this inhibiting mechanism is removed and the subliminal registrations appear in dreams or hallucinations in a delayed manner. I have shown also that such subliminal registrations appear in normal imagery when a person is requested to relax and engage in a sort of free imagery reverie process. In the case of Bobby, the delivery of the subliminal registrations into his hallucinations took place very freely, suggesting that in psychosis the pathway from registration to consciousness is more open and the inhibiting mechanism postulated by Pötzl disinhibited.

Diagnosis in both Bobby and Mrs. H presented difficulties. As has been noted, although Bobby carried a diagnosis of schizophrenia, there was a history of juvenile paresis, so that it is difficult to evaluate the role that organic brain damage played in his condition. In the case of Mrs. H, both the blindness and the hallucinations must have been caused by the pressure of the expanding pituitary tumor. The several experiments that were carried out on her indicated that she was registering subliminal visual stimuli that quickly emerged in her hallucinations and, in at least one instance, in her dreams. Although clinically she appeared to be nearly totally blind, these experiments suggest that there was some residual vision, and the assumption seems to be warranted that enough visual pathway was intact to permit the registration of subliminal stimuli and the incorporation of these into her dreams and hallucinations. It has been demonstrated how astonishingly extensive subliminal registration is, and that far more is registered than appears in consciousness. Experiments with Mrs. H suggest that such registration may take place in the presence of a markedly damaged visual system. If this observation can be confirmed, it will have significant implications for neurophysiology.

The few experiments done with Bobby that utilized the paper-masking technique of Urbantschitsch provide suggestive evidence of the emergence into images and hallucinations of the stimuli made subliminal by this technique. Some rough threshold determinations were made by removing the sheets of paper one by one. Bobby was not able to identify the stimuli until all but one sheet of paper was removed. The effect of stimuli made subliminal by the Urbantschitsch technique will have to be validated in the future by more carefully designed and controlled experiments.

In Bobby it was found that conscious, reality-oriented perception was markedly disturbed. There seems to be a direct relationship between the extensiveness of the utilization of subliminal registrations in hallucinations and the degree of disturbance of supraliminal, conscious perception.

LSD Experiment

The second state of altered consciousness whose effect on the Pötzl phenomenon was investigated is that produced by administering LSD. It is a well-known fact that in many experimental subjects LSD produces vivid hallucinations. I was interested in ascertaining whether subliminal registrations emerge in the imagery or hallucinations of subjects under LSD. The subject of the experiment was a physician who volunteered for the experiment because he wished to study the effect of the drug on himself. In this experiment the stimulus was made subliminal by using the paper-masking technique. In a control experiment in the undrugged state a picture was covered with five sheets of translucent paper until nothing could be discriminated, and the subject was instructed to look at it for one minute. He was then asked to produce a series of 10 images and to draw them. The subject produced images with difficulty, showed much constriction in his capacity for fantasy, and produced images that were largely nonhuman geometrical forms with little associative content. Some of these may possibly have been derived from the stimulus, especially one described as two things meeting that looked like green sharks.[2] This image may have some relationship to the package of Life Savers candy balancing on the nose of the tightrope walker.

At a later session, 80 mg of LSD were administered by mouth. About $2^{1}/_{2}$ hours after the drug was administered, when the subject was showing marked effects of the drug, largely in the form of distortions in time sense and some symptoms of derealization, the stimulus of the tightrope walker was again exposed under five sheets of paper, and the subject asked to produce and draw images. The first was the image of an old Indian face like an Aztec, split in the middle. The second was the image of a little boy with a long nose. This image kept returning to the subject throughout the experiment, the nose getting longer and longer. About 3 hours after the experiment was begun, it was terminated by injecting 50 mg of thorazine intramuscularly into the buttock. The

---

[2]The stimulus picture was of a little man high up on a tightrope, balancing a package of Life Savers on his nose.

subject then had a vivid feeling of the flesh of his buttock "ballooning out" as the injection was carried out.

A number of experimental images that developed, as well as the images of the dream that the subject had the night of this experiment, revolved around a swelling, growing mass of flesh. The most significant images of this sort that developed during the imagery experiment were those involving the little boy's long nose that kept growing. These appear to have been transformations of the cylindrical package of Life Savers balancing on the nose of the tightrope walker; this idea was confirmed by the subject himself. The image of the ballooning mass of flesh on the buttock that appeared during the thorazine injection is another version of this idea. It is important to note that during threshold determination, the subject was not able to discriminate the package of Life Savers until only one sheet of paper remained. Although no human faces appeared in the control or experimental images before the injection of LSD, they did develop after administration of the drug. Under LSD, the imagery generally was more structured, vivid, and intense than during the control period. At times, there was an approach to hallucinatorylike experience, but no actual hallucinations developed. The results confirm the findings that LSD is a primitivizing agent. In this subject, although it did not produce hallucinations, it did intensify the vividness of the imagery and also resulted in a schizophreniclike distortion of time sense and other regressive manifestations. The experiments also provides suggestive evidence for, and confirmation of, Urbantschitsch's observation, over 75 years ago, that a stimulus made subliminal by the paper-masking technique can emerge in subsequent imagery.

FIGURE–GROUND RELATIONSHIPS

Pötzl was the first to observe in his tachistoscopic dream experiments that vague, background forms, as opposed to figural elements, appeared to undergo subliminal registration and emerge in a delayed manner in subsequent dreams, images, and hallucinations. These background forms act like concealed and buried figures. It is as though there is a reversal of the usual fig-ure–ground relationships. I have put this idea to the experimental test by using as a stimulus that Rubin double-profile figure shown earlier and found that both profiles undergo registration, are cognized and discriminated, and may appear as two faces in subse-quent dreams and images. Figure 4.16 (see chapter 3) shows some

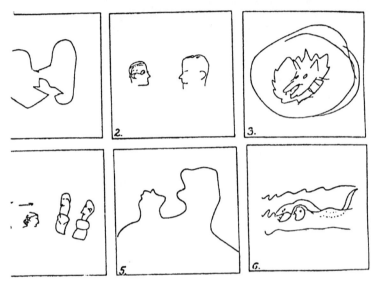

Figure 4.16

of the images elicited during this experiment. Note especially Image No. 3, which is supposed to be a picture of a hyena break-ing through a paper hoop. The hyena is in semiprofile, and the upper margin of the outline of the paper hoop appears to form a human profile. A striking detail is the right ear of the hyena corresponding to the triangular eye of the right profile in the stimulus, which simultaneously constitutes the ear of the hyena and the eye of the human profile formed by the margin of the hole in the paper. It is as though the head of the hyena bursting through the paper left the outline of a human profile.

These experiments suggest that while the figure–ground effect holds for conscious perception, it appears to be suppressed or becomes fluid during subliminal registration or the subsequent preconscious imagery process. They indicate further that the Ge-stalt laws of good continuation, closure, figure-ground, and so forth hold only for the state of consciousness mobilized during experimental laboratory procedures when the intention of the subject is to master, communicate, and evaluate the properties of things, but that these laws do not hold for subliminally registered forms.

THE USE OF PRIMARY PERCEPTUAL AND IMAGERY PROCESS IN MODERN ART

Examination of the paintings of certain modern artists has suggested the possibility that these artists have managed, through a controlled regression in the service of the ego, in Kris's (1952) sense, to make available to consciousness the preliminary, preconscious phases of the perceptual and imagery process. It was thought that it might be interesting to make a comparative study of modern paintings, and the art productions of children, primitives, and psychotics for evidence of the utilization of the same perceptual imagery mechanisms that appear to play such an important role in the formation of normal dreams and images. The present study represents the beginnings of such a project.

George Klein (1956) has pointed out that the artist continuously explores latent form properties of objects. He learns to perceive against the normal principles that govern figure-ground, good form, continuation, closure, and so forth. He destroys in order to discover new forms. The peripheral or background nature of a form lends to it certain positive properties that it no longer has when in awareness. These properties are analogous to those of dream images, making forms fluid and easily fused, tending away from the precision, simplicity, and singleness of meaning of adaptive conscious vision.

Ehrenzweig (1953) is of the opinion that there must be an unconscious perception, which he calls gestalt-free perception, that is not bound by the conscious gestalt, and during which competing form combinations such as background negatives are registered. He believes that every perception, even the shortest, has to pass through many levels of unconscious integration. He speaks of a "structural" repression as opposed to repression

brought about by the activity of the superego. By structural repression, he refers to the "inarticulate," gestalt-free, unconscious
perceptual and imagery mechanisms of the "depth" in mind that
ordinarily remain out of awareness. This structural repression of
"inarticular perceptions" he believes may be more fundamental
and older than the human superego and its censorship of mental
contents. It is these gestalt-free modes of perceiving and imaging
that creative artists are able to make use of. These modes appear
to be identical to the preliminary stages of perception and imagery that we have described.

An examination of several of Picasso's paintings will help to
illustrate this kind of utilization of gestalt-free perception and
imagery. Figure 4.17 is a reproduction of Picasso's *Three Dancers.*
At first glance, the dancer on the right is represented by the
figure in gray with the small head in profile against a black background. On further examination, however, it can be seen that
the background behind the head is painted in the shape of a
profile with a stylized, tapering head. That is, there is a head
within a head, a background head coming into the foreground
when the attention is shifted. The dancer on the left appears to
be bent backwards with her left leg flexed. One breast seems to
be drawn in the shape of an eye. If looked at from another angle,
this figure resembles the head and forepart of some sort of bovine
animal. The structure that serves as the breast of the dancer simultaneously is the eye of the animal. This is identical to the image of
the hyena jumping through the paper hoop, previously described,
where the same structure simultaneously serves as the ear of the
hyena and the eye of the human profile. The head of the dancer
on the left shows a curious configuration; it is actually composed
of two profile heads at right angles to one another. There are
markings to indicate the hair of the heads. If the figure of this
dancer also contains the head of an animal, as has been suggested, these hairs simultaneously become the hairs on the snout
of the animal. It can also be seen that, although these are supposed to be three dancers, there are actually five faces incorporated into the painting. This is similar to the phenomenon of
multiplication of percepts, as frequently observed in the dream
and imagery experiments.

Figure 4.17. Pablo Picasso. *Three Dancers*. The Tate Gallery, London.
© 2002 Estate of Pablo Picasso/Artists Rights Society (ARS), New York.

A second painting, Figure 4.18, *The Seated Woman,* shows some additional mechanisms of gestalt-free perception. One is first struck by the profile of the woman with a large nose facing toward the right. On shifting attention, however, a second profile figure can be seen to the right; the face is black and the small circle constitutes an eye. As a matter of fact, this painting very much resembles the double-profile figure used as a stimulus in our experiments. By making figure-ground fluid, Picasso produces the effect of multiple aspects of the seated woman, and firm figure–ground relationships are abolished. Ehrenzweig has pointed out that modern art shows background forms throughout, that is, a failure to differentiate between figure and ground, or figure and ground interpenetrate.

Still other gestalt-free mechanisms can be observed in Picasso's paintings. It has been shown that the memory images of subliminally registered percepts may lose their original meaning and be apperceived as something else; thus, a face may emerge into consciousness as a mountain peak, an elephant as a fireplace, or a human figure as a cactus plant. This is very similar to the perceptual processes shown by children in their play, where any object may become another, such as a stick becoming a gun, so long as there is some formal resemblance. In Picasso's bronze, *Baboon and Young* (Figure 4.19), the face of the baboon is composed of a child's toy automobile, which was incorporated into the head. The hood of the toy car and the sloping windshield resemble the nasobuccal region, eyes, and brow of a baboon. In his painted bronze, *Goat Skull and Bottle* (Figure 4.20), Picasso has utilized a pair of bicycle handlebars for the horns of the goat. Imaginatively, the percept of the handlebars loses its original meaning and takes on the meaning of goat horns.

Summarizing, we can see that Picasso's works show the following mechanisms of gestalt-free perception and imagery:

1. Abolition of the usual figure–ground relationships, the reversal of figure-ground, and the utilization of concealed figures.
2. Fusions and condensations—for example, the eye of one figure is fused with the breast of another into a single structure which represents both.

Figure 4.18. Pablo Picasso. *The Seated Woman*, 1927. Oil on wood. Gift of James Thrall Soby. © 2002 Estate of Pablo Picasso/Artists Rights Society (ARS), New York.

Figure 4.19. Pablo Picasso. *Baboon and Young.* 1951. Bronze (cast 1955), after found objects. Mrs. Simon Guggenheim Fund. © The Museum of Modern Art/Licensed by SCALA/Art Resource, NY, Museum of Modern Art, New York.

Figure 4.20. Pablo Picasso. *Goat Skull and Bottle.* 1951–1952. Painted bronze (cast 1954). Mrs. Simon Guggenheim Fund. © The Museum of Modern Art/Licensed by SCALA/Art Resource, NY, Museum of Modern Art, New York.

3. Multiplications of percept such as the five profiles utilized in the painting of three dancers, and the head of the seated woman duplicated in the double-profile drawing.
4. Frequent displacements—for example, a much-used one is the displacement of both eyes to one side of the head.
5. Extensive fragmentation of the percept.
6. Loss of percept's meaning and taking on another.
7. Frequent rotations and spatial translocations.

I do not wish to imply that we have given an explanation of Picasso's work or artistic genius, but only that one aspect of his art is the availability to him of the dreamlike mechanisms of ge-stalt-free perception and imagery. This does not imply an enhanced availability of unconscious processes in the dynamic psychoanalytic sense. I am referring to the preliminary phases of the perceptual and imagery process that take place outside of consciousness (see chapters 1, 3). These represent unconscious phases of the functioning of the ego apparatus of perception and imagery; they are something inherent and autonomous in the apparatus itself. It may be that Picasso also was able to represent unconscious, dynamic content as, for example, in his more surrealistic productions. But the paintings we have discussed do not show any particular evidence of this. Rather, there is a utilization of the thought-forms of the primary process and of the gestalt-free perceptual and memory mechanisms subserving it that are involved in the discharge of instinctual drive content, but need not necessarily always be so. They may be brought into play in artistic creation relatively independently of the expression of unconscious content. Christian Zervos is reported by Barr (1946, p. 272) as stating that a fruitful approach would be to make a photographic record of the transformations of his pictures. He stated, "Possibly one might discover the path followed by the brain in materializing a dream."

My contention that Picasso, as well as other modern painters, has made available to himself primitive and preliminary preconscious forms of perception and imagery is in agreement with Ehrenzweig (1953), who stated that the European painter has managed to penetrate to the:

> Gestalt-free, thing-free modes of vision in the last phases of his centuries' old withdrawal from external reality. In this sense, Picasso's play with space would represent yet another advance of unconscious modes of vision. It is probably due to the half-automatic method of working ascribed to Picasso and other modern artists that such deeply repressed modes of vision enter the structure of modern art [p. 120].

SUMMARY

Additional observations on the Pötzl phenomenon, that is, the effects of subliminal visual stimulation on dreams, images, and hallucinations, have been reported.

1. Some preliminary experiments have demonstrated that supraliminal, consciously perceived percepts, contrary to Pötzl's findings, are utilized in dreams. It has been shown that the supraliminal stimuli set off preconscious trains of thought, direct derivatives of which appear in secondary process form in the manifest content of the dream. The subliminal stimulus appears in the dream in sensory image form in relation to the wish-fulfilling drive aspect of the dream and as an indirect, transformed, and disguised derivative.
2. Pötzl's observation that subliminal registrations are extensively utilized in hallucinations has been confirmed. In addition, some suggestive evidence that the subliminal registration can take place when the Urbantschitsch masking technique is utilized has been presented.
3. Some data were presented showing that at subliminal levels, the usual figure–ground relationship becomes fluid or reversed.
4. The use of primary perceptual and imagery processes in modern art was discussed, utilizing some of the works of Picasso as illustrations.

ADDENDUM I

Subsequent to the experiments reported above, I completed a pilot study (Fisher, 1960b) in which the snake was made supraliminal and the vase–swastika subliminal. The formulation that I had made in regard to the manner in which the two stimuli are handled by the dream work turned out to be only partially correct and more complex than I had envisioned. At least three factors appeared to influence the relationship of the stimuli to the primary and secondary processes: (1) the degree of indifference of the stimulus, that is, whether it was subliminal or supraliminal; (2) the meaning content of the stimulus; and (3) the personality characteristics, conflicts, and defensive operations of the subject.

The most striking finding was that when the snake was made supraliminal, it did not appear to be represented in the manifest content in any form. For example, one patient had a dream that he was watching some men open a wall safe that revealed secrets involving a scandal in which six men raped a teenage girl (cf. the image in Figure 4.7—the rape of Europe). The dream ended with the subject being pursued by and hiding from a man who was after him. His associations to the dream led him to childhood memories of his uncle cleaning out a well and killing snakes. His uncle picked up a snake and threw it at him; he screamed and ran into the house. Ever since this traumatic experience, he has had a severe phobia for snakes. The snake incident served as a screen memory against a repressed group of fantasies associated with homosexual fears and wishes relating to the uncle and to his "secret" that he had overt homosexual tendencies. It is clear, further, that when the snake was made supraliminal, it did not behave in the same manner as the swastika and did not activate preconscious trains of secondary process thought. It seemed that the stimulus being a snake was more important than its being supraliminal or subliminal. The snake is a highly charged phallic symbol, suitable to resonate with the drive organization of memories and repressed unconscious wishes. The role of supraliminal stimuli of varying meaning content and affective charge is in need of further investigation.

ADDENDUM II: SUBSEQUENT HISTORY OF SUBLIMINAL RESEARCH

The research on subliminal perception in the United States was carried out by a large group of psychoanalytically trained psychologists. All of them, including myself, were influenced by David Rapaport (1951) and his program for investigating psychoanalytic theories of thinking, memory, and perception. These included a large group from the Research Center for Mental Health, New York University, directed by George Klein and Robert Holt and their coworkers: Spence, Paul, Pine, Goldberger, Eagle, Bach, Wolitzsky, and Fiss. At the Menninger Foundation, Howard Shevrin and Lester Luborsky confirmed and extended the work on the Pötzl phenomenon. In England, Norman Dixon, a psychologist, began working on subliminal perception in the early 1950s and has been one of the most persistent defenders of this controversial work; he has continued to be productive up to the present time. Smith and his coworkers in Sweden have continued their work for many years (cf. Fisher, 1960a, for historical review).

In this country subliminal research was at its height from the early fifties to the early sixties. It overlapped with very active research that was being carried out by a large and prominent group of academic psychologists on what came to be known as "perceptual defense." This work became known as the "New Look." Perceptual defense held that verbal stimuli that are emotionally disturbing or threatening tend to require a longer recognition time than neutral words. It was believed that perception of external stimuli is not free from the influences of such internal events as emotions, needs, attitudes, values, and expectancies. Perceptual defense presented a dilemma that in order *"not* to recognize a stimulus, it must first be recognized." It was believed that a defending agent implied a manikin theory or homunculus situation, or what Allport (1955) called the specter of a "subconscious pre-perceiving perceiver" (p. 45). Finally, the New Look was discredited by destructive and critical arguments from the very same prominent psychologists who had supported it in the first place. At the same time, the work on subliminal perception was subjected to similar criticisms, the most important of which was the contention that there could not be cognition without awareness.

A third, seemingly trivial, event helped to bring about a decline in the work on subliminal perception. Seldom has anything in psychology caused such an immediate and widespread furor as was precipitated by the claim of a commercial firm that the subliminal presentation of the words *Eat popcorn* or *Drink Coca-Cola* during the showing of a motion picture fantastically stimulated the sales of these products to the viewers. Though this event raised the hopes and venality of American advertising firms, the hue and cry led to the banning of the procedure by the British Advertising Council and alarmed reactions within Congress and the Federal Communications Commission; fears of Big Brother, of brainwashing, and of "hidden persuaders" reached phobic proportions.

By about 1960 there was a precipitous decline in subliminal research. However, a few of the analysts continued their work in the field. Most important is Howard Shevrin, who initiated and continued his neurophysiological work using average evoked potentials. Donald Spence wrote on the constricting effects of awareness and other important matters.

According to Erdelyi (1985), the failure of experimental psychology to corroborate the existence of unconscious processes was taken to reflect the failure of the concept rather than the failure of the extant methodology.

A new theoretical revolution was brewing within mainstream experimental psychology. This new perspective, usually known as the *information-processing approach* or the cognitive revolution, involved the adoption of the computer as a model of human information processing. This approach is associated with the names of such prominent psychologists as Broadbent, Haber, Miller, and Neisser.

Although the cognitive revolution had no contact with psychoanalytic theory, the adoption of the computer metaphor generated a host of theoretical constructs that came close to constituting rediscoveries of basic Freudian notions. For example, the term *censorship* became *filtering selectivity*, ego executive control processes became *conflict decision nodes, cathexes,* became *force,* and so on. Because these new concepts had direct counterparts in the computer, there was nothing remotely mystical about them. The concept of unconscious processes was not only not controversial but an obvious and fundamental feature of human information processing. Independent of each other, numerous experimental psychologists reintroduced to cognitive psychology, under new labels, Freud's own distinction between the unconscious, on the one hand, and the conscious or preconscious, on the other. They used such euphemisms as "unavailable" versus "available" memories, "trace storage" versus "trace utilization," and "availability" versus "retrievability."

Erdelyi (1985) states:

> The introduction of new terms rather than the readoption of the older *Unconscious* is probably symptomatic of a continued nervousness on the part of experimental psychology about making its peace with the Unconscious. The modern literature is replete with synonyms such as automatic, inaccessible, preattentive; only rarely

does the Unconscious itself make an appearance. There is no explicit discussion of the reason for this avoidance though informal querying usually turns up a disinclination on the part of authors to be associated with Freud's Unconscious, not any misgivings about nonconscious mentation. The psychoanalytic Unconscious, it is usually claimed, carries excessive theoretical baggage to which the typical modern investigator does not wish to give the appearance of subscribing [pp. 59–60].

Although cognitive psychologists accept the concept of the preconscious in its relationship to consciousness, they assiduously avoid the idea that preconscious processes may resonate with the dynamic Unconscious in Freud's sense. There are a few exceptions. One is Norman Dixon, who wrote an extremely valuable book entitled *Preconscious Processing* (1981). In this book he reviews in some detail the work of the New York psychologists-analysts around George Klein and the Research Center for Mental Health. This extensive work has been largely ignored in the now vast literature on cognitive psychology. Another book, *Psychoanalysis: Freud's Cognitive Psychology* (Erdelyi, 1985), makes a serious attempt to interpret pyschoanalytic concepts in information-processing terms and in many instances is successful and impressive. For example, Erdelyi rearranges Freud's model of the psychic apparatus as presented in the seventh chapter of *The Interpretation of Dreams* in such a way that it becomes a linear rather than a circular model, and he does not equate perception with consciousness as does Freud, but recognizes that there is an unconscious phase to the perceptual process. Cognitive psychologists are given to constructing graphic models of their concepts. Erdelyi presents such a model as a correction of Freud's model in a way which is comparable to the essence of the model presented in chapter 3. Erdelyi also presents a more complex flowchart in terms of the basic features of the model of censorship/repression of both external and internal events. In contemporary information-processing flowcharts, "censors," or "filters," usually are rendered as "decision nodes." A final work I wish to mention is a book by Goleman entitled *Vital Lies, Simple Truths* (1985). A man with a good understanding of psychoanalysis, he makes an attempt to reconcile information-processing theory with psychoanalysis.

Another important line of research in neurophysiology adds some rather decisive evidence for perception without awareness. I refer to the investigation by Howard Shevrin (Shevrin, Smith, and Fritzler, 1971), who has been working with average evoked potentials in relation to subliminal stimulation and has been able to show changes in the evoked potential aroused by subliminal stimuli. Libet (1965), also working with evoked potentials, has reported that a rather long period of activation, 1/50 to 1 sec, is a requirement for conscious experience at near liminal levels, constituting a latent period between the onset of activation and the appearance of the conscious experience. Shevrin has confirmed Libet's finding.

As I have commented, cognitive psychologists, with the few exceptions noted, have almost completely ignored the older work of the American and British investigators. On the other hand, psychoanalysts appear to be almost totally ignorant of the vast literature of the cognitive psychologists providing evidence of cognition without awareness. This is one area where an interdisciplinary convergence is in order and might be very fruitful.

References

Allport, F. H. (1955), *Theories of Perception and the Concept of Structure*. New York: John Wiley.
Barr, A. H. (1946), *Picasso: Fifty Years of His Art*. New York: Museum of Modern Art.
Dixon, N. (1981), *Preconscious Processing*. New York: John Wiley.
Ehrenzweig, A. (1953), *The Psychoanalysis of Artistic Vision and Hearing*. New York: Julian Press.
Erdelyi, M. (1985), *Psychoanalysis: Freud's Cognitive Psychology*. New York: W. H. Freeman.
Fisher, C. (1960a), Introduction. In: Preconscious Stimulation in Dreams, Associations, and Images, by O. Pötzl, R. Allers, & J. Teler. *Psychological Issues*, Monogr. 7. New York: International Universities Press.
——— (1960b), Subliminal and supraliminal influences on dreams. *Amer. J. Psychiatry*, 116:1009.
Goleman, D. (1985), *Vital Lies, Simple Truths*. New York: Simon & Schuster.
Klein, G. S. (1956), Perception, motives, and personality: A clinical perspective. In: *Approaches to Personality*, ed. J. L. McCary. New York: Logos Press, pp. 123–199.
Kris, E. (1952), *Psychoanalytic Explorations in Art*. New York: International Universities Press.

Libet, B. (1965), Cortical activation in conscious and unconscious experience. *Perspectives Biol. Med.*, 9:77–86.

Pötzl, O. (1915),Tachystoskopisch provozierte optische Halluzinationen bei einem Falle von Alkoholhalluzinose mit rückgebildeter zerebraler Hemianopsie. *Jahrb. Psychiat. & Neur.*, 4:141–146.

Rapaport, D. (1951), *Origin and Pathology of Thought.* New York: Columbia University Press.

Shevrin, H., & Luborsky, L. (1958), The measurement of preconscious perception in dreams and images: An investigation of the Poetzl phenomenon. *J. Abnorm. Soc. Psychol.*, 56:285–294.

——— Smith, W. H., & Fritzler, D. (1971), Average evoked response and verbal correlates of unconscious mental processes. *Psychophysiology*, 8:149–162.

Urbantschitsch, V. (1907), *Über Subjektive Optische Anschauungsbilder.* Leipzig: Deuticke.

PART II

EXPERIMENTAL COLLABORATIVE STUDIES

The four studies comprising part II are well-designed experiments, the kind that Khilstrom (1996) had in mind when he observed that subliminal research would have died in the 1960s were it not for the efforts of psychoanalytic investigators who performed studies that met "reasonably stringent methodological standards" (p. 26). The first two chapters report two studies done in collaboration with Irving Paul, a psychologist then on the New York University faculty and on the staff of the Research Center for Mental Health. These studies are systematic and better controlled investigations of the dream and imagery explorations that Fisher had previously reported. The last two chapters range beyond the confines of the dream and imagery experiments to new scientific territory. The collaboration with Howard Shevrin, then at the Menninger Foundation where the research was conducted while Fisher was a visiting professor, resulted in the first investigation combining the subliminal method with the sleep–dream cycle. By this time Fisher had already been devoting most of his research to the sleep–dream cycle so that he welcomed the opportunity to bring together his two major research interests. Finally, research in the concluding chapter (chapter 8) advanced in still another direction by using a newly developed apparatus for tracking eye movements in investigating the relationship between eye movements and subliminal stimulation. This research was undertaken in collaboration with Lester Luborsky, widely known for his important contributions to psychotherapy research.

In the first of the two studies with Paul (chapter 5) for the first time control images were obtained before the stimuli were presented. Two stimuli were compared (the Rubens Double Profile and a schematic version of a clock), and perhaps most important, an objective check list was developed for the Rubens Double Profile. The checklist demonstrated that a clear subliminal effect emerged in images and dreams. In the second study with Paul (chapter 6) there were two notable findings anticipating later discoveries. The first concerned the relationship between consciousness of the stimulus and the strength of the subliminal effect. Paul and Fisher administered a detection procedure in which the stimulus and a blank were presented subliminally and the subject asked to say whether something or nothing had been shown. They reported a negative relationship between success at detection and the emergence of subliminal effects. Those subjects who scored high on detection tended to score low on emergence. The relationship was highly suggestive, although because of relatively few subjects (N=13) statistical significance was not achieved. In much more recent work in our laboratory, we have confirmed in two studies that there is a negative relationship between detection and subliminal effects (Bernat, Snodgrass, and Shevrin, 2001; Snodgrass and Shevrin, 2002). This relationship has special methodological importance as well as casting light on the relationship between conscious and unconscious processes. The fact that there is a negative relationship rules out the possibility that the subliminal effects are simply a function of some degree of consciousness, the so-called partial cue hypothesis advanced originally by Eriksen (1960); in fact if some consciousness is present, the subliminal effect is smaller rather than greater. Theoretically, the finding suggests that some consciousness of the stimulus inhibits unconscious effects and opens the door to a consideration of the role of defenses and other personality factors.

The second finding of note reported in chapter 6 concerns the role of individual differences. Paul and Fisher noted that subjects who showed greater subliminal effects were more capable of reflectiveness and psychological mindedness. They further observed that assuming a passive attitude also seemed to enhance subliminal effects. As already cited in the Introduction we have demonstrated that brain responses can be used to detect the registration of subliminal stimuli related to individual unconscious conflicts. We have also shown that people high in repressiveness inhibit the effect of these subliminally activated unconscious conflicts from appearing consciously (Shevrin, Bond et al., 1996). In other research we have found that a passive attitude results in facilitation of subliminal effects, while an active effort to see the stimulus results in inhibition of these effects (Snodgrass, Shevrin, and Kopka, 1993).

Reported in chapter 7 for the first time is a study of the effects of a subliminal stimulus on reports from REM and N-REM sleep awakenings. The use of the sleep–dream cycle takes the original Pötzl phenomenon from daytime reports of dreams to the time of the actual occurrence of dreaming and adds the further important factor of sleep state unknown to Pötzl (or Freud). Relying on the rebus technique cited earlier that makes it possible to track primary and secondary process transformations of the same subliminal stimulus, it was shown as hypothesized that primary process transformations occurred after REM awakenings and secondary process transformations after N-REM awakenings. More recently Leuschner, Hau, Brech, and Volk (1994), a group of German investigators at the Sigmund Freud Institute in Frankfurtam-Main, have taken up this model by presenting prior to sleep subliminal visual stimuli not unlike Pötzl's but containing easily traceable formal elements, and tracking their effects following REM awakenings. On the basis of their findings, they make a distinction between whole object level effects and those of part object features, which they refer to as "radicals." Of interest with respect to the rebus effects reported in chapter 7, they find that these part object features, or "radicals," are more likely to appear in dream reports. These effects are more clearly primary process in nature. They did not collect reports following N-REM awakenings so that no comparison is possible; however, they did find that in daytime free images, whole object level effects were more prominent, distinguishing them from the more fragmented recoveries characterizing dream reports. The Pötzl phenomenon lives on in the work of these German investigators, and, as in the report in chapter 7, fruitfully combines the subliminal method with explorations of the sleep–dream cycle.

The final chapter reports a pioneering effort to relate eye movement fixation to subliminal registration. In order to accommodate the requirement for tracking eye movements, brevity of stimulus presentation was replaced by faintness. In this respect the study was different from previous studies. The intention was to determine if eye movements began to fixate on the faint targets before anything was reported as seen. It was found that in fact eye movements did begin to center on the targets just prior to the subject reporting that "something" was seen. But of more interest was the finding that massing of eye movements on the faint stimulus prior to awareness of something being present was positively correlated with associations to the target word.

On the whole, these four experimental studies bear out the empirical/clinically based findings Fisher reported in the first four studies. At the point at which Fisher finished his subliminal studies he had imparted to the field a considerable momentum that other investigators have since carried forward.

REFERENCES

Bernat, E., Shevrin, H., & Snodgrass, M. (2001), Subliminal visual odd ball stimuli make a P300 component. *J. Clin. Neurophysiol.*, 112:159–171.
Eriksen, C. (1960), Discrimination without learning without awareness: A methodological survey and evaluation. *Psycholog. Rev.*, 67:279–300.
Khilstrom, J. F. (1996), Perception without awareness of what is perceived, learning without awareness of what is learned. In: *The Science of Consciousness: Psychological, Neuropsychological and Clinical Reviews*, ed. M. Velmans. London: Routledge, pp. 23–46.
Leuschner, W., Hau, S., Brech, E., & Volk, S. (1994), Disassociation and reassociation of subliminally induced stimulus material in drawings of dreams and drawings of waking free imagery. *Dreaming: J. Assn. Study of Dreams*, 4:1–27.
Shevrin, H., Bond, J. A., Brakel, L. A. W., Hertel, R. K., & Williams, W. J. (1996), *Conscious and Unconscious Processes: Psychodynamic, Cognitive, and Neurophysiological Convergences*. New York: Guilford Press.
Snodgrass, M. (in press), *Unconscious Perception: Theory, Method, Evidence*. Amsterdam: John Benjamins.
——— Shevrin, H. (2002), Unconscious inhibition and facilitation at the objective threshold: replicable and qualitatively different unconscious perceptual effects. Manuscript submitted for publication.
——— ——— Kopka, M. (1993), The mediation of intentional judgments by unconscious perceptions: The influences of task strategy, task preference, word meaning, and motivation. *Consciousness & Cognit.*, 2:194–203.

5

THE EFFECT OF SUBLIMINAL VISUAL STIMULATION ON IMAGES AND DREAMS: A VALIDATION STUDY (1959)

CHARLES FISHER and I. H. PAUL

Replications and extensions of the classical experiments of Pötzl (1917), demonstrating the effects of unnoticed and unreportable parts of a tachistoscopically presented picture on subsequent dream formation, and the work of Allers and Teler (1924) on spontaneous imagery, have been discussed in earlier chapters. These experiments have recently aroused renewed interest in the problem of subliminal perception among workers in and out of the behavioral sciences, and the far-reaching theoretical and practical implications are becoming more widely discussed. It is therefore vital that the phenomenon be subjected to careful scrutiny both to evaluate its validity and to assess its limits.

The research reported to date has been preliminary in nature and has suffered from a number of serious methodological shortcomings. The present experiment is part of a project whose main aim is to overcome these shortcomings in order to study the phenomenon systematically and with as much scientific rigor as possible.

Acknowledgments. This research was aided by a grant from the Foundations' Fund for Research in Psychiatry. The authors wish to acknowledge the valuable assistance of Adele Edwards, who participated in many aspects of this investigation.

251

In a typical dream or imagery experiment based on a combination of Pötzl's and Allers and Teler's model, a stimulus was made subliminal by tachistoscopic presentation. Then the subject was requested to make a series of drawings depicting subsequent spontaneous imagery or the manifest images of his dreams of the same night. These drawings were evaluated, first by the subject himself, who by that time had been shown the stimulus, and later by the experimenter, who knew what the stimulus was all along. The evaluation focused on the comparison between the images and the stimulus and a search for elements of correspondence or similarity in forms, in spatial relations, and in meanings was made. In addition, evidence for particular transformations or distortions was sought.

The presentation and description of the above data were largely in anecdotal form without systematic or statistical analysis. The experimenter selected instances in which the influence of the stimulus seemed patent and put aside those drawings which manifested no correspondences.[1] The findings were often striking and generally convincing. However, this procedure is open to the serious criticism that the proof advanced depends upon post hoc subjective judgments on the part of both subjects and experimenter. It does not provide a check on the selective attention and bias of the experimenter in evaluating the data. Since his conclusions are all after the fact and result from a concerted and motivated search for similarities and identities, it is inevitable that he should stress certain features and overlook others. Moreover, the experimental procedure itself leaves no leeway for the purely chance occurrence of correspondences and it does not inform us about the spontaneous imagery of the subject, i.e., the imagery that emerges without any specific stimulus.

To illustrate with greater clarity the methodological problems involved, we present two specific findings derived from such an experiment. The picture shown in Figure 4.12 (p. 220) was tachistoscopically exposed to a subject. He reported seeing nothing

---

[1] The fact that negative instances were usually overlooked may reduce but does not vitiate the demonstrative value of previous research. Its purpose was to demonstrate the effect, but there was never the claim that it was clearly demonstrable in every case. A single and isolated but unmistakable instance was sufficient to establish the effect as a real phenomenon.

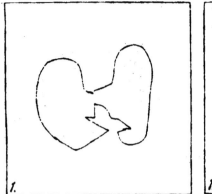

Figure 5.1. Images following tachistoscopic exposure of the double profile.

aside from some gradations of gray and white. Immediately afterward he was requested to close his eyes, to produce mental images, and to make drawings of them. Among the images he produced are the two shown in Figure 5.1. Before making the drawing on the left, the subject said, "I am reminded of an advertisement about the Rorschach test showing a picture of a boy and girl kissing. Their noses seemed to be attached." He described the drawing on the right as a "specimen of plastic in a testing laboratory." The crucial issue of this investigation was to demonstrate whether or not, and in what manner, the images were derived from the tachistoscopically presented picture.

The picture on the left bears an unquestionable resemblance to the stimulus, since it consists of two profiles facing each other and partly joined together. However, the subject had recently seen this picture and it might be argued that the appearance of its memory image in the experiment was accidental or merely the result of an extraordinary coincidence.

The second image presents other difficulties; it does not represent human faces at all, but rather a plastic specimen. Nevertheless, it seems to bear certain striking resemblances to the stimulus. Most remarkable is the torn-out piece displaced to the right, the top of which has a facelike character. If replaced in its original position, it would exactly fit into the area from which it was torn in the same manner that one profile fits into the other in the stimulus picture. Furthermore, it may not be stretching the point to note that the larger segment of the plastic resembles in its general form the profile face on the right of the stimulus. Another correspondence is that the image consists of two objects "facing" one another.

In this discussion, we have proposed that a number of transformations and distortions of the stimulus took place. The problem, therefore, of demonstrating that images incorporate elements of tachistoscopically presented pictures must meet a serious challenge: *by assuming a sufficient number of transformations, almost any image can be alleged to correspond to almost any tachistoscopically exposed picture.* Therefore, a proper research design and appropriate measures of the effect of the stimulus must be directed at meeting this challenge.

The main aim of the present research was to institute experimental controls and checks at as many points in the procedure as possible: from the point where the stimulus is subliminally exposed to the subject, to the point where the drawings depicting his imagery are evaluated. The goals were to evaluate the role of chance, to reduce the role of extraneous factors, and to remove the post hoc and subjective method of judging the results.

RATIONALES AND METHODS FOR COLLECTING THE DATA

Three major innovations were made in the experimental design: (1) the institution of a control session in which the subject provided samples of his spontaneous imagery[2] following no subliminal exposure; (2) instead of just one subliminal stimulus, the use of two where the second one differed substantially from the first in both its formal and conceptual properties; and (3) the institution of more than one recovery condition.

The purpose of the control images was to provide a sample of each subject's usual images which could then serve as a standard or base against which to compare his poststimulation productions. Such a comparison can permit the evaluation of any specific

---

[2]*Imagery* refers to both the subject's drawing and his spoken or written comments about it.

influence of the stimulus free from coincidental, chance, or habitual factors.

As persuasive as such a finding may be, it still does not attain the power that can be secured from a further control over chance correspondences and over extraneous factors. This further control involves an attempt to vary the stimulus conditions and to predict the consequences of such a controlled variation. In previous work, only a single stimulus was used in any given experiment. Therefore, even when elements of the stimulus appeared in the images, it was not possible fully to evaluate the role of chance or coincidence. In order to do this, we decided to use two stimuli that differed markedly from each other and see whether they led to correspondingly different images and dreams. Such a procedure places sharp restrictions upon the operation of chance.

The basic design of the investigation called for subjects to produce four sets of images corresponding to four experimental conditions: (1) *control* images preceding exposure of stimulus *A;* (2) postexposure images following stimulus *A;* (3) *control* images preceding exposure of stimulus *B;* and (4) postexposure images following stimulus *B.* We reasoned that if the postexposure images could be shown by some objective scoring method to differ from the preexposure *control* images and to contain elements of the tachistoscopically exposed stimuli, we could conclude that the subliminal stimuli had had an effect. Furthermore, if, by the same method, it could be demonstrated that the images following stimulus *A* differed from those following stimulus *B,* then the proposition that the stimuli had had an effect would be greatly strengthened.

In addition to manipulating the effect in this manner, we were also interested in methods of enhancing it. Frequently the images reveal properties of the stimulus, but not in a clear-cut, unequivocal, and uncomplicated way. Techniques for magnifying the emergence of subliminal stimulation would be most useful, therefore, in helping us study the phenomenon as well as of interest in their own right. We thought that an altered state of consciousness (see chapter 4; Klein, 1959) might afford more propitious conditions for subliminally registered stimuli to "appear" in imagery.

Klein (1956) has pointed out that the most congenial position for effective perceptual discrimination in the human species is the upright position which involves complex muscular supports. Any condition, such as the supine position, that alters or eliminates these postural supports may affect reality-oriented perceptual discrimination or imagery and encourage the intrusion of primary process modes of perceiving and imaging. Klein reminds us that one of Freud's great intuitive insights is that the supine position is conducive to fluid associations and to the emergence of primary process drive-organized contents into conscious thinking. It may also be conducive to the emergence into consciousness of the memory traces of subliminal registrations. We thought that an attempt to approximate the external conditions of the dreamer by having the subject lie down in a totally darkened room might enhance the emergence.

SUBJECTS

Eleven male, volunteer paid university students in their early twenties served as subjects. They were not preselected and all who volunteered were used. Two subjects dropped out after the first two sessions; the other 9 participated in all four sessions and in each of the experimental conditions. Most of the subjects appeared to fall within the range of "normal" personality structure, judging from clinical impressions, although two seemed quite disturbed and were under psychiatric treatment. All were majoring in either one of the natural or social sciences; only one was a psychology major. The stated motivation of the subjects was to make a little extra money.

APPARATUS

The simple tachistoscope utilized in previous experiments was used in the present investigation. A description of this instrument and an account of the experimental conditions and setting is given in detail elsewhere (see chapter 3). The stimulus was exposed for 1/100 sec. It should be emphasized that the *duration* of the tachistoscopic exposure is not the only factor involved in making a stimulus subliminal. Other factors are the intensity of illumination, the density of the lines with which the picture is drawn, and the distance of the tachistoscope from the screen. With intense illumination a figure drawn with heavy lines can be consciously perceived with tachistoscopic exposures far briefer than 1/100 sec. In the present experiment, we used moderate illumination and a stimulus picture drawn with very light pencil lines and found that the stimulus was well below the threshold for recognition or for discriminating any of its parts.

THE STIMULI

Two simple figure drawings were used as subliminal stimuli: the Rubin double profile (Figure 4.12) and a line drawing of a clock (Figure 5.2). These two figures differ from each other in many formal and conceptual ways which can be objectively specified, and thus their differential effects upon imagery and dreams can readily be distinguished.

The double profile figure was devised by Rubin (see Hebb, 1949) to study figure–ground relationships. In addition to its simplicity,[3] it was selected because we were interested in exploring how figure–ground relationships are dealt with in subliminal registration. Pötzl (1917) noted that vague, sometimes barely perceptible background details of a picture became registered and subsequently emerged as important and central elements in dream images. Under these conditions, the figure–ground effect, contrary to its marked emergence in conscious perception, seems to be obliterated. Schilder (1953) demonstrated that what was ordinarily in the background of experience emerged under certain pathological conditions, as well as in normal dreams, as foreground.

In order to investigate this problem, we carried out some preliminary explorations using the Rubin figure, which is a square divided by a wavy line that separates it into two profiles. Depending upon the focus of attention, an observer notices just one

[3]It has been found that very simple stimuli are most effective in such studies. The desirability of simplicity of stimulus is further discussed below.

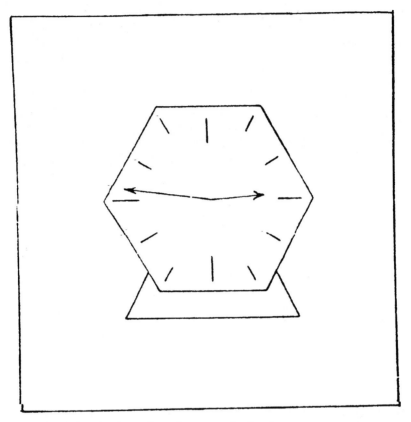

Figure 5.2. The clock used as the second stimulus.

of the profiles—either the right or the left—and they alternate, first one becoming figure while the other remains ground, and vice versa. The results of the preliminary explorations suggested that when subliminal registration of this figure occurs, it does so as two more or less equivalent figures, not as figure and ground. Subsequent dreams and images often showed the influence of not just one profile or element, but of two. We thought that this indicated that figure–ground relationships may become altered and fluid when subliminally registered, and so, to further study this interesting problem, used the Rubin picture in the present experiment.

Procedure for Collecting the Data

Session I

Subjects were seen individually by one or the other of the writers in a small laboratory on the psychiatric ward of Mt. Sinai Hospital in four separate hour-long sessions. As the beginning of the first contact, the experimenter chatted informally with the subject in order to set him at his ease and to gain a measure of rapport with him, to ensure his confidence and willingness to cooperate. The only information given about the experiment was that it had to do with perception and that the subject would be required to make drawings. The subjects were told that they would be informed about the nature of the experiment when it was completed.

The control images were obtained first. Aside from furnishing control data, they served the additional purpose of affording the subject a brief warm-up and training period in the task peculiar to the experiment, namely, that of getting spontaneous images and then drawing and describing them. Relaxation and passivity were stressed: "Just sit back, shut your eyes, and see what pictures come to mind." When a subject found this task difficult and unproductive of images, he was urged to "look into the darkness and see what picture appears there. Try not to think of anything in particular, but just relax and see what comes." We encouraged images of "things" where possible, and discouraged perseveration.

About five images were produced in this way before any stimulus exposures were given. After these control images were obtained and we were reasonably sure that the subject was relaxed and operating in the desired way, his attention was directed to the screen and he was told simply that "something" would be put there. Some subjects, however, were told that the exposure would be very brief and that they might not see it.

The experimenter counted to three and then flashed the double-profile picture. The exposure usually evoked some response —bewilderment, irritation, startle, etc. Immediately following exposure no subject reported seeing the whole or *any part* of the stimulus. They regularly described and drew a vague pattern of light and dark, usually light in the center. After obtaining the

verbal report and drawing of what was consciously perceived following tachistoscopic exposure, the subjects were instructed to
return to imaging in exactly the same way as before. Some subjects
asked whether they should think of what they were able to see
on the screen. We discouraged them from doing so. "Just close
your eyes and let whatever comes to mind come to mind."[4] They
were allowed to produce about five images in this way, sitting
upright behind a desk in the lighted room.

Following this, the subject was asked to lie down on a couch
and the lights were turned off.[5] He was requested to produce five
more images in the supine position in the dark. A dim blue light
was turned on after each image at the subject's demand, to provide enough illumination for him to make a drawing. This recovery condition will be referred to as the *supine-dark* condition: the
first as the *upright-light.*

Before the end of the first session, the following dream suggestion was given: "If you should have a dream tonight, please make
every effort to remember it and report it to me." The subject was
given a pad of paper and advised to keep it near his bed so that
in case he should happen to wake up after the dream he could
note it down right away; if not, then he could do so in the morning. The subject was requested to make drawings of any part of
the dream that was pictorial. Finally, he was asked to mail the
dream to the experimenter.

Session II

At the beginning of the second session, approximately one
week later, some time was spent discussing any dream that was
reported and eliciting associations to it. Next, the approximate
threshold of the stimulus was obtained by successively exposing
it for increasing exposure times until the subject, who drew what
he saw after each exposure, was able correctly to identify the
stimulus. Two thresholds for the double-profile figure were obtained: the first at the point where the subject identified the stimulus as a human head or profile; the second at the point where

---

[4]On occasion, when a subject became blocked or perseverated on objects in the room,
we suggested that he think of the flash and see what picture came to mind.

[5]The room was made almost totally dark by painting the window black. However, a
small amount of light came through small spaces around the door of the room.

he could recognize that the figure was in fact two profiles formed of the same contour line.

Following this, the experimenter and the subject together reviewed the subject's images of the previous session and his dreams. The subject examined his drawings and reported any similarities or identities between them and the stimulus now exposed for a prolonged period on the screen. Such evidence was useful in a corroborative way and sometimes revealed things that might otherwise be missed, but played no direct role in the present experiment since it is post hoc and involves subjective judgments.

Sessions III and IV

About 2 months later,[6] sessions III and IV were conducted duplicating sessions I and II, except that, instead of the double profile, the clock was the subliminal stimulus. It should be noted that by this time the subjects were "sophisticated" about the nature of the experiment. Nevertheless, they were told not to try to guess what the stimulus might be (i.e., whether we were still using the double profile or another stimulus)—and to try and perform in exactly the same manner as before.

SUMMARY OF EXPERIMENTAL DESIGN

Each subject was seen for four separate, approximately one-hour-long sessions during the course of 2 months.

Session I

Step 1. Control period—subject produced about five spontaneous images.
Step 2. Tachistoscopic exposure of double-profile stimulus.
Step 3. Subject produced about five images in the *upright-light* condition.

---

[6]We chose such a long interval because experience with the phenomenon has taught that the effects of subliminal stimulation on imagery appear to linger for a long time, sometimes weeks.

Step 4. Subject produced about five images in the *supine-dark* condition.

Step 5. Dream suggestion.

Session II (about one week after Session I)

Step 1. Report of and associations to dream.

Step 2. Threshold determination.

Step 3. Reexposure period. Subject searched for similarities and identities between his drawings and the stimulus.

Session III (about 2 months after Session I)

Step 1. Control period—subject produced about five spontaneous images.

Step 2. Tachistoscopic exposure of clock stimulus.

Step 3. Subject produced about five images in the *upright-light* condition.

Step 4. Subject produced about five images in the *supine-dark* condition.

Step 5. Dream suggestion.

Session IV (about one week after Session III)

Step 1. Report of and associations to dream.

Step 2. Threshold determination.

Step 3. Reexposure period. Subject searched for similarities and identities between his drawings and the stimulus.

METHODS FOR EVALUATING THE DATA

EVALUATION OF THE IMAGES

The main purpose of this evaluation was to ascertain whether the images were related to the subliminally presented stimuli. We approached the problem of relatedness in terms of identities and correspondences between the images and the stimuli by applying an objective scoring technique. The search for identical or corresponding elements between the images and the stimuli was complicated by the fact, noted earlier, that very rarely does a photographic replica of the stimulus as a whole emerge into the imagery, though often there are apparent replicas of fragments or details of the stimulus. More characteristic was the finding that the image appeared to represent a transformation or distortion of the stimulus either in its figural properties or its meaning, or both. At least 10 types of transformations, such as condensations, displacements, rotations, etc., previously described (see chapters 3, 4, 5), may complicate the evaluation. In addition, the subliminal stimulus appears to fuse with either recent or remote memories. It is difficult, or probably impossible, to work out an objective scoring technique capable of picking up and evaluating all these complex transformations. However, by collecting many images from a number of subjects and applying a simple and objective measuring technique, we hoped that at least part of the postulated influence of the stimuli on the images might be demonstrated. We thought that by utilizing sufficient data and precise and sensitive statistical methods, the overall or major effect could be captured.

A Checklist Technique for Scoring Images

In order to measure the degree of identity and correspondence between the images and the stimulus, we decided to use a checklist furnishing an exhaustive description of the double-profile stimulus. The checklist that we prepared is reproduced in Appendix I. It contains 30 individual items grouped into six general categories, each containing four to seven items. The six major categories and a sample item from each are:

A.   *Content:* e.g., It is primarily a person or persons.
B.   *Form:* e.g., It has one or several important wavy or zigzag lines.
C.   *Movement:* e.g., It is something that ordinarily does transform or change its form.
D.   *Number:* e.g., It is two main things.
E.   *Content and Form:* e.g., It is composed of the profile(s) of thing(s).

F.   *Number and Position:* e.g., It is two things which are interlocked or joined to each other.

The checklist contains some items which, strictly speaking, do
not directly describe the primary properties of the stimulus and
also a number of items within any one category that are mutually
exclusive. For example, the first item under the category *Content*
is, "It is primarily a person or persons." The second item is, "It
is not primarily a person(s) but it contains a person or persons."
Only the first of these items is strictly descriptive of the stimulus,
but any image containing humans bore enough correspondence
to the stimulus to be worthy of a score. These two items are also
mutually exclusive and the wording prevented both items from
being checked off for any one image.

The checklist was devised before the experiment was conducted, but the preparation was influenced to some extent by
some earlier exploratory data that had been collected using the
double profile as a subliminal stimulus. For the most part, deci-
sions as to what constituted a property of the stimulus were not
influenced by these data with the following exceptions: If the
exploratory data suggested properties that otherwise might not
have been thought of and if these properties could be considered
objective and truly applicable, then they were included. The following are two items that arose in this way: (1) "It has an important component at the center, a central line, division, or
element." (2) "It is seen by the subject as transforming or changing into something else." These items are descriptive of the stimulus, although the second is not objective in quite the same sense
as the first: It can be considered quasi-objective because it refers
to the figure–ground alternation.

The checklist was applied to *all* the images collected in the
present experiment, 5 for each of the six conditions, a total of
30 for each subject. The scorer checked off those items that he
considered descriptive of each image and bypassed those that
failed to apply. By adding up the number of items checked off
for any particular image, a score was obtained representing the
degree of identity or correspondence with the double-profile figure. Because many of the 30 items are mutually exclusive, a perfect replica of the double-profile figure could earn a score of
only 18.

The checklist was applied by two sets of judges. The first group was composed of three psychologists[7] who were uninformed about the nature of the experiment, had no way of identifying any of the data, and therefore did not know from which of the experimental conditions any particular image derived. These judges scored the data independently of each other. We will refer to them as the "blind" judges. The second group consisted of the two experimenters and their assistant, all of whom knew the nature of the experiment and the source of each of the images to be scored. These three judges—we call them the "biased" judges—also scored the images independently of each other. The scoring procedure, therefore, provided six separate scorings of the data and yielded two important subsidiary results: (1) It gave an estimate of the reliability or objectivity of the checklisting technique because it revealed how well the scorers agreed with each other. (2) It revealed whether the "biased" judges allowed their knowledge of the nature of the experiment and of the source of the images to prejudice their scoring in favor of the hypotheses. Moreover, they scored the data before the "blind" judges did; therefore, their scoring was not influenced by that of the "blind" judges.

QUANTITATIVE RESULTS

Threshold Results

No subject identified either of the stimuli at 1/100, 1/50, 1/20, 1/10, or 1/5 sec. Half a second or more represented the recognition threshold in all cases, except one in which parts of the stimuli were recognized as 1/5 and 1/10 sec. Most subjects were able to recognize the clock at 1/2 sec, and some could also recognize a human profile at that exposure. However, the majority needed one full second to recognize the face and to detect the features of the clock. No subject recognized that the double-profile stimulus consisted of two alternating profiles below

---

[7] We wish to thank Goldie Kass, Leon Laski, and Evelyn Seklar for their assistance.

a full second and most needed up to 5 sec for full recognition. The threshold data prove unequivocally that the stimuli were completely subliminal.

CHECKLIST RESULTS

Figure 5.3 shows the average checklist scores obtained by each of the three blind judges. These scores represent the average

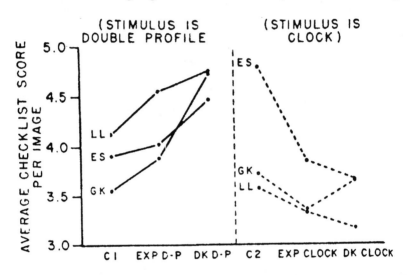

Experimental Conditions

Figure 5.3. Average double-profile checklist scores of all images given under the following six experimental conditions:
1. Preexposure 1 (C1)
2. Postexposure of the double profile (EXP D-P)
3. Postexposure of the double profile in the dark (DK D-P)
4. Preexposure 2 (C2)
5. Postexposure of the clock (EXP CLOCK)
6. Postexposure of the clock in the dark (DK CLOCK)
Three sets of results are shown. These scores were obtained by the three scorers working blindly and independently of each other.

number of checks each judge gave the images from each of the six experimental conditions. The combined average of the scores of the three judges for the preexposure control 1 (called *C1*) was 3.85.[8] These images reflect the baseline or spontaneous imagery of the subjects with respect to the double-profile checklist. The postexposure scores conform to the predicted pattern and thus fully support the hypothesis underlying this experiment. The specific predictions and the results pertinent to them are:

1. The prediction was made that the scores of the images postexposure to the double-profile stimulus (called *Exp-DP*) would be higher than those of *C1*. Each blind judge's score conformed to the prediction. The combined average score of the three judges rose from 3.85 to 4.16.[9]
2. The prediction was made that the scores of the images postexposure to the double profile in the supine-dark condition (called *Dk-DP*) would be higher than both *C1* and *Exp-Dp*. Again, the three blind judges gave results that conform to this prediction. Their combined average score rose to 4.66.
3. The prediction was made that the postexposure control 2 scores (called *C2*) would be approximately the same as *C1*, though possibly somewhat higher because of lingering effects of the double-profile stimulus. The combined average score of 4.03 is in line with this expectation.
4. Since the clock stimulus was very different from the double-profile stimulus, the prediction was made that the average scores for the postexposure clock images in the upright-light condition (called *Exp-Clock*) would score lower than any of the preceding images. Each of the three blind judges gave results fully in line with this prediction. The combined average score was 3.52.
5. The prediction was made that the supine-dark condition would further enhance the above effect, hence decreasing the checklist scores even more so that the postexposure clock images in the supine-dark condition (called *Dk-Clock*) would score

---

[8]The *reliability* of the blind judges (the degree to which they agreed with each other in all of their scoring) was 0.72, a statistically significant and satisfactorily substantial figure that attests to the objectivity of the checklisting method.

[9]All of the results were statistically treated by means of the *analysis of variance* (ANOVA) technique. Each of the positive findings reported in this section achieved statistical significance at a confidence level beyond 0.05. For a detailed analysis of the statistical data see chapter 6.

the lowest of all. Two of the three blind judges gave data supporting this prediction; one judge's score rose, though not beyond the C2 level. The combined average score for the three judges dipped to its lowest point, 3.48.

It is of interest to see how the biased judges scored the data and to compare them to the blind ones. Figure 5.4 closely resembles Figure 5.3 and fully bears out the major predictions in every detail. Though they obtained, on the whole, lower scores than

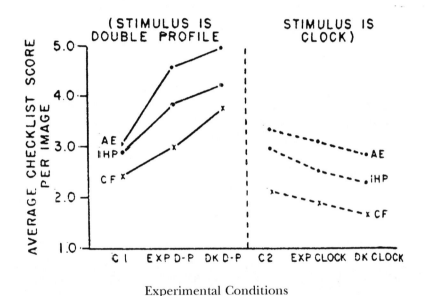

Experimental Conditions

Figure 5.4. Average double-profile checklist scores of all images given under the following six experimental conditions:
1. Preexposure 1 (C1)
2. Postexposure of the double profile (EXP D-P)
3. Postexposure of the double profile in the dark (DK D-P)
4. Preexposure 2 (C2)
5. Postexposure of the clock (EXP CLOCK)
6. Postexposure of the clock in the dark (DK CLOCK)
Three sets of results are shown. These scores were obtained by the three experimenters working independently of each other.

---

[10]Reliability of the biased judges was slightly higher than that of the blind judges: 0.83.

did the blind judges, the biased judges produced results that demonstrate the major effects more clearly. The largest discrepancy between the two groups of judges was in their scoring of the control images. This suggests that a bias occurred in scoring these images by those judges who knew the nature of the experiment and the source of the images; but this did not interfere with the overall results. The fact that the so-called biased judges gave results that so closely resembled the blind ones attests to the objectivity of the technique and the judges.

The fact that the postexposure scores for the double profile in the upright-light condition were higher than those for *C1* indicates that the stimulus had the effect of increasing the number of human faces and other elements of the stimulus in the postexposure imagery. The further increase in the average postexposure scores for the supine-dark condition indicates that the supine position in darkness had an enhancing effect as compared to the upright-light condition. Since the average scores for the postexposure clock images in the upright-light condition were lower than the postexposure double-profile scores, it is justifiable to conclude that, as the clock stimulus had the effect of making the postexposure images more like the clock, they perforce bore less resemblance to the double-profile stimulus. For example, the postexposure clock images contained more inanimate mechanical elements as compared to the double-profile postexposure images which showed an increase in human forms. Further, the score for the postexposure clock images was lower than the score for the control images for the following reason. Although human faces appear with some frequency in any series of control images, following exposure of the clock stimulus, it would be expected that, if the stimulus had an effect, the images that emerged would tend to show an increase in inanimate forms but a decrease in human forms as compared to the control series. Since the average scores for the postexposure clock images in the supine-dark condition were even lower than those for the upright-light condition, we may assume that the supine position in the darkness produced an enhancing effect of the clock stimulus on the subsequent images as compared to the upright-light condition.

It is of interest to examine the checklist results in detail to see which categories and items within the categories contributed most to the results, i.e., to determine in what particular respects the images showed the influence of the subliminally presented stimulus. Did it influence the form of the images, the contents, movement, number, etc.? Figure 5.5 gives a breakdown of the scores of the six main categories of the checklist obtained by IHP, one of the biased judges. It shows that all but one of the categories reveal the effect to a greater or lesser degree. For example, the images elicited in the experimental conditions *(Exp-DP* and *Dk-DP)* following exposure of the double profile show an increase of human or animal figures, as compared to the control condition, *C1,* while the images that were produced following exposure of the clock stimulus show a decrease in this category as compared with the control condition *C2.* The small graph *A* labeled "Content" shows this result graphically. The most marked effect produced by the subliminal stimulus is shown by the "Content plus Form" category: In small graph *E* there is the steepest rise following the exposure of the double profile and the sharpest fall following exposure of the clock stimulus. It is of significance that the

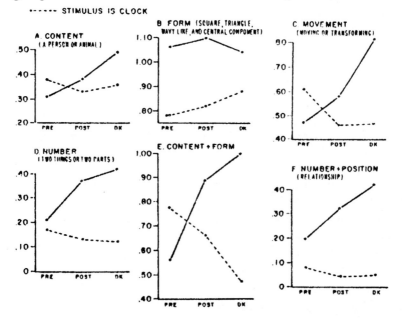

Figure 5.5. A breakdown of the checklist categories showing the average scores per image of the six experimental conditions for each of the six main categories of the double-profile checklist.

"Content plus Form" category contained the checklist items that refer in detail to elements of the double profile.

The one category that did not show the effect is "Form" (small graph *B*). Six of the seven items in this category refer to square or triangular parts, or to a wavy line. These forms are very common and occurred with high frequency in all drawings; perhaps for this reason this category failed to show a differential effect. A detailed analysis of the seven items of this category, not shown here, revealed that some positive effect was shown by the last item, "central line, division, or element." This refers to the crucial double-profile line and is the one item of the category that does not refer to a common form. Incidentally, detailed analysis also shows that a good effect was shown by the items in category *C*, "seen by subject as moving or transforming." These two items refer most pointedly to the figure–ground property of the stimulus—the one to the crucial double-profile line, the other to the shifting characteristic of the phenomenon—and indicate that the figure–ground property showed the subliminal effect.

Although we did not investigate individual differences on the part of the subjects in their susceptibility to the effect, the analysis revealed that the effect was greater on some subjects than on others even though it demonstrated some degree of significance on eight of the nine subjects who completed the experiment. In other words, all but one of the subjects showed the effect to some extent, though some did so more than others.

EVALUATION OF THE DREAMS

The dream suggestion was effective for about two-thirds of the subjects.[11] They submitted 18 dreams, 10 of them following the double-profile stimulation and 8 following the clock. Of these, 11 were dreamed the night of the experiment and 7 were delayed for several days. Four subjects submitted 2 dreams, one following each of the stimuli. We excluded 2 dreams from the sample because we doubted their authenticity (one was reported in over

---

[11]We have regularly found that the dream suggestion is effective in about two-thirds of the cases; this corresponds to the findings of Luborsky and Shevrin as well (1956).

2000 words), and 2 others were so fragmentary that they were also discarded. Therefore, the sample of dreams numbered 14, 11 of which were accompanied by drawings.

We thought that the checklisting technique would not be optimally suitable for these data because even those dreams with drawings consisted largely of a narrative protocol. Therefore, in addition to the checklisting technique, we applied another method of analysis consisting of a paired-choice matching: requiring judges to guess which dreams followed which stimulus, i.e., which stimulus was implicated in or influenced the dream. Ten psychologists were given 7 pairs of dreams, each pair consisting of a double-profile dream and a clock dream, and they were required to judge which was which. Four of the pairs were from the same subject, the others were paired randomly.

All of the judges were informed about the nature of the experiment, but, naturally, they had no way to identify any of the dreams. Seven of the judges were highly experienced in dealing with such data; they were all personally engaged in experimentation in subliminal phenomena at the Research Center for Mental Health at New York University. This fact proved to be important since of the 10 only those 7 were able to match the dreams better than chance. The 7 "experts" scored 30 "hits" and only 19 "misses." This performance achieves significance at only the 0.2% level of confidence which is not high enough for statistical significance. Nevertheless, the fact that all 7 of them did better than chance, i.e., got 4 or more of the 7 pairs right, supports the hypothesis that, to some extent at least, the subliminal stimuli revealed themselves in the dreams.[12]

The 11 dreams (5 double profile and 6 clock) that were accompanied by drawings were checklisted by one of the biased judges and one of the blind judges. The biased judge obtained an average score of 6.0 for the double-profile dreams and only 3.8 for the clock dreams. The blind judge obtained similar scores: 5.8 for the double-profile dreams, and 4.2 for the clock dreams. Since

---

[12]Before we conducted this paired-matching technique, we submitted all of the 14 dreams to 6 graduate students in psychology, informed them of the nature of the experiment, and asked them to guess in each case which stimulus preceded each dream. In their choices, these judges performed no better than chance.

there are so few cases, a statistical test of these scores is not feasible: Nevertheless, the fact that they were both in the predicted direction can be taken as supportive of the hypothesis.

QUALITATIVE RESULTS

Against the background of the encouraging positive objective results, we will now present and discuss some of the raw data illustrating the various ways in which the subliminally presented stimuli were transformed and distorted in their emergence into consciousness in the form of free images and dreams. This presentation will be limited to the images following the double-profile stimulus. It bears mentioning that the images following the clock stimulus often took the form of mechanical objects, such as wheels or springs. There were also many arrow-shaped figures (derived perhaps from the arrow-shaped hands of the clock), and several striking instances of human hands (probably also a transformation of the clock hands). One interesting image consisted of a heart, related by the subject to the clock because it beats rhythmically and is often referred to as a "ticker." A clock per se appeared only three times during the experiment, once during C2, and twice following the clock stimulus.

We tried to classify the data into a number of categories that indicate emergence in progressive degrees, from the most complete and undistorted to the least complete and most distorted. There was not a single instance in which the double profile appeared in subsequent imagery in a photographic way, and even in those instances where there seemed to be a remarkable correspondence, some transformations and distortions were also present.

A number of images from the preliminary exploratory experiments and a few dream images are included in this survey.

EMERGENCE OF TWO HEADS IN PROFILE (FIG. 5.6)

In general, these six images show two human heads in profile or a human head in some relationship to an animal head.

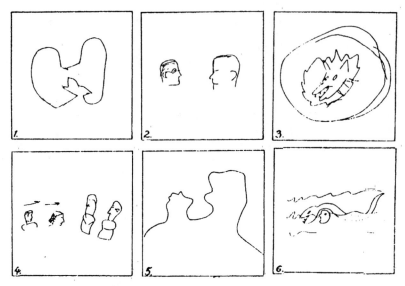

Figure 5.6. Images showing emergence of two heads in profile.

Image No. 1 has already been discussed. The probability is that this was not an accidental phenomenon but represents a fusion of the stimulus picture with the recent memory of the Rorschach card.

Image No. 2 shows two faces in profile confronting one another. The profile on the right has a high forehead and flat head, corresponding to similar details of the right profile in the stimulus.

Image No. 3 shows an unusual transformation. It is supposed to be a picture of a hyena breaking through a paper hoop. The hyena is in semiprofile and the upper margin of the outline of the hole in the paper hoop appears to form a human profile. A striking detail is the right ear of the hyena corresponding to the triangular eye of the right profile of the stimulus. It simultaneously forms the ear of the hyena and the eye of the human profile formed by the margin of the hole in the paper. It is as though the head of the hyena bursting through the paper left the outline of a human profile.

Image No. 4 shows the interesting phenomenon of multiplication of the memory image of the stimulus; there are four heads instead of two. The bulging forehead of the profile on the extreme left, the prominent noses of the three remaining figures, the flat head on the second figure from the right, and the high foreheads on the profiles of the two men correspond to details in the stimulus.

Image No. 5 is a dream picture taken from one of the preliminary, exploratory experiments. The dream image was of two mountain peaks. The subject drew them in one continuous line. While drawing the peaks he became aware that he had drawn two heads facing each other and had an impulse to draw an eye in each figure. The mountain peak on the right especially bears a striking resemblance to the right profile of the stimulus, with its prominent nose, concave forehead, and flat head.

Image No. 6 is also taken from one of the preliminary experiments. It represents a dream image of a man in the water with his head turned toward a sea monster. The profile of the man has a rather prominent chin and nose. The sea monster may represent a transformation of the left profile of the stimulus.

INCOMPLETE EMERGENCE OF TWO HEADS (FIGURE 5.7)

Image No. 1 is a drawing of "Kilroy" looking over a fence. This image, looked at from a certain point of view, can be thought of as representing the emergence of parts of the two profiles of the stimulus. There is a dividing line represented by the fence with the nose on one side of it and the rest of the head on the other.

Image No. 2 represents the subject's eye looking at his own profile and was so described. The image can be thought of as showing the emergence of the right profile of the stimulus along with the emergence of the eye of the left profile. The profile on the right shows the prominent nose and high forehead. The image also contains the implication of a profile facing another profile, i.e., the subject looking at himself.

Image No. 3 represents a "doctor's silhouette." The subject began to draw the upper figure, then drew the oblique line and completed the lower figure. Although it was not the subject's conscious intention, the final picture represents two heads facing one another separated by an oblique line. The redrawing of a figure, resulting in an unintentional reproduction of the stimulus, is not an infrequent occurrence in these experiments.

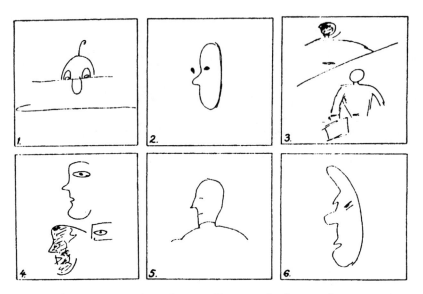

Figure 5.7. The upper three images illustrate the incomplete emergence of two heads. The lower three images show emergence of a single profile.

Emergence of a Single Profile (Fig. 5.7)

Image No. 4 might also be included in the category just discussed. The subject drew an eye, then the lower profile, and then combined the eye and the profile in the upper drawing. Note the prominent chin, nose, and forehead. The subject who produced this image is the same one who had the image of an eye looking at his own profile. The present image may well represent elements of both profiles of the stimulus, ultimately combined into a single one.

Image No. 5, representing Simón Bolívar, shows the prominent nose and high forehead. Note also the absence of the ear, a frequent occurrence in these drawings—the stimulus lacks any ear markings.

Image No. 6 is a picture of the man in the moon taken from the label on the "Admiration Cigar." Note the prominent chin and nose, the concave forehead, and the absent ear. This is another example of a fusion of the memory image of the stimulus picture with a remote memory image.

EMERGENCE OF HUMAN HEAD FACING A NONHUMAN OBJECT
(FIGURE 5.8)

Image No. 1 shows a man facing his dog. The subject initially visualized the dog on ground level, but as he drew it, it moved upward. It is highly probable that this represents an attempt to approximate the profile of the dog to that of the man. Note the absence of features, including the ear, on the profile of the man, and its tendency toward concavity as compared with the convexity of the dog's profile.

Image No. 2 represents the last scene of "All Quiet on the Western Front" where the hero reaches out for the butterfly on the flower. The helmet on the soldier may well have been derived

Figure 5.8. Images showing emergence of human head facing nonhuman object.

from the rounded, bulging forehead of the left profile and has appeared in at least one other subject's images.

Image No. 3 is of a girl holding a lollipop. She was described as facing to the left, as having an immense head, and a large lollipop exaggerated in size. It is probable that the profile on the left was transformed into the large lollipop.

EMERGENCE OF TWO INANIMATE OBJECTS IN SOME KIND OF RELATIONSHIP TO EACH OTHER (FIG. 5.9)

Images of this kind were quite frequent and are of interest because they seem to indicate that an important element, namely, the notion of "twoness," was abstracted from the stimulus. Thus the images shown in Figure 5.9 contain *two* pieces of plastic, *two* cars colliding, *two* paintings on the wall, *two* cars going in the same direction, *two* circles overlapping, and *two* houses. The use of the word *two* in describing the images appeared to be significant. In the following descriptions, it will be seen that several other elements of the figure–ground property of the stimulus

Figure 5.9. Images showing emergence of two inanimate objects in some kind of relationship to each other.

also seemed to emerge in some of these images, e.g., derivations of the central profile line and the idea of the transformation of one object into another.

Image No. 2 shows two cars colliding. It is probable that the two cars were derived from the two profiles and the idea of collision from the alternating central profile line which emerged as movement or a central force.

Image No. 5 shows two perfect circles overlapping. The subject described them as "like breasts," stating that he always imagined them like this, overlapped as if not attached to the body. The transformation of the stimulus into two breasts or buttocks had been fairly common. The idea of overlapping may have been derived from the changing central profile line.

Image No. 6 shows a country house suddenly transformed into a city garage. The house bears some resemblance to a human head. Most significant is the idea of the sudden transformation of the house into the garage, an idea that we believe is based on the transformation of one profile into another. This impression is heightened by the fact that the country house resembles a head, and that the subject compared the exaggerated size of the door of the garage to a human mouth.

EMERGENCE OF COMPONENTS OF THE STIMULUS PICTURE IN ABSTRACT FORM (FIGURE 5.10)

These images illustrate an extremely interesting transformation of the stimulus, and strongly suggest that registration of the alternating figure–ground aspect of the stimulus often took place. The figure–ground relationship was represented in the images in a number of ways. For example, the division into light and dark halves (Image No. 1), a feeling of force in the direction of the arrow (Image No. 2), the impression of streaming or flowing toward the center (Image No. 3), the wavy line and light and dark halves (Image No. 4), and the sensation of movement (Image No. 5). The concept of movement, force, flowing or streaming was probably derived from the double-profile line in the stimulus.

Image No. 1 was described as "just a pattern." The right side was dark and the left gray, the gray becoming more prominent

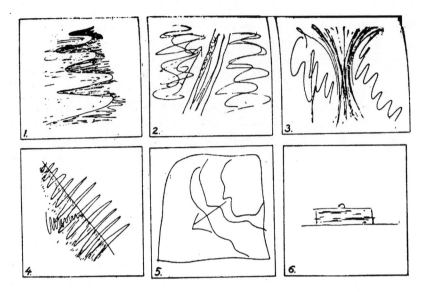

Figure 5.10. Images showing emergence of components of the stimulus picture in abstract form.

as the subject looked. The dark side reminded the subject of a Christmas tree. The wavy line resembles the profile line in its general form. The increase in the intensity of the gray probably relates to the shifting figure–ground relationship.

Image No. 2 represents the cross-section of a branch. There was a "feeling of force" in the direction of the arrow; it was as if food were moving through the canal in the center. The wavy lines on either side are probably distorted representations of the two profiles.

Image No. 3 was described as a "vague amorphous thing," as tending to get black and then gray, and there was an impression of streaming or flowing toward the center. The wavy lines on either side appear to be distorted representations of the double profile.

Image No. 4, like Image No. 1, was described as looking like a Christmas tree, the left half as black and the right as gray. The zigzag line appears to be a representation of the double-profile line.

Image No. 5 was described as meaningless, moving forms which were colored, the arrow showing the direction of movement. Note

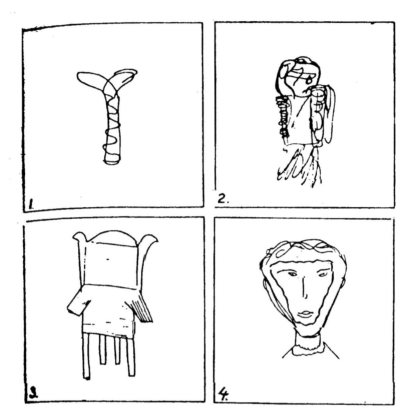

Figure 5.11. Drawings showing relationship of image to subsequent dream.

the resemblance of the wavy lines to human profiles, especially the line at the extreme right. The right half of the image was described as being black and the left as yellow.

Image No. 6 was described as the profile of a cake. This unique description probably represents a derivation from the double profile of the concept of "profileness."

RELATIONSHIP OF IMAGE TO SUBSEQUENT DREAM (FIGURE 5.11)

As has been noted, the objective analysis of the subjects' dreams did not yield results sufficiently positive to demonstrate in a clearcut fashion that the dreams were influenced by the subliminally registered stimuli. However, certain of the individual results were very striking, as illustrated by the following examples. In addition, these two experiments are presented because they confirm earlier work (chapter 3) showing the relationship between the images that develop during the imagery experiment and the manifest dream pictures of subsequent dreams into which they appear to be incorporated.

Image No. 1 was described as a doctor's symbol, a sort of medical caduceus showing two snake heads with a wavy line down the center. The two heads of the stimulus appear to have been transformed into snake heads and the wavy line is probably a derivation of the double-profile line. That night the subject had a dream about a "royal-like chair," which had on its top posts ornate carvings of "lions' heads" (Image No. 3). The heads the subject drew do not at all resemble lions' heads but look much more like the snake heads that had appeared earlier in the image of the doctor's symbol. This was a transference dream, the royal-like chair being a distorted representation of the couch upon which the subject was lying during the imagery experiment.

Image No. 2 represents a deceased friend of the subject's, who died when he dove down to take pictures of a sunken ship. The drawing shows the friend with the diving apparatus over his face. The image is as close as any subject came to reproducing two profiles in juxtaposition, if we think of the diving apparatus as representing a second head in profile.

Image No. 4 shows the manifest dream that this subject had on the night of the imagery experiment. The dream figure had a gray face with a smear of whipped cream covering it. The smear of cream, as represented in the drawing, resembles a mask. The associations to the dream connected this mask with the diving apparatus on the face of the imaged friend. In this instance, however, the face and mask are frontal and not in profile.

DISCUSSION

The positive results of the present experiment provide proof of its main hypotheses. The fact that the design included control data in addition to two different stimuli adequately ruled out chance results and checked the influence of extraneous and habitual factors. The methods for evaluating the data were objective and wholly before the fact, and the statistical techniques used to analyze these data further ruled out the possibility that the results could be due to chance alone. It seems safe to conclude that we have demonstrated that elements and aspects of the subliminal stimuli emerged in the subsequent images and dreams, and, therefore, subliminal registration must have taken place.

However, one possible source of contamination by extraneous factors remained uncontrolled in the present experiment: the fact that the experimenter himself knew what stimulus was being presented. It is possible that, by his words, actions, and responses, the experimenter somehow influenced the subjects' images in the direction of the stimulus. After all, in line with the thesis of this project, we must be especially sensitive to the possibility that, even though the experimenters made a strong effort to be wholly unselective and nondirective in their administration of the procedure, very small, unwitting cues were communicated to the subject while he was imaging and drawing.

We see this as the only barrier to a full acceptance of the phenomenon and hence, in a recently completed experiment, we strove to control this factor. In this experiment, to be reported in detail elsewhere (see chapter 6), subjects were tested in a large group, half of them exposed to one stimulus and the other half receiving another stimulus. All subjects drew their imagery while in a group under conditions where the experimenter could not see their drawings. Since this experiment also yielded positive results, it confirms our impression that our behavior as experimenters while administering the procedures played no role in the outcome.

An additional objection that has frequently been advanced is that in these experiments there are subtle conscious cues or partial information of the true nature of the stimulus that are responsible for the effect. As we have noted, immediately following exposure, no subject reported seeing the whole or any part of the stimuli. We are convinced that the stimulus exposures were well below conscious recognition threshold. However, more careful psychophysical methods will have to be employed to settle this matter definitively. There are a number of methodological difficulties involved in ascertaining whether or not the subjects, even though they reported seeing nothing, may have recognized more than they reported. It is of interest that Shevrin and Luborsky (1958), who obtained three consecutive reports of what was seen after exposure, spread over a 24-hour period, found that their subjects added a little more to each report. They did not, however, ascribe this to cues or partial information but explained their findings by assuming that some impressions that had been subliminally registered gradually emerged into consciousness during the waking state.

In the following discussion we will take up three points and discuss pertinent theory and literature: (1) the effect of subliminal stimulation on dreams and images; (2) the efficacy of the supine-dark condition in enhancing it; and (3) the figure–ground phenomenon in subliminal registration.

The Effect of Subliminal Stimulation on Dreams and Images

The results of the present experiment cannot be accounted for unless some process like subliminal registration is assumed. In addition to the large body of exploratory demonstration that has already been reported, recent studies conducted at New York University by Klein, Holt, and their coworkers (Klein, Spence, Holt, and Gourevitch, 1955; Smith and Henriksson, 1955; Klein, 1956; Bach and Klein, 1957; Smith, Spence, and Klein, 1959), and at the Menninger Foundation by Luborsky and Shevrin (1956; Shevrin and Luborsky, 1958), have succeeded in demonstrating the phenomenon in the framework of rigorously designed and well-controlled experiments. These investigations have not only shown that sublimination registration is a genuine phenomenon but have also demonstrated that it can influence subsequent dreams, imagery, and conscious thinking.

In a well-designed and controlled investigation, Shevrin and Luborsky (1958) have been able to validate the Pötzl phenomenon as well as the effect of subliminal registration on subsequent imagery in the waking state. Their findings support the so-called "law of exclusion" formulated by Pötzl, but only if the law is somewhat modified. The law holds that those parts of the tachisto-scopically exposed pictures that are not perceived appear in the manifest content of subsequent dreams, while those parts that are consciously noted are excluded from the dream. In confirmation of our own findings, and contrary to this form of the "law of exclusion," Shevrin and Luborsky found that elements of the exposed picture that were consciously perceived did appear in subsequent dreams and images. They concluded that Pötzl's law is only relative and was intended mainly to emphasize that the dream is a better vehicle for the unintentional emergence of subliminal registrations into consciousness than is intentional re-call in the waking state. On the other hand, they found that dreams and images are relatively inefficient means as compared with intentional recall in the waking state for recovering con-sciously perceived elements of the tachistoscopically exposed picture.

The degree of emergence of subliminal registrations into dreams and images reported by Shevrin and Luborsky was not very great. As a matter of fact, the degree of emergence of *con-sciously* reported items was almost as great as that of the unre-ported subliminally registered items. We believe that this slight degree of emergence of subliminal registrations was a conse-quence of the method used. For one thing, the authors employed for tachistoscopic exposure a highly complex picture containing many elements. One of the striking things about the picture is that it contains many vague and shadowy background forms, simi-lar to the picture of the three kings used in an early investigation (see chapter 1, p. 42). In our experience, it is just these ground forms, as opposed to figural elements, that are subliminally regis-tered, undergo various distortions and transformations, and emerge in the manifest content of dreams and images. Shevrin and Luborsky's objective method of measuring the emergence of subliminal registrations was not designed to evaluate and trace the possible utilization of these ground forms. The authors identi-fied instances of "emergence" in terms of a conceptual similarity between dream and picture elements. Thus, if a subject did not report seeing trucks in the exposed picture but dreamed about cars or wagons, he was credited with the "emergence" of the vehicles in the picture. They assumed that the meaning of the percept, in this case "mode of transportation," was more constant than any of its visual components which might have been affected by the particular memories of the individual. However, they were aware of the limitations of their method and the probability that conceptual similarity might constitute a limited method of measuring emergence of subliminal registrations.

The rather narrow type of conceptual similarity the authors attempted to measure could not, in our experience, be adequate to detect the complex and subtle kinds of conceptual transformations that take place. We have demonstrated in the present study the complexity of the representation of figure–ground relationships in images and dreams. For example, in the double-profile experiment we were able to detect such remote emergences of the stimulus as the concept of twoness, a central moving force, transformation of an object into another, and the like. We believe that if Shevrin and Luborsky had been able to devise a means of detecting the emergence of background forms and the more subtle kinds of conceptual transformations, they might have found a greater emergence of subliminal registrations into dreams and images. It is, nevertheless, impressive that they were able to validate the Pötzl experiment, even with the rather crude measure that they applied.

Shevrin and Luborsky believed that their findings confirm Freud's (1900) conception of the role of indifferent impressions as day residues in dream formation. Freud stated that preconscious impressions that had not been requisitioned by waking thought activity could more readily serve as a "cover" for unacceptable thoughts than fully developed conscious perceptions; for reasons of censorship the dream process transfers psychical intensity from what is important but objectionable to what is indifferent. This suggests a reason for the operation of Pötzl's law of exclusion. We may add that there is another and perhaps equally important factor. The traces of subliminal registrations are highly unstable and undergo a number of primary-process-like transformations such as condensation, displacement, multiplication, metamorphosis of meaning, etc., making them suitable for the expression of instinctual wishes in terms of psychic reality divorced from external reality; these transformed and distorted traces cease to reflect external reality or do so in a limited way.

The Pötzl and Allers and Teler experiments were offered as demonstrations of the extraordinary efficiency of perceptual registrations without awareness. Highly complex processes involving the ego apparatuses of perception, memory, and consciousness are implicated in the phenomena brought to light in these investigations. No single term such as *preconscious perception* is adequate to convey the complexity of these processes. Use of the phrase "the Pötzl phenomenon" is not very satisfactory but may serve, for the time being, so long as we bear in mind that it comprises at least four phases: (1) a phase of sensory registration outside of awareness (subliminal registration); (2) a phase of cognitive working over, also occurring outside of awareness, in which the registration becomes a memory trace or is recruited into a preexisting memory schema; (3) a phase of delayed emergence of the memory image of the subliminal registration into subsequent dreams and images; (4) a reproductive phase: the verbal report and drawing of the dream or image.[13] In the tachistoscopic dream and imagery experiments the normal perceptual process may be fragmented and slowed up, coming to a premature close, and passing only through the first two phases. The third phase is represented by delayed afterdelivery of the memory image of the subliminal registration into subsequent dreams and images in the absence of the stimulus object, i.e., the tachistoscopic picture.

The first phase, sensory registration outside of awareness, cannot be considered preconscious in the psychoanalytic meaning of the term. By definition, *preconscious* refers to contents not in consciousness but which may, with varying degrees of difficulty, emerge into it. It must be emphasized that in our experiments the subject never recovers the memory of the actual event of sensory registration outside of awareness. When he compares the drawings of his dreams and images to the tachistoscopically exposed picture, there is still no conscious memory of the experience of sensory registration. The subject merely concludes that

---

[13]It has been suggested (see chapter 3) that normal, instantaneous, conscious, reality-oriented perception also involves several phases; that it is an event extended in time even though it appears to take place instantaneously (Smith, 1957). The three phases are: (1) a phase of sensory registration outside awareness; (2) a phase of recruitment to a preexisting memory schema during which meaning is attached to the developing percept; and (3) the developing percept emerges into consciousness, seemingly instantaneously, without delay and in the presence of the stimulus object.

registration must have taken place by virtue of the similarity between his drawings of dreams or images and the tachistoscopically exposed stimulus picture. Sensory registration outside of awareness is, therefore, not preconscious in the psychoanalytic sense, but "unconscious" in the somatic sense suggested by Schilder (1953). The term *preconscious*, however, can properly be applied to the events of the second phase, that is, the cognitive working over of the memory trace of the subliminal registration. Shevrin and Luborsky (1958) designated as *preconscious recall* the emergence of these preconscious memory traces in dreams or images; this corresponds to our third phase. The *unintentional recall* of preconscious images is a more accurate description than *preconscious recall.*

Further investigation will be necessary to determine in what phase of the Pötzl phenomenon the various transformations and distortions take place. We have suggested that the most likely possibility is that they occur during phase 2, during the cognitive working over of the memory trace. It has not been ruled out, however, that they may occur during registration, during the phase of emergence into consciousness, or even during the reproductive phase. Another problem for future investigation is whether the initial registration of the stimulus is total or partial. Some of the data suggest that there is an initial total registration of the stimulus with subsequent fragmentation, perhaps in phase 2, with afterdelivery of fragments of the stimulus into consciousness. The evidence for this consists of the finding, in certain experiments, that although the images that emerged consisted of only fragments of the stimulus, when all the images were combined together, they could be shown to reconstitute the total stimulus (see chapter 3).

Both normal perception and the Pötzl phenomenon have been explained by Klein (1959) in a manner very similar to the above in the following formulation:

> [T]he traditional summary of responsiveness to stimulation, based on the narrow perspective of events in the "waking state" of the laboratory requires revision. The sequence seems rather to be: the organism's sensory surfaces are stimulated; registration occurs;

followed by a cognitive "working over" of this registered stimulation, through its recruitment to various conceptual schema; leading to an emergence of the reaction, partly in a particular mode of
awareness (perception or imaging) and partly on other behavioral
levels [pp. 22–23].

Klein suggests that the term *preconscious perception* should be
dropped because modes of awareness can differ in different states
of consciousness and, therefore, it is necessary to specify preconscious in respect to what state of consciousness. Ordinary conscious perception is a quality of experience distinct from other
presentational modes of awareness; i.e., we are able to become
aware of registrations in different presentational modes such as
images, dream images, hallucinatory images, in contradistinction
to percepts. Klein (1959) suggests that the recent term *subception*
perhaps more adequately conveys the idea of a psychic representation not yet committed to a particular quality of experience, i.e.,
a sensory registration not yet developed into a percept, image, or
dream image. However, the term *subception* does not adequately
describe the complex perceptual, memorial, and cognitive factors
involved in the Pötzl phenomenon, but stresses only the first
phase, namely, sensory registration without awareness.

Transformations and distortions of the subliminal registrations
present some interesting problems. Although some subjects produced highly individual transformations, there appeared to be a
certain degree of repetitiveness and uniformity in the types of
transformations reported by different subjects, e.g., some of them
extracted out from the double-profile stimulus the concept of
"twoness" or of a central moving force. However, the problem
of individual differences was not elucidated in this study and we
gained no clear idea of why some subjects received high scores
and others low scores. Very rarely was there a photographic replica of the stimulus as a whole, and there was a variety of intricate
transformations and distortions of the stimulus both in its many
figural properties and in its meaning. It remains to be determined
why certain subjects show one type of transformation and others
different types, and further research might well find such study
profitable.

The effect of the subliminal stimulus seems to be highly complex and many variables undoubtedly enter into it. Some of them

may determine the individual differences noted, e.g., the capacity for free fantasy, the nature of the emotional relationship between subject and experimenter, the unconscious meaning of the particular stimulus as well as the experimental situation to the subject, differences in cognitive organization and style, variations in the defensive and adaptive characteristics of the ego, the state of consciousness, etc.

In spite of individual differences the data indicate that subliminal registration and its influence upon imagery and dreams is probably a universal phenomenon. In the present experiments it was demonstrated in all but one of the nine subjects and in previous experiments it has been demonstrable in a high percentage of cases. It is a problem for future research to investigate the many variables entering into the phenomenon that may intensify or diminish or bring about individual variations in its expression.

Some work on individual differences had already appeared in the investigations of the New York University group (Smith et al., 1959) and in the experiments of Luborsky and Shevrin (1956). Using the so-called masking technique (the exposure of a subliminal stimulus immediately followed by the exposure of a supraliminal stimulus), Smith et al.(1957) investigated the effect of subliminal exposure of the words *angry* and *happy* on the perception of a supraliminal stimulus, a neutral or ambiguous face. They were able to demonstrate that meanings were aroused by the subliminal words which directly affected the response to the consciously seen stimulus, altering the subjects' impressions of the face in directions congruent with angriness and happiness. They found that these meanings were highly varied and were affected by the characteristic adaptive and defensive resources of each subject. Those subjects who had a more disturbed and confused contact with reality were more sensitive to the subliminal stimulus. Those who showed the least effect frequently manifested a form of paranoid rigidity and a stubborn clinging to the most obvious, most confirmable details. The greatest effect was evinced by those with a readiness and ability to give themselves up to fantasy, to accept passivity, to enter into an empathic involvement with story characters; they also showed greater conflict regarding hostility.

Smith (1957) also noted that perceptual processes of compulsive individuals seem to be controlled by an all-or-nothing principle, by avoidance of all stages between a blank report of the stimulus and a correct one. Such individuals tend to suppress the emergence into consciousness of the primary-process-like preliminary stages of perception that develop outside awareness.

THE FIGURE–GROUND EFFECT IN SUBLIMINAL REGISTRATION

Our findings on the apparent elimination of the figure–ground effect may have important implications for perceptual theory. In normal conscious perception, one face of the double–profile stimulus is seen as figure and the other as ground. The results of our experiments seem to indicate that there was a total subliminal registration of the double-profile figure with subsequent recognition of the nature and meaning of the stimulus. In addition to the fact that there were instances of the appearance in conscious imagery or manifest dream pictures of two profiles facing one another, the preconscious recognition that there were two profiles was also suggested by the rather frequent emergence into images of *two* objects, such as circles, pictures, houses, etc. It was as if different aspects of the stimulus such as twoness, the idea of transformation, or a central moving force were subliminally registered and subsequently emerged into conscious imagery. Some of these images were of an abstract nature where, for instance, the alternating figure and ground were represented by light and dark halves of a field which tended to change their shading. At the same time these images contained actual elements of the stimulus, such as a wavy line resembling the central profile line.

Even though there was evidence that following subliminal registration there was recognition of the true nature of the stimulus, with elimination of the figure–ground effect, during the subsequent threshold determination the subjects saw only one of the profiles, i.e., the figure–ground effect was present. This suggests that while the figure–ground effect holds for conscious perception, it appears to be suppressed in registration or the subsequent preconscious imagery process.

Relevant to this discussion is Klein's suggestion (1959) that:

> [T]he laws of perception developed in the academic experimental laboratories are specific only to a particular state of consciousness, and that the functional importance of these states must be understood in terms of the structure and dominant orientations of that particular state. It is a state of consciousness characterizing behavior when one's conscious intentions are to master, to communicate and to evaluate the properties of things—a state mobilized to an extreme in the usual laboratory perceptual task [p. 27].

Such laboratory tasks are always carried out in a state of consciousness that guarantees an effective appraisal of reality and sharp distinctions between wish and reality. Klein stresses the fact that it is about this state of consciousness that perceptual theories have been formulated and that most of the laws thus far formulated for perception may have restricted validity for this state alone. It may be argued, therefore, that the Gestalt laws of good continuation, closure, figure-ground, etc., may hold only for this state but may not be valid for subliminally registered forms, as our results on figure-ground seem to indicate.

SUPINE-DARK AS A CONDITION FOR RECOVERY

The results demonstrated that in the supine-dark condition there was a more extensive emergence of elements and aspects of the subliminal stimuli into imagery than occurred in the upright-light condition. One factor, however, was not controlled and ruled out: The images in the supine-dark condition were always elicited following those obtained in the upright-light condition. Therefore, it is possible that the increased delivery was a function of time lapse, i.e., the images produced later in the experimental session may have shown greater emergence irrespective of the recovery condition. Further experimentation is therefore called for to separate this time or order factor from the condition of recovery.

There is good reason, however, both in theory and in the work of other investigators to believe that the recovery condition itself was efficacious. For example, the important work on sensory deprivation has demonstrated that individuals subjected to vigils of sensory deprivation show marked interference with organized, logical, reality-oriented thinking along with manifestations of primary process intrusions which sometimes take the form of hallucinations (Bexton, Heron, and Scott, 1954; Heron, Doane, and Scott, 1956). It may be noted that Pötzl (1915) demonstrated that subliminal registrations are extensively utilized in hallucinations. Although our subjects were not subjected to anything like such an extreme vigil as in the sensory deprivation experiments, they nevertheless may have suffered a mild form of it, resulting in an intensified intrusion of the memory traces of the subliminal stimulus into consciousness.

Recent refinements of psychoanalytic ego psychology, particularly by Rapaport (1958), suggest that by reducing stimulus intake, the supine-dark condition may have interfered with the ego's relative autonomy from the id. This interference, according to the theory, can lead to increased reliance on primary process thinking which may include the emergence of subliminal registrations into consciousness. We believe that the supine-dark condition may have enhanced the delivery of subliminal registrations into consciousness for two reasons: first, because the supine-dark condition involves the reducing of postural supports as mentioned earlier; and second, because the darkness constitutes a form of sensory deprivation.

Klein (1959) has formulated the problem in a similar manner when he states:

As reality contact and reality requirements are minimized, so attention cathexis can be deployed to registrations, and they can be brought to awareness in a *passive eidetic-like* manner. It is possible that all ways of minimizing reality-adaptive intentions, e.g., by reducing postural supports for discrimination, by inducing distractions, by producing a state of passive receptiveness in which thoughts "take over" the subject in contrast to an active, attentive condition which is conducive to "producing" thoughts, etc., may facilitate emergence of subliminally registered contents in general and in *perceptual* form in particular [p. 23].

To the ways of minimizing reality-adapted intentions listed by Klein we may add the reduction of illumination to the point of darkness. The intensification of imagery in the hypnagogic state while lying in bed in darkness before sleep is a well-known phenomenon.

SUMMARY

1. The present investigation represented a validation of the Pötzl dream experiment and the Allers and Teler imagery experiment, i.e., to demonstrate the effect of subliminal visual stimulation on subsequent dreams and images. The methodological deficiences of previous research were corrected by instituting experimental controls and checks at as many points in the procedure as possible: from the point where the stimulus is subliminally exposed to the subject to the point where the drawings depicting his imagery are evaluated.
2. The following major innovations were made in the experimental design: (a) a control session in which the subject provided samples of his spontaneous imagery following no subliminal exposure; (b) more than one recovery condition, namely, the upright-light and the supine-dark; (c) a checklist, based upon an objective description of the stimulus (double profile) for scoring and evaluating the data; (d) the scoring of the data by blind judges who did not know the nature of the experiment; (e) the use of a second subliminal stimulus (clock) that differed substantially from the first in both its figural and conceptual properties; (f) a statistical evaluation of the results.
3. The major hypotheses of this experiment were confirmed. The average checklist scores for the postexposure images following the tachistoscopic exposure of the completely subliminal stimulus (double profile) were considerably higher than the scores for the control images, indicating that elements and properties of the stimulus appeared in subsequent imagery with a frequency far greater than chance alone would allow. The average checklist scores of the postexposure images following subliminal stimulation by the second stimulus (clock) showed predictable decreases

as compared to the control images and the images following the first stimulus (double profile), proving that, not only was it possible to produce the effect, but it could be manipulated in predictable ways.

4. Evidence was obtained strongly suggesting that the supine-dark recovery condition had an enhancing effect on the emergence of subliminal stimuli into imagery. These results were discussed in relation to the effect on the imagery process of removal of postural supports, stimulus deprivation, and interference with the autonomy of the ego.

5. Qualitative analyses of the results were made revealing a variety of transformations and distortions of the subliminal stimuli. Evidence was obtained that during subliminal registration the figure–ground effect became fluid or was eliminated. The results were discussed in terms of the possibility that the Gestalt laws of good continuation, closure, figure ground, etc., may hold for the particular state of consciousness mobilized in the usual laboratory perceptual task but may not hold for subliminally registered forms.

6. Although this study was primarily concerned with demonstrating the effects of subliminal stimulation on imagery, some data were presented which also bore on the Pötzl phenomenon, e.g., showing that subliminally registered stimuli emerge in the manifest content of subsequent dreams.

7. The conclusion is drawn that subliminal visual registration is a genuine phenomenon and that subliminal visual stimulation may influence subsequent dreams and images.

APPENDIX I

CHECKLIST

A.   *Content*
    1. It is (or is so described by *subject*) primarily a person or persons.
    2. It is not primarily a person(s), but it contains a person or persons.

3. It is, or else contains, an animal or animals.
4. Though not drawn or described as one, it, or its parts, bears a striking resemblance to a human or animal head.

B.   *Form*
1. It is square.
2. It is not square, but it has a square part or parts.
3. It is triangular.
4. It is not triangular, but it has a triangular part or parts.
5. It has one or several important wavy or zigzag lines.
6. It does not have one or several important wavy lines, but rather is made up, or consists, of wavy or zigzag lines.
7. It has, or its parts have, an important component at the center (a central line, division, or element).

C.   *Movement*
1. It is something, or else it is composed of an important part(s), which can or does ordinarily move.
2. It is something, or else it is composed of an important part(s), which is seen by *subject* as moving.
3. It is something, or else it is composed of an important part(s), which can or ordinarily does transform or change its form.
4. It, or an important part(s) of it, is seen by *subject* as transforming or changing into something else.

D.   *Number*
1. It is two main things.
2. It is only one thing, but consists of two main parts.
3. It is composed of pairs of things.
4. It has an important part(s) which consists of two things or parts.

E.   *Content and Form*
1. It is, or else it is composed of, only the head(s) of something(s) (of persons, animals, or objects).
2. It is, or else it is composed of, the profile(s) of thing(s) (of persons, animals, or objects).

3. It has a high or bulging "forehead" line (especially if it is human or animal, though also possibly if it is an object or abstract design.

4. It has a prominent "nose" line (especially if it is human or animal, though also possibly if it is an object or abstract design).

5. It has a big "chin" line (especially if it is human or animal, though also possibly if it is an object or abstract design).

6. It is "flat-headed" (especially if it is human or animal, though also possibly if it is an object or abstract design).

F. *Number and Position*

1. It is two things which "face" each other (it is only necessary that one of them have a clearly defined "front" and that it be directed toward the second thing).

2. It is composed of a part, or parts, in which two things "face" each other.

3. It is two things which are interlocked or joined to each other.

4. It is composed of a part, or parts, in which two things are interlocked or joined.

5. It is two things (or has a part or parts with two things) which, though not "facing" each other or interlocked with each other, are nevertheless in, or else are seen by *subject* as in, some sort of relationship to each other.

REFERENCES

Allers, R., & Teler, J. (1924), Uber die Verwertung unbemärkter Eindrücke bei Associationen. *Zeitschr. f. Neurol. & Psychiat.*, 89:492–513.

Bach, S., & Klein, G. S. (1957), The effects of prolonged subliminal exposures of words. *Amer. Psychologist,* 12:397–398.

Bexton, W. H., Heron, W., & Scott, T. (1954), Effects of decreased variation in the sensory environment. *Can. J. Psychol.*, 8:70–76.

Freud, S. (1900), The Interpretation of Dreams. *Standard Edition*, 4. London: Hogarth Press, 1953.

Hebb, D. O. (1949), *The Organization of Behavior.* New York: John Wiley.

Heron, W., Doane, B. K., & Scott, T. H. (1956), Visual disturbances after prolonged perceptual isolation. *Can. J. Psychol.*, 10:13–18.

298 SUBLIMINAL EXPLORATIONS

Klein, G. S. (1956), Perception, motives and personality. In: *Psychology of Personality: Six Modern Approaches,* ed. J. L. McCary. New York: Logos Press, pp. 123–199.

——— (1959), Consciousness in psychoanalytic theory: Some implications for current research in perception. *J. Amer. Psychoanal. Assn.,* 7:5–34.

——— Spence, D. P., Holt, R. R., & Gourevitch, S. (1955), Cognition without awareness: Subliminal influences upon conscious thought. *Amer. Psychologist,* 10:380.

Luborsky, L., & Shevrin, H. (1956), Dreams and day residues: A study of the Poetzl observation. *Bull. Menninger Clin.,* 20:135–148.

Pötzl, O. (1915), Tachystoskopisch provozierte optische Halluzinationen bei einem Falle von Alkoholhalluzinose mit rückgebildeter zerebraler Hemianopsie. *Jahrb. Psychiat. Neurol.,* 4:141–146.

——— (1917), Experimentell erregte Traumbilder in ihren Beziehungen zum indirekten Sehen. *Zeitschr. f. Neurol. & Psychiat.,* 37:278–349.

Rapaport, D. (1958), The theory of ego autonomy: A generalization. *Bull. Menninger Clin.,* 22:13–35.

Schilder, P. (1953), *Medical Psychology.* New York: International Universities Press.

Shevrin, H., & Luborsky, L. (1958), The measurement of preconscious perception in dreams and images: An investigation of the Poetzl phenomenon. *J. Abnorm. & Soc. Psychol.,* 56:285–294.

Smith, G. (1957), Visual perception: An event over time. *Psychol. Rev.,* 64:306–313.

——— Henriksson, M. (1955), The effect on an established percept of a perceptual process beyond awareness. *Acta Psychol.,* 11:346–355.

——— Spence, D. P., & Klein, G. S. (1959), Subliminal effects of verbal stimuli. *J. Abnorm. & Soc. Psychol.,* 59:167–176.

6

SUBLIMINAL VISUAL STIMULATION: A STUDY OF ITS INFLUENCE ON SUBSEQUENT IMAGES AND DREAMS (1959)

I. H. Paul and Charles Fisher

Introduction

It is commonly acknowledged that perception is the resultant of interacting forces which are themselves not perceived and not conscious. In this sense few psychologists would question the existence of an "unconscious" which has an important influence on perception. The novel question currently being asked by investigations into the consequences of subliminal sensory stimulation, though perhaps rooted in this position, takes it considerably further in asking: Can complex and organized sensory stimuli, which are effectively prevented from being perceived, nevertheless be *registered*, and then proceed to influence cognition?

In other words, let one visually stimulate a person with a simple figure, but prevent him from perceiving it. He can only report that he didn't see what was shown him—the exposure was too

This investigation was supported by a grant from the Foundation's Fund for Research in Psychiatry. The authors wish to acknowledge the valuable assistance of Adele Edwards.

brief, the figure too faint, another stimulus masked it, or the like. Was that figure nonetheless registered? Did it attain a palpable status beyond the level of awareness? Will it show itself subsequently in the person's conscious cognition?

A substantial amount of exploratory work as well as a few validating experiments have already been reported in answer to these questions. The effects of subliminal visual stimulation upon dreams and images have been studied extensively by Fisher (see chapters 1, 2, 3) who derived his interest in this area of study from the ground-breaking work of Pötzl (1915, 1917), and of Allers and Teler (1924). Until recently, Fisher's efforts to demonstrate the phenomenon have been confined to exploratory experiments that relied largely upon clinical methods. But recently, rigorously controlled experiments have been conducted in this area by Klein, Holt, Spence, and others at New York University (Klein, Spence, Holt, Gourevitch, 1958; Klein, 1959), by Shevrin and Luborsky at the Menninger Clinic (Luborsky and Shevrin, 1956; Shevrin and Luborsky, 1958) and at Mt. Sinai Hospital by the present writers (see chapter 5).

While providing positive empirical evidence of the phenomenon and showing that it is not an artifact of the methods used to produce and evaluate it, each one of these studies illustrates how unstable and small-scale it usually is. Under the experimental conditions that have been used, there are relatively few instances of a clear-cut and unequivocal emergence of a subliminally presented stimulus into subsequent imagery and dreams. Such emergence, for the most part, appears to be piecemeal and fragmentary, and seems frequently disguised by means of transformations. Appraised by objective criteria, its effects can often be detected only by subjecting a sizable amount of such data to statistical analysis. A major hurdle to the detection of any effect is the fact that people's images and dreams are so complex, and so multiple and variously determined, that it is especially difficult to single out the effect of an experimentally presented stimulus while at the same time allowing for, and assessing, chance correspondences, as well as the effects of habit and of extraneous factors. Consequently, further work still is needed to pursue the search for techniques of obtaining, enhancing, and reliably evaluating this intriguing phenomenon.

Purpose

This experiment is part of a larger project, the overall goal of which is to isolate and study the consequences of subliminal visual stimulation upon imaging and dreaming. Fisher's earlier demonstrations (see chapters 1, 2, 3), though generally persuasive and often striking, relied heavily upon (1) a post hoc approach to the data; (2) emphasis upon selected examples; and (3) a quasi-clinical contact with subjects. The present experiment is the second of two in which a concerted attempt was made to overcome the shortcomings of these studies, to establish the phenomenon on a sounder empirical footing, while at the same time exploring variables that may give clues about the underlying processes.

Encouraged by the positive results which are described in chapter 5, the present experiment continued along the same lines but made further modifications in the design. Most important of all, it abandoned the quasi-clinical technique, dealt with subjects as a group, and strove for a more complete balancing of conditions and influences. One of its important goals was to control any possible influence by the experimenter himself who, since he knew which stimulus was being used and was in contact with the subject while he produced his images, may unwittingly have influenced the imagery.

In addition, a number of strategies of handling the data were explored in the present experiment. Each of them was objective and precisely controlled, and was directed toward testing a basic proposition centering on the validity of the subliminal effect. The proposition: *Exposure of a figured visual stimulus at a level beyond awareness (i.e., where there is no possibility of conscious perception and report to even a fragmentary degree) will be followed by the production of images and dreams which reflect, both directly and in transformed ways, the influence of the stimulus, its meanings and forms.*

Collection of the Data

Subjects

The subjects were 16 students: 10 men and six women about 20 years of age, seniors in the graphic arts department of a school of design. They were chosen not only because of their ability to draw, which helped overcome the hurdle of making graphic representations of images and dreams, but also because of the possibility that artists, with their experience in free and fanciful imagery, might more conspicuously show the effects of subliminal stimulation.

STIMULI AND EXPERIMENTAL CONDITIONS

The experiment was conducted in a moderately sized classroom which was dimmed by turning out the lights and partially shading its windows. Each subject sat and worked alone at a drawing table. During the presentation of the stimuli, subjects arrayed themselves in a straight row across the front wall of the room and faced the rear of the room. They were about 20 feet from the rear white wall upon which the stimuli were exposed.

The stimuli were exposed by means of an SVE slide-projector, attached to which was a Rapax camera shutter which permitted exposures varying from 1/200 sec to 1 sec. It projected an area about 2 sq ft. By means of pretesting, it was found that an exposure of 1/100 sec, slightly out of focus, and at a constant (but unmeasured) illumination, gave an adequately invisible exposure. This setting was such that *the experimenter himself could not detect whether he was exposing the figured slide or the completely blank slide.* Threshold-determining procedures were conducted after the main procedures (necessarily so), and they attested to the fact that the exposure level under the specific experimental conditions assured that the stimuli were truly subliminal (see below, pp. 305–309).

The figured stimulus (figure) consisted of a lightly drawn, thin line-drawing of the Rubin figure–ground profile-reversal figure, shown in Figure 6.1. The blank stimulus (*blank*) consisted of a square frame of light. The Rubin figure, which has been used before with good results (see chapters 4, 5), is interesting, though simple, and seems more readily recovered by subjects in their imagery than other less interesting stimuli. An additional purpose for using it has been to explore the nature of figure–ground relationships in subliminally registered stimuli.

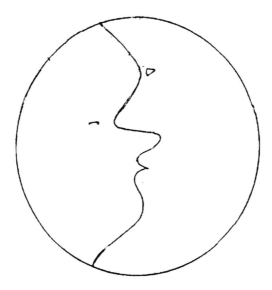

Figure 6.1. The Rubin double-profile figure: The figure stimulus.[1]

Images were produced and drawn by each subject under three experimental conditions: (1) following instructions to image (*control*); (2) following subliminal exposure of a blank slide (*blank*); (3) following subliminal exposure of a figured slide (*figure*).

A warm-up period initiated the experiment. During this period the experimenter was able to convey to the subjects the best approach for them to adopt: namely, to try for a passive attitude and merely to watch for whatever mental image occurs spontaneously; and to be quick and uncritical in the drawing of it. Subjects had a chance to have questions answered and doubts cleared up about their task. Moreover, this period enabled the setting of a suitably subdued, slightly mysterious and reverielike atmosphere. This "regression-inducing" atmosphere, which in a sense corresponds to the clinical-like contact with subjects of the previous research, may be important in facilitating the phenomenon.

---

[1]This figure was copied from Hebb (1949, p. 20). One major change has been made: Instead of a square frame, the profiles are enclosed in a circular frame in order to contrast it with the *blank* which consists of a square frame of light.

The warm-up period was followed by the control condition. Its main function was to provide examples of the kinds of images and drawings these particular subjects give spontaneously. These images then served as a base against which were compared those images produced under the subsequent two conditions of subliminal stimulation.

The blank and figure conditions were balanced off against each other so that each subject, during the course of two separate sessions, participated in both. This was achieved as follows: Following the control condition subjects were divided randomly into two equal groups; one group had the blank condition to begin with (i.e., during session I) while the second had the figure condition; later on (session II), the second group had the blank and the first, the figure condition. To minimize the persisting effects of stimulation, 5 weeks intervened between the two sessions. Every effort was made to duplicate the procedure of the first session during the second. Subjects were requested, at the end of each of the two experimental sessions, to record and submit the dreams they might have that night.

A third session ended the collecting of the data. It consisted mainly of a determination of the thresholds for the stimuli. In the case of the figured stimulus, two thresholds were located: (1) the point at which a "face" or "faces" was recognized; and (2) the point where the subject grasped its reversible, figure–ground characteristic. The threshold for the blank stimulus was the point where the subject realized that there was no figure being exposed. To provide further assurance that the figure was exposed at a subliminal level, a discrimination procedure was then carried out. Ten exposures at the experimental rate (1/100 sec) of the figure and blank intermixed in a random order were presented, and the subject was required to say or guess after each presentation whether it was the figure or the blank. Only 13 of 16 subjects participated in this final phase of the experiment.

Throughout all three sessions, the subject remained completely anonymous, identifying himself by means of an arbitrarily assigned code number.

EXPERIMENTAL CONDUCT IN DETAIL

The experiment was conducted in three one-hour sessions. The following are the procedural steps, excerpts of the instructions given, and some description of the subjects' behavior and the way the procedures fared.

Session I

Step 1, The Warm-Up: The initial session began with the warm-up period. The experimenter introduced the research with the following remarks:

> You are being asked to participate in a psychological experiment on imaging or imagining. Let me assure you, and I'll be saying this again: This has nothing at all to do with your training program nor any connection with school. This is in no way a test of you either individually or as a group. You will each remain completely anonymous.
>
> This is part of a study of the kinds of mental images people get. We've chosen you for subjects, because, being art students, you are more likely to get pictorial images and, moreover, you'll probably be able to draw them easily.
>
> The main thing you will be asked to do is: to shut your eyes; to relax; and to let an image come to mind; and then, when one does, to draw it and label it. Try to relax as much as possible and not work too hard at it. Just see if a simple picture comes into your mind; and when one does, look at it so to speak with your mind's eye and then draw it. The drawings should be quick and as simple as possible. Try not to use much critical judgment on it, it needn't be a *good* drawing. Remember, this is not a test of drawing ability—in fact, it's not a test of any kind; just relax and don't worry about your performance. When the drawing is finished, don't tamper with it; don't pretty it up, but just label it and its parts.

A brief question period followed in which the experimenter again stressed relaxation, passivity, and a "nonvoluntary" attitude. Subjects seemed at this point to have already become intensely involved in the experiment and also appeared a little awed and anxious. They worked in complete silence with little moving or fidgeting.

To obtain the warm-up images, the experimenter said:

> Now please shut your eyes. Relax, and then see what image comes to mind. When there is an image, open your eyes and draw it. Then label it, comment on it, and number it. After that, shut your eyes and start again. Please do this at least five times; that is, try to get a minimum of five images. When you've done five, look up.

One individual soon complained quietly but anxiously that he was not getting any images, and was reassured by the experimenter. After 10 minutes, the experimenter interrupted the warm-up (only one or two subjects were finished) with the following comments:

> Fine. Now I want to get some idea of how you are doing. Do you find that you're drawing objects that you've seen recently? Like things or people in this room, or things at home, or what you've seen in the streets? Try to avoid that kind of thing by not thinking voluntarily of anything specifically. Just let whatever comes into your mind come. Be passive, and wait for something to come, by itself, so to speak.

One subject made the point that the same image kept coming up again and again and asked whether he should simply draw it over and over. The experimenter advised that he try to avoid this and pointed out that this might be the only really active thing they should do. Another subject pointed out that very small stimuli seemed to influence his imagery, for example, when someone coughed. The experimenter said this would probably be true but that the students should try as much as possible to shut out their surrounding world. The experimenter then asked the subjects to write down how they were finding the task.

Step 2, The Control Images: The experimenter went on to the control procedure with the following:

> Fine, let's do another five images now. Begin on a fresh page and start numbering from "one". When you've done five, look up. If there is still time and you want to do more, go ahead. But do at least five. Shut your eyes and begin.

It was 15 minutes before all subjects had finished. Some subjects finished earlier and occupied themselves with sketching and doodling (the experimenter collected these drawings at the end of the session).

Step 3, The Tachistoscopic Presentations: Next came the subliminal stimulation. The experimenter said the following:

> Fine. You can stop relaxing for a moment. Now, for the next part I want you each to have a code number so that I can divide you into groups. Would you please number off beginning in the front row. (The subjects numbered off.)
>
> Now, please remember your number because it will be a kind of identification mark. Your anonymity will still be preserved while there will be some way of identifying the various work you do. Please write your number on the cover of your pad, and then memorize it. Number all of the work you have done so far.
>
> Now, I'm going to flash something on the wall. (The experimenter pointed out the place where the exposure would occur.) You are to watch it very carefully. I will flash it on for only an extremely brief period and probably no one of you will see anything at all. The flash will be too quick. But please watch it closely anyway.
>
> Now, will all of you whose code number is an *even* number, please rise and come to the front of the room. (Half of the subjects arrayed themselves along the wall. The experimenter then asked all the subjects to shut their eyes and described how he was going to flash the stimulus.) I will go 1, 2, 3, in about that rhythm, and then I'll flash it.
>
> Now, will only those people who are standing, please open your eyes. The rest keep them shut and covered. Only the even numbered people open your eyes and look up at the wall. Here we go, 1 2 3!

The experimenter exposed the double-profile figure. The subjects, with a slight murmur of what appeared to be perplexity, returned to their seats, and the remaining subjects took their place. The experimenter repeated the instructions and then exposed the blank slide.

It should be noted that the subjects who were sitting and supposed not to be watching the exposure, had their backs to it—additional assurance that they did not cheat and look at it.

(The experimenter continued by soliciting another set of images.) Would you all shut your eyes. Now, see what images come to mind and draw them. Do it just as you did before; relax and see what image comes to mind, then draw it and label it and comment on it. Just as we've been doing all along. Please make sure you start on a new sheet and begin numbering from "one." When you've done five, look up. If there's time and you wish to do more, go ahead.

Everyone returned to work in the same cooperative spirit as they did earlier, and within about 15 minutes all had finished.

Step 4, The Dream Instruction: After the subjects had completed their images the experimenter gave the dream suggestion in the following way:

Thanks for your cooperation. There's one more thing. If you should happen to have a dream tonight, please make a big effort to remember it. Be sure and remember your dream. It might help to remember it if you take this pad that I will give each one of you and keep it beside your bed with a pencil. If you should happen to wake up after your dream and you feel like it, write it down and draw it—that is, draw all parts of the dream that are pictorial, and you can make more than one drawing if you wish. Otherwise, if you remember it in the morning, write it down, and make sketches of the pictorial parts. Finally, if you care to, write down anything about the dream that seems important—whether it's a sort of dream that you usually have, whether it has some particular meaning to you, what the different parts might mean, etc. (After some questions, the experimenter arranged to collect the dreams on the following day.)

Session II

The second session took place after an interval of 5 weeks. The procedure duplicated the first session except that the warm-up period was omitted and was replaced with some informal discussion of problems brought up by the subjects, e.g., the difficulties of labeling images.

The experimenter repeated, with only an occasional modification of wording, the original instructions and began by soliciting control images. The same amount of time, about 15 minutes, was given to obtaining control images.

Then the experimenter called the even-numbered subjects to the front and exposed the blank slide to them. Next he exposed the figure to the odd-numbered subjects. The last series of images was completed in a little over 15 minutes. Finally, the dream suggestion was given.

Session III

The final session occurred one week after the second. Only 13 subjects were present. The main procedure was the threshold determinations.

The experimenter began by explaining the threshold procedures. He pointed out that the purpose of the procedure was to determine how long the slides had to be exposed before the subjects could accurately see what was on them. The experimenter stated that he would show each slide eight times, each time for a little longer, and that each time the subjects were to draw what they see.

All subjects arrayed themselves at the front of the room. The experimenter began with the figure[2]. It was flashed eight times in the following sequence: (1) $1/100$ sec; (2) $1/100$ sec; (3) $1/50$ sec; (4) $1/25$ sec; (5) $1/10$ sec; (6) $1/5$ sec; (7) $1/2$ sec; (8) 1 full second. Just before the final exposure, the experimenter asked: "Would you note down if you see anything unique about this figure." After the final exposure, the experimenter put the slide on for 10 sec and instructed the subjects to examine it for "something interesting." After this, the experimenter pointed out what it was—the reversible double-profile.

Then this procedure was repeated with the blank. At the end the experimenter asked each subject to indicate at what point he became quite sure that the slide was a blank one, "Exactly when did you realize there was nothing on it?"

Next the experimenter said he was going to flash, 10 times at the very rapid rate, either the figured or the blank slide and

[2]A question may be raised concerning the level of dark adaptation of subjects during the threshold determining procedure: Was it the same as during the experimental sessions? The room was in approximately the same dim state during all three sessions (no measurements were taken). During the first experimental session, the first subliminal exposure occurred after subjects had been in the room approximately half an hour. During the second, the interval was approximately 25 minutes. During the threshold determining session this interval was probably 15 minutes. Whether these differences could have affected the thresholds substantially enough to cast doubt on the results is a moot question.

subjects were to guess after each which one was flashed, the blank one or the one with the figure on it. The slides were exposed in the following order: F, F, B, F, B, B, B, F, F, B.

APPRAISAL OF THE DATA

THRESHOLD RESULTS

The threshold data were examined first in order to deal with the crucial problem: What did the subjects actually see? Were the stimuli truly and wholly subliminal?

Threshold of the Figure
During the eight successive presentations of the double-profile figure (the first two at 1/100 sec and then each exposure a step longer in duration), no subject recognized its content until the seventh 1/2 sec exposure. Of the 13 subjects who participated in the threshold procedures, only four were able to do so at this point. Two others recognized the stimulus at 1 full second, the final exposure in the series, while the remaining seven subjects failed to do so even then. Only three of the six subjects who were able to identify the content of the figure grasped the nature of the stimulus and reported not one but two faces.

These data certainly indicate how difficult it was for subjects to identify the stimulus even with a relatively long tachistoscopic exposure. However, the question may be raised as to whether there was partial recognition of the stimulus, i.e., perception of parts of it that might have gone on to influence the imagery and dreams. The first two exposures of the series are of special pertinence to this question, since they duplicated the 1/100 sec exposure conditions of the experiment itself.

Three of the 13 subjects drew nothing following the two 1/100 sec exposures of both the figure and the blank, merely writing "nothing" each of the four times (one of them wrote "nothing but black-and-white tones"). The remaining 10 subjects made drawings following these exposures. These drawings are all pre-sented in Figure 6.2, which gives some indication of the extent

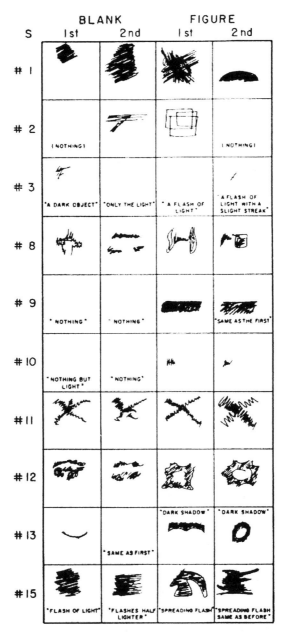

Figure 6.2. Drawings made after 1/100 sec exposures in the threshold-determination procedure.

of their "perception" of the stimuli. Inspection of the drawings in Figure 6.2 reveals that no more than four subjects saw something that might, albeit remotely, be related to the double-profile figure. Two drew circles, another drew two vague masses joined like an "H," while the last drew a form which he labeled "spreading flash." However, the two subjects who apparently "saw" the circle of the figure also drew round figures following the blank. Evidently they were reporting not the actual figure but the growth of the flash of the tachistoscopic exposure. The same may or may not be true of subject 15 whose "spreading flash" may be based on the profile line of the figure and whose drawings following the blank are more formless. However, the fact that this subject achieved a chance score (5 out of 10) on the discrimination procedure (see below, Table 6.1) suggests that his perception was only of the flash, and that his drawing was primarily fortuitous.

Subject 8's performance, however, seems less controvertible. The fact that he scored 9 out of 10 on the discrimination procedure (see Table 6.1) lends weight to his drawing of two interconnected figures and indicates that this subject may well have been able to secure some appreciable amount of information from the exposure of the figure.

Threshold of the Blank

It is difficult to evaluate the threshold data on the blank. Most subjects reported seeing "nothing" right from the start of the eight successive exposures, but they did so on the figure also. Their report was not one of seeing a positive something, but of not seeing anything. After a certain level of exposure was reached, however, they began to realize that "nothing" was really there. At this point, some subjects spontaneously made a note of this. Immediately following the last exposure, the experimenter asked subjects to note down at what point they thought there was a blank being exposed. Naturally, these data cannot be highly reliable since they relied on subjects' recall and trustworthiness.

Two subjects still gave evidence of seeing "something" at the final exposure of a full second. Two others reported "nothing" for the first time at 1 full second; one subject so reported at 1/2; seven claimed it at 1/5th; and one subject reported it at 1/10th. However, no subject reported seeing the "blank" at less than the 1/10 sec exposure, the fifth exposure of the series. We may therefore conclude that the blank also afforded subjects no distinctive clue regarding its nature during the experimental exposures.

Discrimination Threshold

The final and most stringent test of the subliminality of the two stimuli was the final procedure in which 10 exposures at 1/100 sec were given, and the subject had merely to write down which was flashed, the figure or the blank; if they were not sure they were required to guess. Half the exposures contained the figure, half were blank, and their order was random.

No subject was correct on all 10 trials, but one (subject 8) was correct on nine. Two subjects (4 and 13) got eight correct hits[3], four got seven, one got six, four performed at chance (five hits), where 65 is chance[4], and thus performed significantly better than chance, and one was below chance with three hits. Altogether, the subjects got a total of 82 hits. However, a trial-by-trial analysis indicated that their ability to discriminate figure from blank improved as the sequence of 10 exposures proceeded. On trials 1 and 2 the subjects did poorer than chance, while on trials 3 to 10 their performance was better than chance. Table 6.1 presents

TABLE 6.1

Percentage of Subjects Successfully Discriminating Figure and Blank in Each of the Ten Trials (50% is Chance Expectancy)

					Trials				
1	2	3	4	5	6	7	8	9	10
F	F	B	F	B	B	B	F	F	B
38%	31%	85%	77%	85%	77%	54%	54%	61%	69%

[3]It is instructive, at this point, to consult Table 6.12 which shows the relative ranking of the 13 subjects on the degree of "emergence"—the extent to which they displayed the subliminal effect and so contributed to the positive outcome of this study. If it was perceptual information that brought about the effect, then these three subjects should rank high among the "emergers." Table 6.12 shows that, except for subject 8 who ranks fourth, these subjects rank quite low. Subjects 4 and 13 provided data that regularly went in the *opposite* direction (see Tables 6.2, 6.7, and 6.9). If these three subjects are excluded, the results of the experiment actually improve. On the other hand, the best three subjects—the highest "emergers"—obtained the lowest discrimination scores (3, 5, and 5 out of 10, in that order). These findings are considered below on p. 332 and pp. 335–338.

[4]Chi-square is 4.45, 1 d.f., $p = 0.05$.

these results, and also shows that subjects made more errors on figure than on blank, preferring to guess "blank" or most often seeing "nothing." They responded "blank" 61.9% of the time, and "figure" 38.1%.

The fact that the subjects received only two subliminal exposures during the experiment proper, and the fact that the first two trials of the above threshold test were well within the range of chance, gives support to our assumption that not only were the two stimuli presented well below the level of recognition threshold, but that the level was low enough to prevent subjects from perceiving any part of the stimulus. The threshold test shows, incidentally, that had we continued to present the stimuli for more than two consecutive exposures we might have established a summation effect with the consequent reception by the subjects of some cues and information about the stimulus. However, we can take assurance from these data, together with the drawings in Figure 6.2, that the stimuli presented during the experiment were truly subliminal and afforded the subjects no appreciable amount of cues and information about the stimulus.

METHODS OF ASSESSING THE IMAGES AND RESULTS

The main data of this experiment were the images[5] and the reported dreams. Each subject provided images under three experimental conditions: *Figure, Blank,* and *Control (Control 1* and *Control 2)*. In addition, 10 dreams were secured; four following *Figure* and six following *Blank*. These dreams will be considered in a later section of this report. The present section deals with analysis of the images.

Each of the analyses was designed to reveal whether the images show the influence of the subliminal stimulation. Two different kinds of analyses were used: one in which the images were objectively examined for the presence of distinctive elements of the double-profile stimulus; the second in which experienced and trained judges blindly matched the data to the three experimental conditions. The latter analysis will be presented first.

---

[5]"Images" refers to the subject's drawings, with the comments made on them.

Sorting Analyses

The question asked by this kind of analysis is, simply, whether experienced and trained judges[6] can detect evidence of the subliminal stimuli in the images. A graduated series of four matching or sorting procedures was applied. They varied from a "free" sorting, in which the most experienced judge (CF, one of the writers) was required to assign each image to either *F*, *B*, or *C*, i.e., to decide whether it showed the influence of the double-profile, the blank, or neither; to a constrained sorting in which a large group of judges was shown two sets of images from one subject, one actually from figure and the other from blank, and asked to match them to figure or blank. These procedures and their results will be presented in the order they were administered; from the freest to the most constrained.

The first step in preparing the images for analysis was to remove (by actual excision to prevent any possible cues) all identifying marks from them, and to code them. A private coding system was written lightly in pencil on the back of the drawing.

Sorting I: An Expert's Free Sorting

CF (an expert in the sense of having had long experience with the influence of subliminal stimulation upon imagery and dreams, and particularly with the influence of the double-profile figure in this way) served as judge in the first sorting. The total output of images numbering 385[7] was mixed and shuffled thoroughly and presented for him to sort into three piles: figures, blanks, and controls. (This was, incidentally, his first contact of any sort with these data.)

The pile of images consisted of 95 figures (24.7% of the total), 107 *Blanks*s (27.8%) and 183 Controls (47.5%). For the purpose of this analysis, which uses the statistical method for matching data presented by Mosteller and Bush (1954), this is called the *target deck*. CF's sorting is called the *matching deck*. He was told the approximate composition of the target deck (percentage of

---

[6]Their experience and training was acquired before this experiment took place, eliminating possible contamination by the present data.

[7]This number is inflated by images from subjects who participated in only one of the sessions and hence are not among the 16 subjects whose data were treated by the later analyses.

figures, blanks, and controls) but was not required to make his matching deck correspond exactly to that distribution.

In his matching deck this judge selected 92 images which he labeled *Figure*, 80 *Blanks* and 213 *Controls*. He was found to be correct in 180 of these choices; achieving 28 hits on *Figure*, 31 hits on *Blank*, and 121 hits on *Control*. According to the Mosteller-Bush technique the overall number of hits expected by chance alone was 146.2; the difference between this and the 180 hits yields a *z-score* of 3.81 which is significantly beyond the 0.001 level. Therefore, we can safely conclude that CF was able to sort the images significantly better than chance.

Which category was he most successful in matching? In his choice of figure he achieved 28 hits or 30.4 success while the target deck consisted of 24.7% figures; in his choice in blank he hit 31 times or 38.8%, while the target deck consisted of 27.8% blanks; in control, he achieved a hit percentage of 56.8 and the target deck was composed of 47.5% controls. In all three categories he exceeded the target deck; his margin being 5.7% in figure, 9.0 in blank, and 9.3 in control. This shows that he was most successful in matching controls and blanks, and least successful in figures.

Sorting II: Free Sorting Subject by Subject

The second sorting was similar to the first except that, instead of dealing with the entire sample of images, the judge dealt with the total output of each of the 16 subjects one at a time. Moreover, he was told in each case what the exact distribution of figures, blanks, and controls was, and instructed to make his sorting correspond exactly to that.

Seven judges were used in this sorting (included among them was CF). The other judges had some personal experience with experiments on subliminal perception at the Research Center for Mental Health, New York University; each was familiar with Fisher's previous work, and, incidentally, each was personally convinced of the validity of the phenomenon.

The present analysis pools the results from the seven judges on the 16 cases. The Mosteller-Bush technique for assessing the significance of matching data was again applied. Table 6.2 presents the results and analysis of the matching. It shows that the

TABLE 6.2

Mosteller-Bush Matching Analysis of the Number of Hits (Correct Matchings) by the Seven Judges in Sorting II

Subjects	N hits	$\overline{m}$ expected by chance)	s^2	z
1	83	55.37	34.44	4.61[a]
2	57	49.70	36.68	1.12
3	85	44.31	28.56	7.53[a]
4	37	53.69	32.27	(3.02)[b]
5	59	48.23	29.33	1.90[c]
6	44	52.08	28.49	(1.61)[d]
7	49	53.20	30.10	(0.86)
8	75	55.37	34.44	3.25[a]
9	49	52.50	29.96	(0.73)
10	62	52.50	29.96	1.65[d]
11	45	37.80	23.66	1.50
12	74	51.66	19.04	5.01[a]
13	35	46.06	30.52	(2.09)[c]
14	61	52.50	29.96	1.46
15	49	52.50	29.96	(0.73)
16	75	52.50	29.96	4.02[a]
Total	939	809.97	477.33	5.89[a]

[a] $= p < 0.0001$
[b] $= p < 0.01$
[c] $= p < 0.05$
[d] $= p < 0.1$

overall matching performance of the seven judges on all 16 cases was better than chance beyond the 0.001 level of statistical significance. A case-by-case examination reveals that 10 of the 16 cases were matched better than chance, 6 of them at a level beyond 0.05 significance. Only 2 cases (subjects 4 and 13) were matched significantly poorer than chance.

The target deck was composed of 26.8% figures, 24.8 blanks, and 48.4 controls. The matching deck of the seven judges was composed of 19.1% figures, 20.1 blanks, and 60.8 controls. In other words, the judges scored more hits on control than they did on either figure or blank. This means that the major sources of misses was failure to distinguish between figure and blank—the judges were better able to discriminate between controls and figures-blanks. Nevertheless, this does not mean that they did not score significantly on figure and blank. Table 6.3 shows the number of hits on each condition that can be expected by chance

TABLE 6.3

Percentage Total Number of Hits by the Seven Judges Compared with the Percentage Expected by Chance in Sorting II

	Figure	Blank	Control
Observed	30.8	35.1	54.4
Expected	26.8	24.8	48.4
Difference	4.0	10.3	6.0

alone and compares it with the actual number of hits on each. It reveals that each condition was matched better than expected by chance. Interestingly enough (and consistent with the other matchings), there are more hits on blank than on figure or control.

A judge-by-judge breakdown reveals that five of the seven scored more hits on figure than would be expected by chance, while all seven judges scored more hits on blank than would be expected by chance. Table 6.4 shows these results.

TABLE 6.4

Total Number of Hits on Figure and Blank Compared with the Number Expected by Chance in Sorting II

Judges	Guessing Figure		Guessing Blank	
	Observed	Expected	Observed	Expected
CF	28	22	27	19
AE	27	22	22	19
DS	21	22	25	19
RH	28	22	26	19
FP	27	22	33	19
GK	20	22	25	19
LG	28	22	31	19
Total	179	154	189	133
	$\chi^2 = 4.06, p = <0.02$		$\chi^2 = 23.6, p = <0.001$	

Sorting III: Subject by Subject Images Arranged in Sets

The next sorting required judges to single out the figures and blanks from the four sets of images produced by each of the 16 subjects. Each judge was shown each subject's four sets of images; each set was in the original order, but the sets were unlabeled and randomly arranged; and the judge had to determine which set was figure, which was blank, and which two were control (*C1* and *C2*).

This sorting was executed in the following way. Each subject's images were arranged into four sets or columns, mounted and installed on the walls of the corridors at the Research Center for Mental Health.[8] Each set or column was randomly numbered from 1 to 4 and each subject's total output was identified by a "block" number (1 to 16). Members of the staff (faculty and graduate students) were invited to participate as judges and the task was set in the form of a "game." In order to enhance their motivation, a prize of five dollars was offered for the best performance. Each judge received the following instruction sheet along with a picture of the double-profile and a set of answer sheets.

> You may have noticed the "art exhibit." Even though each drawing is the work of a serious art student, it is not hanging to be admired but to be judged. Each drawing is the rendering of a mental picture that presumably came spontaneously into the artist's mind while he was a subject in a Pötzl-type experiment.
>
> Each block of drawings is the total production of one subject. You will see that there are four columns in each block and they are numbered 1, 2, 3, and 4. The four columns represent the experimental conditions. One of them is associated with a subliminal exposure of the Rubin double-profile figure, one is associated with a subliminal exposure of a blank slide, and the two remaining ones are drawings made at the outset of each of the sessions.
>
> You are invited to be a judge in this experiment and to "play the game" of guessing which column of drawings from each block followed the two main experimental conditions; the figure and the blank conditions. The columns are of course randomly arranged in the blocks. However the order in which each series of drawings was produced is intact—they begin from the top of each column.
>
> The Rubin figure—a copy of it is attached—was projected within a rectangular patch of light that the tachistoscope projects on a screen. The blank slide consisted of just the rectangular patch of light. Exposure time was 1/100 sec, and the lens was in a half-blurred position. The experimental question is: Did the subliminal stimulation have an effect upon the spontaneous imagery?

[8] We wish to thank Drs. Robert R. Holt and George S. Klein and their coworkers for their assistance and cooperation in this phase of the research.

Your task is twofold: (1) to select the column that followed the figure condition; and (2) to select the column that followed the blank. Please do these two tasks separately and as independently as you can. Begin with the figure condition and go through all 16 blocks of drawings. Then, afterwards, repeat the procedure for the blank condition.

Please "play the game" as follows:

1. Pretend this is a gambling situation where your choices are registered in the form of bets. The size of your bet should represent the degree of confidence you feel about your choice, and the distribution of your bets among the four columns in each block should result in a rank ordering of the four columns.

2. For each block of drawings you have 10 (ten) units or points (or matchsticks or dollars) to bet with. You must use all 10 of them in each case.

3. You are free to distribute your 10 units any way you please. For example, if you want to choose column 3 of a block, you can, say, bet 5 units on it; then, if column 1 also seems a good bet, you might bet 3 units on it; finally, you might want to bet the remaining 2 units on column 2. In this way you have distributed all 10 of your units in each block. Please try to have the distribution of your bets result in a rank ordering of the four columns with as few ties as possible. Try to make each bet accurately reflect the degree of confidence you have in each of your various choices. The distribution of your bets among the columns in each block will be used in the experiment as an index of confidence.

Incidentally, the experiment will also assume that you worked independently, so please do. When all of the betting sheets are in, the "exhibit" will stay up for awhile and the columns will be identified. This will permit discussion and further examination. Nobody should be able to say "I told you so."

Thirteen judges participated in this matching procedure. All judges seemed to apply themselves seriously to the task and many of them spent a good deal of time carefully studying the images and weighing their choices.

The data were processed by adding each judge's score on the four sets of images on all 16 cases for his figure and blank selections. Since there were 10 points distributed in each case, a total of 160 points was assigned by each judge for each matching. Therefore, a perfectly nondiscriminating performance should assign 40 points to each of the 4 sets of images. If, in matching figure, a judge scored 100 points on the figure set and 20 points on each of the other three, then his performance was in the "correct" direction, he clearly discriminated the figure images. In order to transform these data, 40 (chance score) was sub- tracted from each total, yielding an algebraic index of his score, a plus score being better and a minus poorer than chance.

Table 6.5 presents a summary of these findings. The results show that judges were generally successful in selecting the true figures and the true blanks. Eleven of the 14 judges achieved a plus score on figure when they were guessing figure. Even though most of them achieved a very low score, the fact that these scores are so consistently positive makes their performance statistically significant: The judges achieved an average score of +4.15, which is significantly greater than zero at the 0.05 level ($t = 2.33$, d.f. 12). On *Blank* and *Control 1* their score is significantly negative. However, on *Control 2* their score is positive and slightly greater than on *Figure*; +4.38. However, because of the great variability, this value is not significant ($t = 1.59$).

The judges' ability to correctly identify the blanks is highly significant and unequivocal. On blank no judge failed to get a positive score, and their average of +14.54 is highly significant.

It is especially noteworthy how far superior was CF's achieve- ment to that of the other judges, but only in guessing figure—on guessing blank, his performance is average. His experience had been exclusively in detecting the influence of the double-profile figure and not in assessing the influence of a blank stimulus, and this seemingly accounts for his differential superiority. This suggests how important experience may be in detecting the in- fluence of a subliminal stimulus.

Each judge's data sheet was also scored for the number of hits (i.e., the number of instances in which he assigned the highest score to the correct set of images). The total number of hits is also shown in Table 6.5. Since there were 16 cases and four condi- tions, a chance number of hits would be 4. Five of the judges scored more than 4 hits in guessing figure, while six scored 4, and only two scored less than that. The average number of hits was only 4.81, which falls short of statistical significance ($t = 1.65$). However, in guessing blank, the judges scored significantly more

TABLE 6.5

Total Confidence Score of Each Judge in Guessing Figure and Blank on the Four Sets of Images: Sorting III[a]

Judges	Guessing Figures					Guessing Blank				
	F	B	C1	C2	N hits	B	F	C1	C2	N hits
CF[b]	+24	−11	−4	−9	$9^{1}/_{2}$	+14	−20	+1	+5	6
RH	+6	−17	+1	+10	4	+21	0	−8	−13	7
HL	+6	−12	−6	+12	5	+23	+1	−4	−20	7
SB	+5	+1	−12	+6	$6^{1}/_{2}$	+20	+7	−19	−8	$10^{1}/_{2}$
LC	+4	+7	+3	−14	4	+1	+3	−13	+9	4
FP	+4	−13	−3	+12	$3^{1}/_{2}$	+25	+16	−15	−26	$7^{1}/_{2}$
HK	+2	−10	−12	+10	4	+25	+1	−10	−16	8
PL	+2	0	−12	+10	4	+14	+6	−4	−16	5
AP	+1	−3	−2	+4	$5^{1}/_{2}$	+13	−2	−15	+4	7
RS	+1	+5	0	−6	4	+13	−3	−1	−9	7
GK	+1	−5	−3	+8	6	+3	−4	+11	−10	$4^{1}/_{2}$
DS	0	+12	+4	+8	4	+4	+15	−10	−9	5
AW	−2	+3	+3	−4	$2^{1}/_{2}$	+13	−3	+1	−11	7
M	+4.15	−5.15	−3.31	+4.31	4.81	+14.54	+1.31	−6.62	−9.23	6.58
SD	6.17	7.54	5.54	9.37	1.70	7.83	8.74	7.99	9.68	1.65
t from zero	2.33	2.36	2.07	1.59	1.65[c]	6.43	0.52	2.86	3.29	5.38[c]
p	<0.05	<0.05	<0.05	—	—	<0.001	—	<0.02	<0.01	<0.001

[a]Chance score of 40 is subtracted from each score yielding an algebraic index of performance: A plus score is superior to chance, a negative score is inferior to chance. Also included are each judge's number of hits ($^{1}/_{2}$ point for each tied hit).

[b]The most experienced judge.

[c]From 4, the chance number of hits.

hits than would be accounted for by chance alone (an average of 6.58, $t = 5.48$).

TABLE 6.6

Number of Cases Which Judges, on the Average, Guessed to be Figure and Blank

	Guessing Figure				Guessing Blank			
	F	B	C1	C2	B	F	C1	C2
Observed	7	3	1	5	8	3	4	1
Expected	4	4	4	4	4	4	4	4
$\frac{(O - E)^2}{E}$	2.25	0.25	2.25	0.25	4.00	0.25	0	2.25
		$\chi^2 = 5.00$,				$\chi^2 = 6.50$,		
		$p = {<}0.10$				$p = {<}0.05$		

Table 6.6 presents a summary of the number of cases in which the judges, on the average, assigned the highest score on figure and on blank (i.e., guessed it to be figure or blank). Since there were 16 cases (subjects) and four conditions, a perfectly chance performance is to score 4 hits in each condition. In guessing both figure and blank the judges, on the average, hit correctly most often (7 hits on figure and 8 on blank). A chi-square analysis reveals, however, that only the latter achieves a satisfactory level of significance.

Only CF proved able to guess figure at a level well above significance. Table 6.7 presents a breakdown of his performance. Counting ties as $^1/_2$ he guessed correctly in $9^1/_2$ of the 16 cases, guessing 2 blanks as figure, 3 *Control 1*s, and $1^1/_2$ *Control 2*s. This achieves a chi-square of 10.38 which is significant at beyond the 0.02 level. CF did not have difficulty discriminating *Figure* from *Control 2*, as did most of the other judges. His average confidence score on *Control 2* was only 1.94, while on *Figure* it was 4.00; on *Blank* his score was 1.81, and on *Control 1*, 2.25. An analysis of variance shows this to be statistically significant.

Sorting IV: Paired Choice of $F \times B$

For the final sorting, the judges were presented with only figures and blanks, and their task was to discriminate the one from the other.[9] This was done by removing the two control sets from

---

[9]Had the results of sorting III already been analyzed, we would have tested, not *Figure* against *Blank*, but rather *Figure* against *Control 2*. Sorting III showed that the judges were

TABLE 6.7

CF's Performance on Guessing Figure (Sorting III). Each Entry is the Confidence Score Assigned to That Set of Images

Subject	F	B	C1	C2
1	5	0	1	4
2	1	2	3	4
3	5	0	0	5
4	1	6	3	0
5	3	1	5	1
6	7	0	2	1
7	4	0	6	0
8	7	2	0	1
9	1	5	1	3
10	4	2	1	3
11	4	2	4	0
12	7	1	0	2
13	3	2	3	2
14	4	2	3	1
15	4	1	2	3
16	4	3	2	1
Mean	4.00	1.81	2.25	1.94

Analysis of Variance

Source	Sum of squares	Degrees of freedom	Variance	F-ratio	p
Conditions	49.63	3	16.54	5.32	<0.01
Residual	186.37	60	3.11		

each of the blocks of images, and requiring the judges to guess which of the two remaining sets was figure and which was blank.

The following instructions were distributed along with an answer sheet:

> One final task. You will observe that two of the columns in each block are now lettered in red with the letters *A* or *B*. These two columns are the noncontrol columns, and in each case either *A* or *B* is figure and the other is blank. We would like you to make the rounds one last time and choose which of the two lettered columns is figure. Indicate your guess in each block by betting up to 5 points on it in the appropriate space. Please make the size of

---

able to discriminate the *B*s well above chance; their difficulty was in selecting *F* over *C2*. It would therefore have been useful to test their ability to separate *F* from *C2* in this two-choice manner.

your bet reflect your amount of confidence. A bet of *1* point will indicate minimal confidence, *5*, maximum.

Fifteen judges participated in this sorting. Their performance reveals a clear-cut ability to discriminate figure from blank. Table

TABLE 6.8

Number of Hits and Total Confidence Score of Each Judge in the (8-Choice Figure 1–Blank Task (Sorting IV))

Judges	N Hits	Total Confidence Score	Average Confidence Score	
			on hits	on misses
CF	13	+34	3.4	3.3
RH	11	+23	3.3	2.6
HL	10	+15	3.1	2.7
SB	11	+19	3.6	4.0
LC	8	− 2	4.5	4.7
FP	11	+30	4.3	3.4
HK	10	+18	3.8	3.3
PL	7	− 7	1.9	2.2
AP	7	− 3	2.6	2.3
RS	9	+12	4.1	3.6
GK	9	+11	4.2	3.9
DS	7	+ 2	3.6	2.5
AW	8	+ 8	4.0	3.0
Mean	9.47	+14.00	3.63	3.18
SD	1.74	12.24	0.67	0.21
t from 8	3.13	*t* from zero = 4.28	*t* of difference= 1.55	
p	<0.01	<0.001	−	

6.8 presents the results and shows that 10 judges do better than chance (8 hits), two perform at a chance level, and three below. The mean number of hits, 9.47, is significantly greater than chance at the 0.01 level. Moreover, only three judges achieve a negative confidence score; the mean score is +14.0, significantly greater than zero at the 0.001 level. On their hits the judges show more confidence than on their misses; however, this difference fails to attain statistical significance.

It is again noteworthy that CF's performance is the most superior.

The results of the four sortings may be summarized as follows. The judges were clearly able to detect differences in the images that corresponded to the experimental conditions. Moreover, it was not merely a case of distinguishing pretachistoscopic images from post-exposure ones, i.e., *Control* from *Figure-Blank*. They could also distinguish between *Figure* and *Blank*. However, the *Figure* images were matched poorest of all except by one judge, CF, who presumably revealed the benefits of a good deal of personal experience with the effects upon imagery of this particular stimulus.

CHECKLISTING ANALYSIS

The final analysis of the images consisted of scoring each one on the basis of an objective checklist which was designed exhaustively to describe the Rubin double-profile stimulus. This checklist was prepared in connection with the previous study (see chapter 5), and is fully described in the report of that experiment. It proved successful in capturing the effects of the stimulus, subliminally exposed, upon images and dreams.

The checklist contains 30 items which refer to the properties of the double-profile figure, and is divided into six categories: A, Content; B, Form; C, Movement; D, Number; E, Content and Form; and F, Number and Position. The previous study demonstrated that this checklist technique is reliable even when performed by a scorer who knows the source of each image he is scoring (see chapter 5 for these results). Therefore, each of the images of this study was scored on the checklist by one of the writers.

The results are presented in Table 6.9. The average score of the *figure* images was higher than each of the others. An analysis of variance was carried out to test the significance of these results, and showed that the differences between the four conditions are significant, as are the differences between the 16 subjects. However, only figure is significantly superior to the others, while the remaining three conditions do not differ significantly among themselves.

Table 6.10 presents a breakdown of the checklist data according to the six major categories of the checklist. It shows that

TABLE 6.9
Average Checklist Score of Each Image Produced Under the Four Experimental Conditions

Subject	C1	C2	B	F	Total
1	1.2	1.4	1.6	3.4	7.6
2	2.5	3.6	2.6	1.5	10.2
3	1.3	2.6	1.0	1.4	6.3
4	2.4	3.2	2.6	1.7	9.9
5	1.8	0.6	1.0	1.2	4.6
6	1.2	1.0	0.5	1.6	4.3
7	2.2	1.0	2.0	1.8	7.0
8	0.6	0.8	1.1	2.0	4.5
9	0.6	0.9	2.2	0.6	4.3
10	2.2	2.8	2.8	4.4	12.2
11	3.0	2.0	1.5	4.5	11.0
12	1.4	1.2	0.0	3.0	5.6
13	1.8	1.0	1.2	0.7	4.7
14	2.0	1.6	2.6	4.0	10.2
15	1.0	2.6	1.0	2.2	6.8
16	2.2	1.6	2.0	3.0	8.8
Mean	1.71	1.74	1.61	2.31	
SD	0.46	0.83	0.65	1.48	

Analysis of Variance

Source	Sum of Squares	D.F.	Variance	F-ratio	p
Conditions	4.85	3	1.62	2.66	<0.05
Subjects	26.91	15	1.79	2.94	<0.01
Residue (error)	27.70	45	0.61		

TABLE 6.10
Breakdown of Checklist Results: Average Checklist Scores Per Image on the Six Checklist Categories

Category	C1	C2	B	F
A: Content	0.87	0.75	0.94	1.31
B: Form	3.81	4.12	3.87	4.75
C: Movement	1.69	1.69	2.19	2.06
D: Number	0.37	0.37	0.44	1.19
E: Content and Form	1.00	0.87	0.94	1.44
F: Number and Position	0.12	0.50	0.31	0.87

in one category, Movement, the blank images achieved a higher score than did the figure images. In all others the figure images scored highest. This indicates that the figure images contained more of the properties of the Rubin double-profile figure (except for the movement properties) than did the others.

SOME EXAMPLES OF THE RAW DATA

Having shown that the two sets of analyses provide support for the hypothesis underlying this experiment, it may be worthwhile at this point to present and discuss a few examples from the images. Three sets of data have been selected, each of which was more or less successfully matched by the judges, and each of which illustrates a way in which the subliminal stimuli seem to have exerted an effect.

The first example, the images of subject 10 shown in Figure 6.3, contains quite simple concrete images. The same images tend to recur in each of the four sets. However, those following the blank and the figure contain distinctive elements which correspond to the stimuli. A forest scene occurs in all four of the conditions. However, the last contains a new and important element: two people. Two human heads also appear in the second figure image; heads appear also in control 2, but there are three of them.[10] The final image of the figure set contains overlapping circles which may be related to the overlapping components of the double profile stimulus. Notice also that there is a central dividing line. The blank set contains the only instance of abstract forms. Such forms appeared most frequently following the blank and may reflect the fact that an empty square was what this stimulus consisted of.

The next example, the images of subject 12, shown in Figure 6.4, consists of abstract forms which suggest concrete objects to

---

[10]Incidentally, this subject had the figure in session 1. Therefore it is possible that there was some carryover to the second session, especially to control 2 with which this session began. The pair of hands that occurs in control 2 may be a reflection of such a lingering effect.

Figure 6.3. Images of subject 10.

this subject. Even though the images in each of the four sets contain elements which seem related to the double profile, the judges were able to match the figure set correctly because it contains the most compelling correspondences. Three of the four figure images consist of two elements in some appositional relationship to each other. Only one other image (the first of control

330 SUBLIMINAL EXPLORATIONS

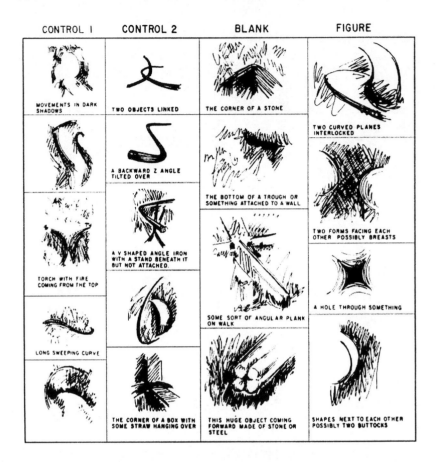

Figure 6.4. Images of subject 11.

2) depicts two interlocked objects.[11] Moreover, the second image of the figure set contains two objects actually "facing" each other. The blank images, on the other hand, are distinctive in their emphasis on angular forms.

The images of subject 3, shown in Figure 6.5, consist of both concrete and abstract forms. Human heads appear only once, three of them in control C2. However, the figure set contains two images which are very impressive; the third and fifth. The former

---

[11]This subject also had the figure in the first session so that this image might well have been a carryover.

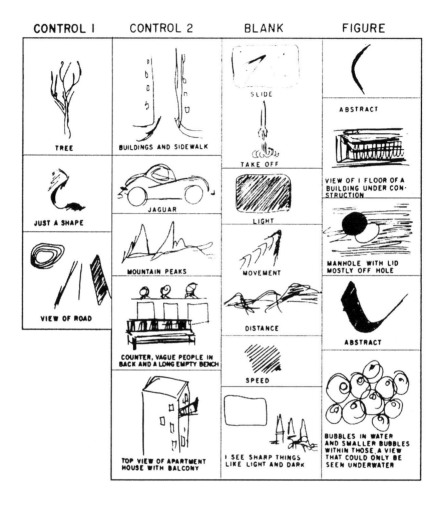

Figure 6.5. Images of subject 3.

shows two overlapping circles, while the latter is a multiplication of such circles each of which contains a second circle. Such multiplication, incidentally, is a transformation that has appeared frequently in previous studies. The blank set of images is conspicuously abstract, consisting of simple impressions of light, movement, speed, and shading. Four of the images seem almost like literal depictions of the blank stimulus.

DREAM DATA

Ten dreams were submitted by the subjects, six of them following the B condition, and four following F. Before submitting them to judges for blind matching, all identifying marks were removed and the dreams were randomly numbered. Fifteen judges were allowed to study all the dreams and then required to guess which were figure and which blank. In addition, they were asked to rate each of their choices along a 5-point scale with respect to their degree of confidence. The judges were not informed of the exact makeup of the target deck, but were merely told that it contained both figure and blank dreams.

The Mosteller-Bush matching analysis was applied to these data, and the results are presented in Table 6.11. The judges scored 97 hits where only 71 could be expected by chance. This achievement is significant at close to the 0.001 level of confidence. Moreover, the average confidence score on the hits is significantly higher (at the 0.02 level) than the average confidence score on the misses. Again, CF is revealed as the most successful judge.

It may be of interest to reproduce here two of the dreams which were submitted following exposure of the figure, and which were matched correctly by all judges.

The first dream (submitted by subject 12) was not accompanied by any drawings and consisted of the following account.

> In the beginning of this morning's dream I can only vaguely remember a few images. There was a very huge snake rolled up in every which way, very uncommon to snakes. It was rolling back and forth balancing something like a little cork on its nose. There was a man seeing that he keeps doing it, and people gathering around, but not too close, to see this show. Later the man came over with his animal on a chain, but it had changed to an old police dog. I was still afraid of it when it came over to sniff me. I was also surprised to see that my little mutt who was lying by me with his chin on the ground, didn't budge. For this was very uncommon to my dog since he was quite a scrapper for his size.
>
> In another part of the dream I remember passing a dumpy hotel bar with two women sitting there. Some other things were going on which I cannot remember.

TABLE 6.11
Results of Guessing F and B on Dreams

Judge	Matching deck		N Hits	m̄ (N hits expected by chance)	σ^2	z	Average Confidence Score	
	F	B					on hits	on misses
CF	6	4	8	4.8	2.56	1.69	4.0	3.0
SB	6	4	8	4.8	2.56	1.69	4.7	5.0
RH	6	4	8	4.8	2.56	1.69	3.3	4.0
SK	5	5	7	5.0	2.67	0.92	4.0	3.0
ME	7	3	7	4.6	2.24	1.27	3.7	3.0
HK	7	3	7	4.6	2.24	1.27	4.3	5.0
AP	7	3	7	4.6	2.24	1.27	4.0	2.5
AE	6	4	6	4.8	2.56	0.44	3.7	1.0
GK	6	4	6	4.8	2.56	0.44	4.5	3.5
FP	7	3	7	4.6	2.24	1.27	3.5	3.0
DS	6	4	6	4.8	2.56	0.44	4.0	3.5
LG	6	4	6	4.8	2.56	0.44	5.0	4.5
RS	7	3	5	4.6	2.24	0.07	3.7	3.0
LC	7	3	5	4.6	2.24	0.07	5.0	5.0
PL	6	4	4	4.8	2.56	(0.81)	4.0	3.0
Total	95	55	97	71.0	36.59	4.22	4.09	3.47
						$p = <0.001$	$t = 2.60$	
							$p = >0.02$	

The Mosteller-Bush statistical analysis of matching data is applied. The target deck consists of 6 Bs and 4 Fs.

In the last part, I was taking a test in a room with the students of my Design class. But the room was elsewhere. When we got to the part of the examination having to do with mathematics, I remember solving the first problem only. The other two problems were full of mathematical symbols I knew nothing about. After struggling over the two problems for a long time and observing the rest of the class doing the same, I decided in irritation to go on with the rest of the test. Then I very vaguely remember a fountain.

The second dream (submitted by subject 2), which is even more remarkable for the degree of apparent emergence of the double-profile stimulus, was reported in fragmentary sentences which accompanied four drawings. Under the first two drawings was written the following:

Some man telling another girl and myself all sorts of fairly short jokes which he never seemed to run out of. Although there were no people in these robes I was aware that one was me and the second a friend, and the third and fourth were twins with identical red and yellow robes on.

Then, under the third drawing, which is reproduced in Figure 6.6, the following was written:

Some two characters from dream from carriage now wearing lavender robes—floating around in space.

The first dream contains much that seems to reflect the subject's experience of taking part in the experiment. The emphasis on looking ("see the show"), on the test, on struggling to solve problems, and so on, seem directly related to the experiment. A number of other reported dreams also showed this influence (sometimes in the form of explosions, flashes of lightning and guns, etc.) that may be related to the flash of the tachistoscopes. However, several of the other features of the dream episodes led judges to detect aspects of the double-profile figure. For one thing the emphasis on twoness, "two women," "two problems", corresponds to the two profiles; the rolling and balancing snake corresponds to the wavy and alternating profile line; and the

Figure 6.6. Drawing accompanying dream of subject 2.

transformation of the snake into a dog might even reflect the figure–ground reversal.

The second dream seems even more striking. Notice the remarkable correspondence of the two ghost figures to the double-profile figure. The transforming and fluid character of the figure–ground phenomenon might be represented in the fluidity of the ghosts.

In passing it should perhaps be remarked that subject 2 who submitted this dream did not do correspondingly "well" on the imagery part of the experiment. In fact this subject showed no signs of having been influenced by the subliminal stimuli and his images were not matched well by the judges, nor did they achieve the appropriate pattern of checklist scores.

RELATIONSHIP BETWEEN THRESHOLD AND DEGREE OF EMERGENCE

In examining the threshold data an interesting finding emerged. Not only were there fairly wide individual differences in threshold, but these differences seemed to correlate with degree of emergence of the subliminal effect.

On the basis of the four sortings, the checklisting, and the dream results, it was possible to rank order subjects on the basis of the extent to which they "showed" the effect of the subliminal stimuli. Table 6.12 shows these data together with the threshold data. The table also shows whether subjects claimed to find the task of imaging and reproducing his images (immediately following the warm-up period) relatively easy or difficult.

Table 6.12 reveals a pattern of negative relationship between the subject's threshold and the degree of emergence he showed in his images: Those who showed the greatest emergence tended to have the highest thresholds (see Figure 6.2, Table 6.1, and the discussion below on pp. 335–338). If we count the eight successive threshold exposures (see above, p. 305) as 1 to 8, and a "no" (i.e., subject did not recognize the stimulus within the 8 exposures) as 9, and if we divide the 13 subjects into two parts, seven emergers and six nonemergers, then the emergers have a higher threshold on figure and blank and score fewer $F \times B$ discrimination hits than do the nonemergers. The emergers have an average threshold on figure of 8.4 and on blank of 7.1, while the nonemergers score 8.2 and 6.3 respectively. On the 10 2-choice discriminations the emergers obtain an average of 5.9 hits while the nonemergers get 6.8 hits. Moreover, the emergers tend to find the task more difficult than the nonemergers do: Five of the seven emergers found it difficult, as compared with only two of the six nonemergers.

The results justify the conclusion that the subliminal stimulation exerted systematic effects upon subsequent imagery and

TABLE 6.12

Threshold Data on Subjects* Rank-Ordered with Respect to Degree of Emergence (Most to Least) of the Subliminal Effect

| Rank | Subject | Thresholds | | F × B (N hits on 10 trials) | Ease or difficulty of task |
		Figure	Blank		
1	12	No	No	3	Easy
2	3	No	No	5	Difficult
3	10	No	$1/5$ sec	5	Difficult
4	8	$1/2$ sec	1 sec	9	Difficult
5	14	$1/2$ sec	$1/5$ sec	5	Difficult
6	6	1 sec	$1/5$ sec	7	Easy
7	1	No	$1/5$ sec	7	Difficult
8	9	No	$1/5$ sec	7	Easy
9	2	1 sec	$1/10$ sec	8	Difficult
10	13	$1/2$ sec	$1/5$ sec	7	Easy
11	15	$1/2$ sec	$1/5$ sec	5	Difficult
12	4	No	$1/2$ sec	8	Easy
13	11	No	1 sec	6	Easy

*This table presents data on those 13 subjects who participated in the threshold-determining session.

dreams that could be detected by experienced judges, and that could be measured by an objective checklist. The experiment was designed to provide a strict test of the phenomenon, and accordingly a careful attempt was made to control contamination from various sources. The main source—which was uncontrolled in the initial experiment of this project (see chapter 5)—was the influence of the experimenter himself. In the first experiment subjects were run singly by one of the experimenters, who knew which stimulus was being exposed and so ran the danger of communicating (by small, unwitting—perhaps subliminal—cues) what kind of stimulus it was. In the present experiment, this possibility was eliminated by the fact that the experimenter ran the subjects in a group where half of them had one stimulus and half the other.

It must be emphasized that, in departing from the original experimental methods, the present investigation ran the danger of employing a methodology disadvantageous for the occurrence of subliminal effects in sufficiently measurable amounts. It is possible that the quasi-clinical contact, with its ingredients of transference and support, is an important condition of the effect, not in giving the subject cues about the stimulus, but rather in facilitating free and truly spontaneous imagery that could surrender to the influence of the *registered* stimulus. There is a strong impression—supported by the recent work of Bach and Klein (1957) and Smith and Henriksson (1955)—that a "guarded" subject may remain nonsensitive to the phenomenon.

The purpose of using a blank stimulus in addition to a figured stimulus was specifically to control for postexposuredness. That is to say, if only a comparison between pre- and postexposure images were made, there would not have been a rigorous test of the influence of the stimulus, since the very fact of the tachistoscopic exposure may appreciably alter images, and it may then be this kind of effect that judges are sensitive to when they guess "figure." By providing images following a blank slide a further control is exerted over this extraneous factor. However, it turned out that this was more than merely a control, for judges were able, with surprising efficiency, to match the blank images. As a matter of fact they performed significantly better on the blank images than they did on the figure images.

Can it be assumed, then, that the blank slide was not really subliminal in the same sense that the double profile was? There is nothing in the threshold data to support such an assumption. In fact these data specifically deny the possibility that subjects saw that "nothing" besides a patch of light was flashed on the screen. After they had been shown both the double-profile figure and the blank slide, subjects could not discriminate a tachistoscopic exposure of one from the other. On the first two trials their guesses were slightly poorer than chance, while on the ensuing trials their guesses improved significantly.

These observations point to the conclusion that the blank slide provided a positive stimulus—one of considerable power. It gave rise to images of more formless character, to emptier and vaguer pictures. Judges selected them because they contained the fewest objects and frequently seemed to reflect merely the tachistoscopic flash. Moreover, they earned the lowest checklist scores, except on the one subcategory "movement" (on which they earned the highest scores). The blank stimulus gave rise to images of objects and forces moving; frequently a subject reported merely that he experienced movement in the abstract, or else the movement of abstract patterns.

Even though the judges as a group matched the images at a level statistically better than chance, for the most part their performance was not strong—their successes were far from overwhelming. Only in the case of one judge was a strikingly good performance observed—CF, one of the authors of this paper and the individual with the greatest personal experience among the participants in relating images and dreams to subliminal stimuli. It is important to remember, however, that CF showed his "ability" only in matching the double-profile figure, while on the blank his performance was only slightly better than that of his colleages. He has had considerable experience with this particular stimulus, but none with a blank. It may therefore be concluded that it was not a special facility with such phenomena that resulted in his superior matching, but rather a greater familiarity with the double-profile figure and the ways it tends to influence imagery and dreams.

This finding also indicates that there must have been a good deal of regularity in the way different subjects showed the effects of the subliminal figure. Transformations are not random; there seems to be a consistency from subject to subject. (A description and discussion of the most common kinds of transformations are presented in chapter 5.) Yet individual differences among subjects were prominent: Some showed the effect substantially, others less clearly, and others showed the reverse. It was not possible to carry out an exploration to determine what individual factors accompanied greater or lesser emergence. However, the threshold data provided an interesting observation in this regard. Those subjects who showed the greatest emergence also showed the highest threshold and tended to find the task of imaging most difficult. Only 13 subjects participated in the final threshold-determining procedure, and the data are too sparse and inconsistent to establish their statistical reliability. Seven of the subjects showed a greater degree of emergence on the various measuring techniques than did the remaining six. These seven had higher thresholds on Figure and Blank, and also did poorest in discriminating the two at the tachistoscopic (1/100 sec) speed. Only two of the emergers reported that they found the imaging task easy, the other five reported difficulty; while four of the nonemergers found it easy and only two, difficult.

Incidentally, the fact that the emergers had the higher rather than the lower thresholds provides a way to counter the suspicion that they must somehow have obtained partial cues, or that they vaguely saw something of the stimuli. However, if it is assumed that none of the subjects got any partial cue or perception and that the stimuli were truly subliminal to all, then these findings suggest two other interpretations.

If the threshold level varies from person to person in a way that corresponds to his sensitivity to external stimuli, then these findings suggest that those people who are the least sensitive may be the most responsive to subliminal stimulation. It is as though there were a reciprocal relationship between sensitivity to external stimulation and sensitivity to internal stimulation in the form of unconscious ideas and forms. Individuals who are more reflective and introspective ought to do better when the task involves a reliance on less conscious ideas than on tasks which require alertness and sensitivity to impinging situations and stimuli.

There is a second possible interpretation of this tentative finding. If it must be assumed that there is no such thing as a universal threshold, but that each individual's threshold varies with his perceptual apparatus, then the differences in threshold indicate that the stimulus was presented at different depths of subliminality for different subjects. Those subjects with low thresholds received the stimuli at a level closer to their threshold, and those with high thresholds got the stimulation at a lower or deeper subliminal level. The finding of differential emergence, then, reveals that (within limits, of course) the deeper the stimulation, the greater the emergence.

The question may be asked: How many of the subjects showed the effect? The answer is complicated by the fact that there was some variation in this regard among techniques of analysis; some subjects showed the effect on one or another of the matching procedures, but not on the checklist, and vice versa. Half of the subjects showed the effect on the checklist, while three others approximated it (ranked higher than chance, but were "beaten" by one of the other conditions). Five subjects had a lower checklist score on figure than on the other conditions. Of these five, however, two were matched better than chance on the figure × blank matching (Sorting IV); a total of nine subjects were matched better than chance in the sorting, while two were at chance level, and five were poorer than chance. CF was able correctly to identify 9 subjects' Figure images.

We may conclude, therefore, that according to the methods of analysis employed, about half of the 16 subjects revealed the effect in their images. Did the others not respond to the subliminal stimulation? This question cannot be answered with certainty; but one interesting fact should be borne in mind. One subject produced dreams in which the extent to which the double-profile figure clearly emerged was remarkable (see Figure 6.6). Every judge correctly matched this dream and it seems difficult to escape the conviction that it was influenced by the subliminal stimulus. Yet this particular subject was among those who showed no effect in the imagery part of the experiment; he consistently fell in the "no effect" group and his images seemed to bear no relationship to the stimuli.

It is unfortunate that so few dreams were submitted, because the possibility should be explored that some subjects who show the effect in their dreams, will not show it in their imagery, and vice versa.[12] One can speculate that the phenomenon is universal; the variable factor is mode of emergence. For some it will be free imagery, for others dreams; and for others it may be some third sort of cognitive process yet unexplored. What is clearly needed in this field of study are methods of eliciting[13] and assessing the possible effects of such subliminal stimulation.

It may be appropriate to close this discussion with a word about theory. Both psychoanalytic as well as contemporary neurophysiological theory furnish a basis for understanding the subliminal effect. The former does so in its distinction between *conscious, preconscious,* and *unconscious* mental processes, in conjunction

---

[12]However, it has been our experience that, in general, subjects who show an extensive utilization of subliminal registrations in their waking imagery also show it in their dreams.

[13]Modes of enhancing the effect have been studied, and some, like putting subjects into a reverielike state, seem moderately successful (see chapter 5). Fisher recently administered LSD to a subject and observed a conspicuous emergence of subliminal stimuli during the drugged state.

with the proposition that there are certain conditions for any percept achieving consciousness. The latter does so in its emphasis on the complexity of the *transmission* of sensory excitation through the midbrain to the higher cortical areas. Each theoretical framework proposes that there are levels short of consciousness at which sensory stimulation can be interrupted, and thus a conscious perceptual experience is an advanced stage of a relatively extended and complex process. The questions arise: What effect, if any, does such an interrupted process exert? Can it have a relatively stable and enduring effect, i.e., arouse a trace or schema? Does it exert pressure "upward" and eventually influence cognition? The weight of the previous studies supports this position. However, they say little about how these effects are achieved—what factors and processes are involved.

In addition to these important ramifications for theory, there is an inherent interest in this area of study since it deals with a wide range of phenomena pertinent to human adjustment and behavior. If the effect is ubiquitous and far-reaching, then our understanding of perceptual phenomena will be enriched by a new class of subperceptual processes, and concepts developed with regard to it will have important implications for perceptual theory.

References

Allers, R., & Teler, J. (1924), Uber die Verwertung unbemerkter Eindrucke bei Associationen. *Zeitschr. ges. Neurol. u. Psychiat.*, 89:392–513.

Bach, S., & Klein, G. S. (1957), The effects of prolonged subliminal exposures of words. *Amer. Psychologist*, 12:397–398.

Hebb, D. O. (1949), *The Organization of Behavior*. New York: John Wiley.

Klein, G. S. (1959), Consciousness in psychoanalytic theory: Some implications for current research in perception. *J. Amer. Psychoanal. Assn.*, 7:5–34.

——— Spence, D. P., Holt, R. R., & Gourevitch, S. (1958), Cognition without awareness: Subliminal influences upon conscious thought. *J. Abnorm. & Soc. Psychol.*, 57:255–266.

Luborsky, L., & Shevrin, H. (1956), Dreams and day residues: A study of the Poetzl observations. *Bull. Menninger Clin.*, 20:135–148.

Mosteller, F., & Bush, R. R. (1954), Selected quantitative techniques. In: *Handbook for Social Psychologists*, ed. G. Lindzey. Cambridge, MA: Addison-Wesley.

Pötzl, O. (1915), Visual hallucinations in a case of alcoholic hallucinosis in a patient recovering from cerebral hemianopsia. *Jahrbuch Psychiat. & Neurol.*, 35:141–146.

——— (1917), Experimentell erregte Traumbilder in ihren Beziegungen zum indirekten Sehen. *Zeitschr. f. Neurol. & Psychiatr.*, 37:278–349.

Shevrin, H., & Luborsky, L. (1958), The measurement of preconscious perception in dreams and images: An investigation of the Pötzl phenomenon. *J. Abnorm. & Soc. Psychol.*, 56:285–294.

Smith, G., Spence, D. P., & Klein, G. S. (1957), Subliminal effects of verbal stimuli. *J. Abnorm. & Soc. Psychol.*, 59:167–176.

Smith, G. J. W., & Henriksson, M. (1955), The effect on an established percept of a perceptual process beyond awareness. *Acta Psychol.*, 11:346–355.

7

CHANGES IN THE EFFECTS OF A WAKING SUBLIMINAL STIMULUS AS A FUNCTION OF DREAMING AND NONDREAMING SLEEP (1967)

HOWARD SHEVRIN AND CHARLES FISHER

The experimental study of dreaming has benefited from two advances in method spaced more than a generation apart. In 1917, Pötzl discovered that parts of a briefly flashed picture not available to immediate report in the waking state appeared in subjects' dreams. In 1953, Aserinsky and Kleitman, and later Dement and Kleitman (1957a,b), discovered that subjects reported dreams

Acknowledgments. This investigation was supported by Public Health Service Research Grant No. MH-2257 from the National Institute of Mental Health, principal investigator, Howard Shevrin, The Menninger Foundation; and Public Health Service Research Grant No. MH-03267, from the National Institute of Mental Health, principal investigator, Charles Fisher, Mt. Sinai Hospital, New York. The research was undertaken while Charles Fisher was Visiting Sloan Professor on the faculty of The Menninger School of Psychiatry. The actual experiment was conducted at the Topeka Veterans Administration Hospital, which was made possible by the invaluable help of R. E. Reinert, chief of staff. The research was designated as Veterans Administration Research Project No. P2-64. The authors would also like to express their appreciation to Vincenzo Castaldo, staff psychiatrist at the Kansas Reception and Diagnostic Center, for his assistance in preparing subjects for the EEG recording and in monitoring their records. They are also grateful to Lolafaye Coyne, chief statistician, Research Department, The Menninger Foundation, for consultation with regard to the statistical analysis of the data, to Benjamin Naylor for his helpfulness in many aspects of the research, to Richard Shackelford for his technical assistance, and to Lorraine Boutwell for her attendance as a chaperone.

when awakened from a state of sleep characterized by electrocortical desynchronization and rapid eye movements (stage 1, or REM sleep), while the incidence of reported dreams was considerably less in three other states of sleep in which rapid eye movements were absent (stages II, III, IV, or N-REM sleep). The Pötzl technique makes it possible to track subliminal stimulus influences on various responses, while the sleep–dream cycle provides ready access to dreams and other phenomena of sleep as they occur. By combining both procedures, one may be able to examine thought processes during sleep.

The Pötzl method has stimulated much research and controversy concerning the existence of subliminal perception which has been reviewed by Fisher (1960). Since Fisher's review, more recent work by Shevrin and Luborsky (1961), Shevrin and Stross (1962), Giddan (1967), Hilgard (1962), Bevan (1964), and Spence (1964) has provided additional evidence, based on a variety of stimuli and experimental conditions, that a stimulus unavailable to report may nevertheless influence a wide range of responses.

Although a considerable number of studies have shown that dream reports are given with much greater frequency after REM sleep than following N-REM sleep, it has been equally evident that mental activity referred to as dreams by subjects also occurs in stages II, III, and IV (Foulkes, 1962; Rechtschaffen, Verdone, and Wheaton, 1963).

Foulkes and Rechtschaffen (1964) have studied the effects of two films, one aggressive and the other heterosexual in content, upon REM and N-REM (stage II) reports. While containing few incorporations of film content, the REM reports following the aggressive film were longer, more exciting, and of greater interest than those following the heterosexual film. No differences were found in N-REM (stage II sleep). The investigators comment on the "dissociation" between the meager incorporation of content and the strong affective influence of the films, concluding that perhaps "the dissociation is only apparent and that the film content is so transformed symbolically that it is no longer recognizable as film determined content in the dreams" (p. 997). The present study begins at the point to which these investigators brought the problem: What are the transformations by which presleep content is incorporated in dreams? It may well be that these transformations are crucial in distinguishing between REM and N-REM sleep.

In psychoanalytic theory the transforming thought processes (dream work) are of central importance in understanding dreams and in distinguishing them from other psychic products. Freud (1900) described a number of transforming mechanisms such as displacement, condensation, and symbolization. He referred to these mechanisms as constituting the primary process of thought which he distinguished from the mechanisms of logical thought constituting the secondary process.

The purpose of this experiment was to see if REM and N-REM sleep could be distinguished on the basis of thought processes paralleling the psychoanalytic concepts of primary and secondary process thinking. A major emphasis was placed on the underlying thought processes rather than on characteristics of content. The same content may arrive in consciousness on the basis of quite different thought processes. Stage II sleep was selected to be compared with REM sleep because dreamlike content has been most frequently reported in that stage. If dreaming characterized stage I thinking, then it should be distinguished from stage II thinking in the use of primary process mechanisms. On the other hand, if stage II thinking is essentially rational in nature, then the usual conceptual level of meaning should predominate in products associated with that stage.

The two stages of sleep may also be compared with the presleep waking state. Insofar as primary process thinking is rarely found in most normal subjects in the waking state, it is likely that responses obtained following stage I REM sleep would be richer in primary process thinking than comparable presleep waking responses. Other work (Stross and Shevrin, 1965, 1968) has suggested that the retrieval of subliminal effects in secondary process form may be enhanced by a change in state of consciousness such as is induced by hypnosis. It may be that secondary process subliminal effects will be greater following stage II awakenings than in the presleep waking state because of the change in state of consciousness brought about by sleep itself.

THE REBUS TECHNIQUE

Language plays an especially important role in dreams (Freud, 1900; Sharpe, 1937; Berger, 1963). Freud cited the example of a man who dreamt of a railway station called *Husyatin*. He was awakened from this dream by his wife's coughing, or *husten,* in German. The verbal trace activated by the stimulus, *husten* (coughing), did not directly appear in the dream, but became the name of a railway station. In an experimental study which yielded data remarkably similar to this clinical illustration from Freud, Berger (1963) showed that proper names played into subjects' ears as they were in REM sleep were incorporated into their dreams most often on the basis of assonantal similarity. For example, Naomi became "An *aim* to *ski,* friend who says 'oh' *show me*" (p. 731). Berger reported that judges were able to detect these incorporations reliably. The limitation of the Berger study is that no comparison was made with N-REM incorporations to determine the nature of the associative process in nondreaming mentation during sleep. Following Wundt, Freud (1900) referred to associations of this kind as "superficial" or "external" because the associative bond was based on a clang similarity rather than on meaning. In dreams, language may seem to lose its referential function and be treated as plastic stuff subject to phonic condensations of the kind just illustrated clinically and experimentally.

The rebus technique (Shevrin and Luborsky, 1961) attempts to take advantage of these changes in linguistic function presumed to take place in dream formation by using a stimulus capable of eliciting three levels of response that are distinguished from each other on the basis of different verbal relationships. A picture of a pen and a knee may give rise to ideas related meaningfully to the objects—words like *ink, paper, leg, bone* (*conceptual* level); or to words such as *pen*nant and ma*ny* which are related by sound but not by meaning to the object (*clang* level); or to a new word, *penny,* formed by a combination of both sounds, which may emerge by way of such related associates as money, coin, round, etc. (*rebus* level). The rebus method thus makes possible the multiple tracking of the briefly flashed stimulus at levels of thought organization related to primary and secondary process thinking. Not simply the thought *contents,* but the associative process by which the contents arrived in consciousness can thus be inferred.

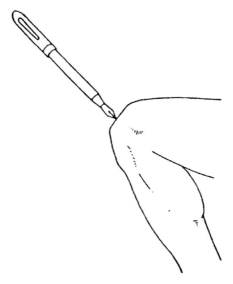

Figure 7.1. The penny rebus.

By using the rebus stimulus as a tracer, it may be possible to detect differences in thought processes between REM, N-REM, and presleep waking mentation.

Specifically, two hypotheses can be formulated: (1) The rebus effect should be stronger in responses obtained after stage I awakenings than after stage II awakenings or during the presleep waking state. (2) The conceptual effect should be stronger in responses obtained after stage II awakenings than after stage I awakenings or during the presleep waking state.

SUBJECTS

Ten women were used for the experiment, ranging in age from 19 to 35. They were nurses and nurses aides who worked the night shift at several local hospitals and could sleep in the laboratory during the day. Each subject was studied during a baseline session to determine that she had a normal sleep–dream cycle. The subject was then scheduled for two experimental sessions a week apart. For participating in the experiment subjects were paid $20.

Experimental Design

The experimental design was based on one developed in previous experiments with the rebus stimuli using hypnosis as the means for inducing changes in states of consciousness (Shevrin and Stross, 1962; Stross and Shevrin, 1962). Each subject was her own control for stimulus effect: Either the experimental stimulus (picture of a pen and a knee) or a blank card was flashed prior to the subject's retiring to sleep. The stimulus order was counterbalanced by assigning five subjects randomly to each of two stimulus orders: penny rebus followed by the blank card a week later (PB order), or blank card followed by the penny rebus a week later (BP order). As an additional control the experimenter who obtained the subjects' responses did not know which stimulus they had seen for that particular session.

Equipment

The stimulus was an India ink outline drawing of a pen and a knee against a white background mounted on a 35-mm slide. The blank side was made by mounting a clear strip of film on a 35-mm slide. A Bell and Howell 300W projector with an attached Eastman-Kodak supermatic mechanical shutter calibrated just prior to the experiment was used to flash the slide on a beaded screen some 11 ft away from the subject. The picture covered an area of 22 × 35 in. Luminance levels were determined with a Standard Electric Instruments photometer. There were three luminance levels: (1) blinds closed with flash, 27.4 ftl; (2) blinds closed without flash (for dark adaptation), .023 ftl; (3) blinds partially opened to permit subject to draw the stimulus, .27 ftl. The stimulus was flashed at 0.006 sec. Electrode placements for the electroencephalogram recording were: (1) left frontal; (2) left parietal; (3) left occipital; (4) left and right outer canthi for detecting eye movements. The ears were used as references. The subject was awakened by a loud alarm clock set off as the experimenter entered the room for the awakening. The subject was encouraged to awaken quickly and to begin responding to the questions immediately. The EEG and tape recorder were in an adjoining room.

EXPERIMENTAL PROCEDURE

The objective was to obtain three paired stage II and stage I awakenings for each subject during an experimental session. If possible, stage II awakenings should immediately precede stage I awakenings. In practice this was difficult to achieve because of unpredictable fluctuations in the duration of stage II sleep periods and the brevity of most early REM periods. After each awakening the subject was asked to perform three tasks in the following order:

1. Sleep Report: Immediately upon awakening the subject was asked the following question: "What was happening just before you were awakened?" If no content was forthcoming, the subject was then asked, "What went through your mind just before you were awakened?" The experimenter could feel free to ask the subject to clarify details of her report because he did not know which stimulus the subject had seen. After describing the sleep content the subject made a drawing of what she reported and described the drawing as she made it. This latter requirement was meant to elicit a greater amplification of the content.
2. Image: The subject was asked to close her eyes and to describe the first picture that came to mind and then to make a drawing of it while describing it for a second time.
3. Free Associations: With her eyes closed the subject was instructed to say all the individual words that came to mind during 4 min. A special instruction was used to induce a passive and uncritical attitude:

Now I'm going to ask you to say all of the individual words that come to mind in the space of several minutes. I will tell you when to begin and stop. It would help if you would close your eyes, so please close them now and let them remain closed until I tell you to open them. Fine; when I tell you to begin I want you to say all of the individual words that come into your mind in the space of several minutes. Let whatever words that want to come into your mind; say all the words that pop into your mind; let your mind roam as far as it wants to—no matter how related or unrelated—no matter how silly or nonsensical the words may seem. It's particularly important that you say all of the words that come into your mind. You can do this best by making yourself so relaxed that the words just come up by themselves; just let it happen and say the words as they come to you. You'll find that it gets easier as you go along. Ready? Begin . . . .

The addition of images and free associations is consistent with the view that the underlying thought process must be the focus of attention. The sleep report describes the end result of that process, but other means may be used to tap the same process. In psychoanalysis, for example, free associations are an essential accompaniment of dream interpretation; in fact, the analyst assumes that the manifest content of the dream may be misleading without free associations which are relied on to open a window upon the latent dream thoughts. Images have been found useful in a number of investigations of subliminal effects (see chapters 2, 3, 5, 6; Shevrin and Luborsky, 1958, 1961). In the presleep waking state, two descriptions and drawings of the flashed stimulus were obtained, as well as an image and free associations. The experimental sections were electrically recorded.

MEASURES

In order to ensure clear and objective scoring for the rebus and conceptual levels, the rebus and conceptual scores were based as normative lists of associates collected from a sample of 200 subjects. The clang measure was determined by counting up all words containing *ny* sounds and all words containing a syllable composed of a *p* followed by a vowel and a final (*p–n*).[1] Since no judgment is involved in identifying these associates and the clangs, reliability is exceptionally high. All protocols were scored by two raters independently and compared for omissions. Combined scoring and tabulating errors were consistently less than 3 percent on all scored responses. In the analyses to be reported below, all scores were corrected for the total number of words in any given response.[2]

RESULTS

In any investigation of subliminal stimulation it is first necessary to show that the stimulus was not available to direct report by subjects following its brief exposure. No subject was able to identify correctly any part of the stimulus following its 0.006 sec exposure at the brightness described above. How far below the recognition threshold the stimulus was flashed was assessed by estimating each subject's recognition threshold at the end of the experiment. Only one subject was able to identify the stimulus at less than 1 sec (.500 sec). Four other subjects took 1 sec and the remaining five subjects needed several 1 sec flashes to recognize the stimulus. The stimulus was evidently flashed considerably below its recognition threshold.

SLEEP REPORTS

There were 51 stage I awakenings out of which 46, or 90%, resulted in the report of some content, usually described as a dream by subjects. There were 47 stage II awakenings out of which 28, or 60%, resulted in the report of some content, occasionally

---

[1]A scoring manual is available on request from the editor, in which the rules for using these measures are fully described—*Progress Report: Preconscious Perception in Dreams and Waking Images*, United States Public Health Service Grant No. M-2257, Appendix A: Manual for Scoring Rebus and Conceptual Associates, Clangs and Rules for Word Counts.

[2]Criteria for statistical analysis are to be found in Appendix C of the Progress Report described in note 1.

354 SUBLIMINAL EXPLORATIONS

described as dreams by subjects. The stage I percentage of content
reports is higher than the 80% usually reported in the literature.
The stage II percentages compare with 35, 72, and 23% reported,
respectively, by Goodenough, Shapiro, Holden, and Steinschriber
(1959), Foulkes (1962), and Rechtschaffen et al. (1963).

TABLE 7.1
Rebus Subliminal Effect and Sleep Stages Free Associations (Penny Associates)

Subject	Waking presleep	Rank	Stage II	Rank	Stage I	Rank
JM	−2.00	2	−4.27	3	0.21	1
CR	0.35	2	−5.36	3	1.52	1
GR	−7.07	3	0.13	2	4.62	1
JD	−1.08	3	0.91	2	1.58	1
SS	−0.99	2	−1.85	3	1.06	1
CW	10.00	1	−1.12	2	−2.82	3
RC	−6.25	3	2.80	1	−0.91	2
MF	−3.95	3	0.10	2	0.44	1
CR	−3.12	2	−5.53	3	2.54	1
MP	−0.01	2	−1.42	3	2.83	1
Total		23		24		13
Mdn	−1.54		−1.27		1.29	

Note. $\chi^2 = 7.40$, $p < 0.03$.

The dreams and other thought contents reported by subjects
immediately following stage I and stage II sleep failed to show
any rebus, conceptual, or clang subliminal effects.

FREE ASSOCIATIONS

Rebus Effect

In order to compare the three conditions (presleep waking,
stage II, and stage I) a Friedman two-way analysis of variance was
performed on the difference scores for each subject between the
experimental and control sessions for the free associations.[3] A

[3]The use of difference scores runs the risk of "building into" the experimental effects
differences which may be largely due to the control level of a given variable. The authors
have taken this possibility into account by first checking to see if the correlations between
the control and difference scores were comparable for the three experimental conditions.
If these correlations were comparable this would indicate that the control variables were
having an approximately equal effect in all conditions; thus any differences among condi-

TABLE 7.2
Conceptual Subliminal Effect and Sleep Stages Free Associations (Pen + Knee Associates)

Subject	Waking presleep	Rank	Stage II	Rank	Stage I	Rank
JM	−6.12	3	2.89	1	0.85	2
CR	0	2	3.28	1	−0.43	3
GR	−12.12	3	−5.78	2	−5.11	1
JD	−0.10	1	−2.04	2	−2.98	3
SS	−0.01	2	3.84	1	−0.42	3
CW	0	3	4.61	1	3.22	2
RC	−1.48	2	0.69	1	−2.32	3
MF	−3.57	3	−1.07	2	1.71	1
CR	−0.09	2	3.60	1	−1.15	3
MP	−0.01	1	−0.79	2	−1.40	3
Total		22		14		24
Mdn	−0.10		0.74		−0.79	

Note. $\chi^2 = 5.60$, $p < 0.06$.

positive score indicates that the experimental session showed more of the effect than the control session; a negative score the reverse. Only one subject (CW) showed a complete reversal of the expected order of effects. The differences among the conditions were significant ($\chi^2 = 7.40$, $p < 0.03$). The individual group comparisons made on the basis of the Wilcoxon test for paired replicates showed, as hypothesized, that the rebus effect was stronger in stage I than in stage II ($p < 0.025$), or in presleep waking ($p < 0.05$).[4]

Conceptual Effect
For the pen and knee associates the same Friedman two-way analysis of variance was performed on the difference scores for the three conditions. The differences among the three medians were associated with a $\chi^2 = 5.60$, $p < 0.06$ (for the 0.05 level, $\chi^2 = 5.99$). Individual group comparisons were then made on the basis of the Wilcoxon test for paired replicates; the conceptual effect was stronger in stage II than in stage I ($p < 0.025$), or in presleep waking ($p < 0.05$). The relationship between the rebus

tions could not fully be accounted for by the control scores alone. Whenever the correlations were significantly different from each other the analysis was not pursued.
[4]A one-tailed test was used because the direction of the difference was hypothesized.

and conceptual effects for the three conditions can best be seen in Figure 7.2.

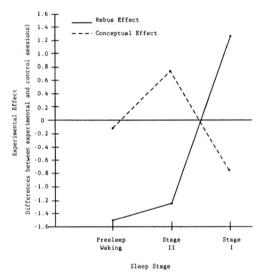

Figure 7.2. Rebus and conceptual subliminal effects as a function of sleep stages. (Median values; $N = 10$.)

No differences were found for the clang effect or for any of the measures in the images.

DISCUSSION

The rebus technique allowed the authors to "track" objectively different levels of thinking associated with presleep waking, stage I, and stage II sleep without the need to resort to subjective evaluations or clinical judgments. Their findings make it necessary to distinguish between the registration of the stimulus, and the conditions under which the registered stimulus will result in identifiable responses. As these conditions change, the kind of influence exerted by the stimulus will vary. Thus, the same pen and knee verbal traces will enter into the stream of thought as conceptual designations of objects in stage II sleep and will participate in stage I sleep as a clang combination. These stages may succeed each other so that these trace formations may change back and forth depending on the prevailing level of sleep. Fisher (1965) suggested that in stage I the thought content in the preceding stage II sleep is "worked over" by primary process mechanisms. When stage I has temporarily abated the same thoughts may revert to their former secondary process relationships.

The free associations were more sensitive to the rebus and conceptual level effects than the dream reports themselves. In another study, investigating the influence of the same subliminal stimulus on recovery in hypnosis and the waking state, it was found that free associations were especially sensitive to the subliminal effects (Stross and Shevrin, 1968).

Of special interest were the findings bearing on the presleep waking state. Both the rebus and conceptual level effects present in free associations were stronger following their respective sleep stages than in the presleep waking state. Sleep as such may enhance the recovery of subliminal stimuli although the subliminal stimuli will elicit markedly different responses depending on the prevailing stage of sleep. These findings point to the importance of states of consciousness with respect to the processing of subliminal information.

Several technical limitations may account for the failure of the sleep reports to show the experimental effects. The 10% absence of scorable responses in stage I and the 40% absence of scorable responses in stage II impose severe limitations on the statistical analyses of the data which may account for the absence of significant differences. In addition, subjects for the most part were relatively inarticulate upon awakening and needed considerable encouragement from the experimenter before they would elaborate their initial brief descriptions of their sleep experiences. On the other hand, adequate free associations and images were obtained after almost every awakening.

Of the three responses, images were the least sensitive to the experimental effects. Images are primarily visual in nature, while the effects measured in this experiment were largely verbal. Perhaps, as primarily visual experiences, images cannot easily reflect these verbal influences, although they may reveal visual effects not studied in this experiment.

REFERENCES

Aserinsky, E., & Kleitman, N. (1953), Regularly occurring periods of eye motility, and concomitant phenomena during sleep. *Science*, 118:273–274.

Berger, R. J. (1963), Experimental modification of dream content by meaningful verbal stimuli. *Brit. J. Psychiatry*, 109:722–740.

Bevan, W. (1964), Subliminal stimulation: A pervasive problem for psychology. *Psycholog. Bull.*, 61:81–99.

Dement, W., & Kleitman, N. (1957a), Cyclic variations in EEG during sleep and their relation to eye-movements, body motility, and dreaming. *Electroencephalogr. & Clin. Neurophysiol.*, 9:673–690.

———— (1957b), The relation of eye movements during sleep to dream activity: An objective method for the study of dreaming. *J. Experiment. Psychol.*, 53:339–346.

Fisher, C. (1960), Introduction: Preconscious Stimulation in Dreams, Associations, and Images. *Psychological Issues*, Mongr. 7. New York: International Universities Press, pp. 1–40.

———— (1965), Psychoanalytic implications of recent research on sleep and dreaming. *J. Amer. Psychoanal. Assn.*, 13:197–303.

Foulkes, W. D. (1962), Dream reports from different stages of sleep. *J. Abnorm. & Soc. Psychol.*, 65:14–25.

———— Rechtschaffen, A. (1964), Presleep determinants of dream content: Effects of two films. *Percept. & Motor Skills*, 19:983–1005.

Freud, S. (1900), The Interpretation of Dreams. *Standard Edition*, 4 & 5. London: Hogarth Press, 1953.

Giddan, N. S. (1967), Recovery through images of briefly flashed stimuli. *J. Personal.*, 35:1–19.

Goodenough, D. R., Shapiro, A., Holden, M., & Steinschriber, L. (1959), A comparison of dreamers and nondreamers: Eye movements, electroencephalograms and the recall of dreams. *J. Abnorm. & Soc. Psychol.*, 59:295–302.

Hilgard, E. R. (1962), What becomes of the input from the stimulus? *J. Personal.*, 30:46–72.

Pötzl, O. (1917), The relationship between experimentally induced dream images and indirect vision. In: Preconscious Stimulation in Dreams, Associations, and Images. *Psychological Issues*, Monogr. 7, Vol. 2. New York: International Universities Press, pp. 41–120.

Rechtschaffen, A., Verdone, P., & Wheaton, J. (1963), Reports of mental activity during sleep. *Can. Psychiat. Assn. J.*, 8:409–414.

Sharpe, E. F. (1937), *Dream Analysis*. London: Hogarth Press.

Shevrin, H., & Luborsky, L. (1958), The measurement of preconscious perception in dreams and images: An investigation of the Poetzl phenomenon. *J. Abnorm. & Soc. Psychol.*, 56:285–294.

———— ———— (1961), The rebus technique: A method for studying primary-process transformations of briefly exposed pictures. *J. Nerv. & Ment. Dis.*, 133:479–488.

———— Stross, L. (1962), The effects of altered states of consciousness on primary-process transformations of briefly exposed pictures. *Amer. Psychologist*, 17:196.

Spence, D. (1964), Conscious and preconscious influences on recall: Another example of the restricting effects of awareness. *J. Abnorm. & Soc. Psychol.*, 68:92–99.

Stross, L., & Shevrin, H. (1962), Differences in thought organization between hypnosis and the waking state: An experimental approach. *Bull. Menninger Clin.*, 26:237–247.

———— ———— (1965), The effects of hypnosis on subliminal perception: A comparison of dream recall in wakefulness and hypnosis. *Internat. J. Clin. & Experiment. Hypnosis*, 15:3–71.

———— ———— (1968), Thought organization in hypnosis and the waking state: The effects of subliminal stimulation in different states of consciousness. *J. Nerv. & Ment. Dis.*, 147:272–288.

Wundt, W. (1874), *Grundzüge der physiologischen Psychologie.* Leipzig.

8

EYE FIXATION BEHAVIOR AS A
FUNCTION OF AWARENESS (1968)

LESTER LUBORSKY, RICHARD RICE, DONALD
PHOENIX, AND CHARLES FISHER

When a stimulus is presented so faintly that the viewer is unaware of seeing it, his eyes should not behave as though he were
inspecting it. This simple supposition has never been tested in
all of the research on waking and sleeping eye movement (Woodworth and Schlosberg, 1954; Fisher, 1965).

A direct way to test this supposition is by exposing a faint stimulus at graded increments of illumination and photographing the
eye fixations at each stage. Inspection patterns of fixations might
occur well before, just before, or only at the moment of awareness. If our method were to reveal "intelligent" tracking behavior
before the reported awareness of seeing anything, it would be
one of the most direct ways for exploring "cognition without
awareness."

Acknowledgments. We owe special thanks to Ira Kaplan and Joe Derman for work with
the pilot group, and to Norman Mackworth for collaboration in planning and running
the pilot group. We are grateful for the critical reading by Donald Spence, Ulrich Neisser,
and John Paul Brady. Barton Blinder gave helpful suggestions for the data analysis. We
relied on Freda M. Greene for her editorial, secretarial, and administrative skills. Reita
Brandt and Mannor Woo assisted with apparatus and data. This investigation was supported by U.S.P.H.S. Grant MH-03654 from the National Institute of Mental Health.

Not only unaware tracking of unseen stimuli may be revealed, but other eye behaviors as well. The fixations may fall on a stimulus by happenstance or by the viewer's naïve preference for looking in a certain area of the field. Whether the viewer's looking is directed or by chance, the more the gaze falls on forms within foveal vision the more registration can occur. Registrations also may take place even without eye fixations directed exactly upon the stimulus—information can be taken in through peripheral vision. Whether the target falls within foveal vision or not, after prolonged subthreshold stimulation sensitive methods of assessing faint registrations might produce positive results. (The word *registration* is used throughout in a most general sense: that is, any form of information about a stimulus which enters the memory system.)

With these formulations in mind, we set up an experiment with two aims: (1) to find the degree of eye fixation clustering before or coincident with awareness of seeing a stimulus; (2) to determine whether a stimulus has registered even though the subject might be unaware of it and cannot directly report it.

After the subject has inspected an apparently blank field containing a faint stimulus, content related to the stimulus which could not be reported directly may appear by means of his free associations or recall of images. Faint registrations also may prime the recall of associates of the below-threshold stimulus. Finally, the *form* of the subject's description of his first discrimination of something on the screen may contain more knowledge than he is aware of having. Block and Reiser (1962) found such an effect when the subject chose the word *uncertain* as his response to a discrimination task.

METHOD

The method provided for an initial absence of conscious perception of the stimulus by means of a very low illumination on the screen. A Kodak 35 mm projector behind the subject projected a word on the screen for 10 sec, but so faintly (and with bright room illumination of about 12 ft candles) that none of the subjects could see it at first, or at least could not report it. The amount of light from the projector was controlled by a variable transformer. The subject was instructed to scan the screen and report anything he saw—*any* differentiation. Five-volt stepwise increases were provided until the subject reported seeing "something," then fragments, and eventually the stimulus word.

A blank slide, or the stimulus slide, was projected. The stimulus slide had the word *cheese* typewritten on two quadrants—the upper right and lower left—of the same kind of transparent paper that was used for the blank slide. Thus, texture and illumination were kept constant for both the blank and stimulus slides. The subject was seated viewing the screen at a distance of 25 in; the dimensions of the projected field were $6^1/2$ by 11 in. Our considerable experience with a 10-sec exposure led us to expect about 25 fixations within that period. After two exposures of the stimulus and two of the blank, the subject was shown 26 hand-held 3×5 in cards, one at a time, each card containing a typewritten word either associated or unassociated with the word *cheese*. Then, recall of the 26 words was requested.[1] To prevent the experimenter from giving any unconscious emphasis to cheese-related words, he held the cards so that he could see only their backs.

Photographs of eye fixations were taken for each illumination level until the subject fully recognized the word *cheese* in both quadrants. We used the Mackworth eye camera (Mackworth and Kaplan, 1963) which operates on a corneal reflection principle and provides a photographic record of the location, duration, and sequence of the fixation. Accuracy of aiming of fixations was $\pm 1°$ of the expected location. The following summarizes the procedure:

Expose stimulus (47 v)[2]
Expose blank (47 v)

---

[1] The stimulus word *cheese* and the words for recall were based upon Spence and Holland (1962), who discovered that subthreshold tachistoscopic exposures of the word *cheese* could prime word associates of cheese, so that recall of these associates minus the number of recalled nonassociates would be greater for subjects shown *cheese* than for subjects shown a blank exposure.

[2] The illumination from the projector was measured by a light meter held *against the projector lens*. The range of illumination was from 7 to 70 ft candles (47 to 87 v). The 5v steps produced an average increase of 8-ft candles with the early steps somewhat less than 8 and the later ones somewhat more.

Expose stimulus (47 v)
Expose blank (47 v)
Show the subject the 26 word cards, then ask for recall
Free association (three minutes)[3]
Expose stimulus (47 v)
Expose stimulus (52 v)
Expose stimulus (57 v)

Continue this ascending series until the subject fully recognizes *cheese* in both quadrants.

SUBJECTS

A pilot group of 9 subjects was run solely to standardize conditions, and those results will not be presented.

The study was carried out on an experimental group of 23 subjects (13 men and 10 women). Fifteen were undergraduate or graduate students at the University of Pennsylvania, the remainder were laboratory technicians, secretaries, and nurses. The stipulations for inclusion were that the subjects have reasonably good eyesight at 2 ft without corrections, and that they could expect to be in the Philadelphia area for 4 or 5 years to take part in future experiments.

Some analyses will be separate for two subgroups of these 23 subjects: Subgroup 1 contains 13 subjects and subgroup 2, 10. After running the first 23 subjects, we wondered whether the word *cheese* was exposed so far below threshold that we could not reasonably expect effects of any sort in our indirect measures of recall. At the lowest illumination step for subgroup, even the experimenters, who knew something was being exposed below threshold, could not discern any stimulus differentiation. Thereafter we began our exposure series one illumination step higher (5 v) for subgroup 2, yet we still could not detect any stimulus differentiation in the target area. No subjects in the pilot or experimental groups reported any differentiation at the initial illumination levels.

---

[3]A free-association period was tried. Because it came after the recall list, the list itself may have stimulated cheese-associated content. Results are therefore not included.

A control group of 14 subjects, comparable in composition to the experimental group, was shown only blank exposures (see *control group* under "Results").

INSTRUCTIONS

Initial Instructions
"This is an experiment in perception. A picture will be exposed several times. Each time it will be exposed very faintly but you will have time to look at it." After the alignment card had been shown, the subject was told: "After this card you are free to look at the next card, wherever you wish." (Said twice.)

Instructions After Exposure
"Fully describe what you saw." If the subject answered in single words such as "nothing," he was asked for more of his experience: "Describe what you saw fully." This was repeated each time. (These instructions were intended to create an attitude of looking carefully and reporting fully.)

Instructions for Recall List
"Now I'm going to show you 26 words, one at a time and one on each card. Later, I'll ask you to reproduce them from memory. This is not a test, for it is quite impossible to remember all the words. Just relax and watch each word as it is shown." After the cards were all shown: "Please write down all words you can remember in whatever order you can. Continue writing as long as you wish, and feel free to guess as often as you wish." (When the subject stopped writing, he was given another minute in which the instruction was repeated: "Feel free to guess and write down all you can recall.")

MEASURES

AWARENESS MEASURES

Following each exposure the subject was asked to describe everything he had seen. Everything he said was recorded on tape.

"Something" Awareness Stage
The exposure number of the first report of awareness of "something"; i.e., the very first visible differentiation on the screen.

"Cheese" Awareness Stage
The exposure number of the first report of awareness of *cheese.*

Accuracy of the "Something" Awareness Statement
The accuracy level of the "something" statement was classified because it might be related to eye behavior before the report of awareness. The first report of awareness of any differentiation on the field varied considerably in its resemblance to the stimulus word *cheese.* The first reports could be rated along a 6-point scale: (1) dark band; (2) angles, lines, patterns, figures; (3) letters, numbers, writing; (4) word; (5) word similar to *cheese*; (6) *cheese.*

Most subjects were rated at 3. Four subjects were rated 4, and five were rated 5. Only one of the 23 subjects reported *cheese* as the first "something" report.

LOOKING-AT-TARGET MEASURES

Fixations-on-Target Areas
These are measures of the concentration of fixations in the two areas of the screen in which the word *cheese* is exposed. The most objective way to define the size of each target area is to examine the subjects' fixations when they have reported seeing the word *cheese* and to determine the area covered by the fixations on and around the word. To the rectangular area of the word we added a narrow border to accommodate for the average error in the fixation-recording equipment. Each of these target areas measured $2^1/_2 \times 5$ in on the screen.

Figure 8.1 shows the way the screen appears to the subject when he has seen the word *cheese,* and the way the screen is subdivided to indicate the quadrants, the target areas within the quadrants, and measures. Measure 1, the principal measure, is: areas 2 + 3 divided by all quadrants. (Other measures tried are listed in Table 8.1.)

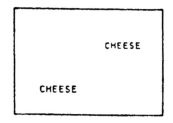
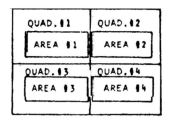

THE SCREEN AS IT APPEARS TO S
WHEN HE HAS SEEN THE WORD

THE SCREEN AS SUBDIVIDED FOR
THE QUADRANTS, AREAS, AND
MEASURES

Figure 8.1. The screen as the subject sees it and as it is subdivided for scoring.

TABLE 8.1

Correlations between Fixation Measures for Target (Cheese) Areas and Recall Preference for Cheese-Associated Words

First Two Exposures	Measure	Total group (N = 23)	Subgroup (N = 10)
Cheese	areas 2+3 ——————— (Measure 1[a] all quadrants)	0.53**	0.72*
Blank	Same	0.48*	0.62*
Cheese	areas 2+3 ——————— (Measures 2[a] areas 1+2+3+4)	0.43*	0.69*
Blank	Same	0.42*	0.65*
Cheese	quadrants 2+3 ———————(Measure 3[a] all quadrants)	0.45*	0.70*
Blank	Same	0.43	0.31
Cheese	areas 1+4[b] ——————	−0.33	−.72*
Blank	all quadrants Same	−0.31	−0.60*

*$p < 0.05$.
**$p < 0.01$.
[a]Measure 1, the principal one used, seemed best; the denominator (all quadrants) includes all fixations and focuses on the two target areas in the numerator (areas 2+3). Measure 2 gave similar results. Measure 3 was insensitive, being based upon all quadrants.
[b]These "noncheese" areas of the screen are introduced as a further control device.

SCATTER MEASURES

"Scatter" measures, i.e., extensiveness of area covered by fixations on the screen, were introduced because they were shown to have many correlates with measures of looking and defense. One of the most striking is with the defense of isolation—under a free inspection set, the more scatter, the more the defense of isolation (Luborsky, Blinder, and Schimek, 1965). Various eye fixation measures and their correlates are described in Luborsky, Blinder, and Mackworth (1963, 1964).

Scatter (Cells Covered)
   A grid was constructed dividing a photograph of the slide into 130 squares. (Each square was 0.007 of the total area.) This area measure is the total number of cells containing one or more fixations.

Scatter per Fixation
   This measure is the number of cells containing one or more fixations *divided by the total number of fixations.* It is the same as the area per fixation and is therefore the inverse of density.

RECALL MEASURES

Recall of Associates
   This is the recall from the 26 cards of words associated with cheese, minus the recall of control words (see note 3).

RESULTS

EYE-FIXATION BEHAVIOR AND AWARENESS

The obvious relationship between eye behavior and awareness of a stimulus can best be seen by means of a graph (Figure 8.2), which plots the mean percentage of fixations in the target areas for each subject in relation to that subject's own awareness threshold for reporting "something" on the screen. This "something" threshold represents the finest and most sensitive discrimination: the point at which the subject first said there is something he sees on the screen but is not able to tell what it is. "Something minus

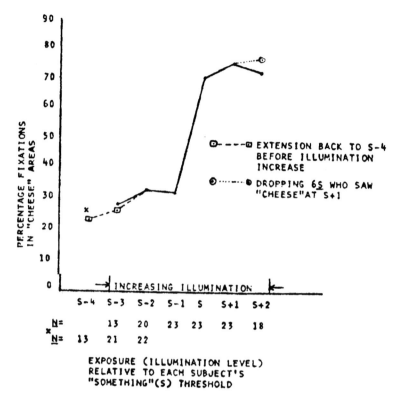

Figure 8.2. Percentage of fixations in target areas before, at, and after each subject's "something" threshold.

one" (s−1) refers to the illumination level just before the subject reported "something; minus two" (s − 2) refers to two illumination levels before he reported something, and so on. The illumination levels, of course, differ for different subjects, since the measures are intraindividual ones.

The subjects' first report of seeing "something" coincided with a large increase in fixations in the target areas. This increment from s − 1 to "something" is the only significant one in the curve ($t = 4.80$, $p < 0.01$). There was hardly any tendency for the fixations to concentrate in the target areas *before* the awareness and report of seeing "something." Before the report of awareness, fixations either did not represent directed looking or, if they did, were part of the broad search to find something on the screen. The s − 1, s − 2, and s − 3 points are all in a relatively flat line; then, when the "something" point arrives, there is a sudden increase in focusing on the target. (Note that we use *awareness* when we mean *report of awareness.*)

From the s + 1 to the s + 2 level the curve shows a slight decrease in fixation concentration, but it is not a significant shift. The subject usually reported seeing *cheese* after either the s + 1 (*N* = 10) or s + 2 (*N* = 6) level. When the slide was reexposed after *cheese* had once been reported, the subject reported *cheese* again, but the fixations were slightly less concentrated (not significantly).[4]

All three of the measures of fixations on the target area reveal similarly shaped curves. This further strengthens the impression that the relationship between reported awareness of the first discrimination of "something" and concentration of fixations is not an artifact of the particular measure used.

Our most intense focus in this study has been on the first discrimination of something on the screen. If, instead, we had looked at the full recognition of the word *cheese*—as in many perception studies—we would have come to a more usual type of conclusion: Concentration of fixations gradually increases from far below report of awareness to awareness (Figure 8.3). To review the main results: There is much looking before full discrimination (i.e., pre-*cheese*), but little or no looking before first discrimination (i.e., pre-"something").[5]

---

[4]This slight lessening of the subject's concentration after he once has seen the stimulus corresponds to findings of Bruner and Mackworth (reviewed by Mackworth and Kaplan, 1963) on deployment of fixations on out-of-focus pictures as they become less and less ambiguous. Fixations tend to be concentrated when the figures are ambiguous, and relatively scattered afterward.

[5]Acuity and motivation play their usual part in individual differences. The higher the acuity, the lower the illumination level at which *cheese* is first reported ($r = -0.42$, $p < 0.05$); the degree to which fixations concentrate in the target area when the subject first reports full recognition of *cheese* is also correlated with acuity ($r = 0.59$, $p < 0.01$). An interesting pattern of change in scatter from s − 1 to s-level was discovered: Six subjects concentrated their fixations, eight stayed the same, and nine dispersed their fixations. Those who first scattered their fixations at the s-level were not looking around much at the s − 1 point, then, at the s-point, they "woke up" and began to strive for further discrimination. The six subjects who concentrated their fixations from s − 1 to the s-point probably had been more motivated from the start to find something. If we combine the six (concentrators) with the eight (stable) and compare these 14 with the nine who dispersed their fixations, we find that the 14 (1) concentrated fixations in the target area; (2) reduced the *number* of fixations from s − 1 to the s-point; and (3) reduced heart rate activity from s − 1 to the s-point. It is as though subjects who either concentrated their fixations or kept them stable settled down when they achieved first discrimination of

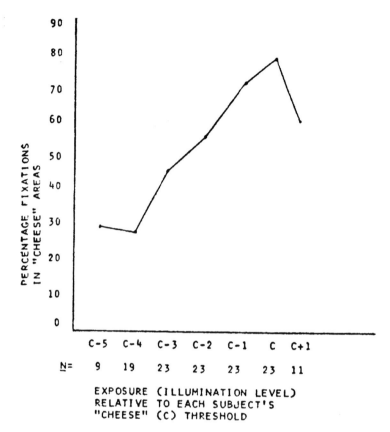

Figure 8.3. Percentage of fixations in target areas before, at, and after *cheese*-threshold.

REGISTRATION BEFORE REPORT OF AWARENESS

The following are five types of data to be considered in deciding whether we have evidence for registration before report of awareness.

1. Fixations in the Target Areas Before any Report of Awareness
A maintained rise in fixations in the target area *at least one sep before* the subject reports "something" on the screen might be

---

something. They showed this in decreased heart rate and in greater density and lengthening of their fixations.

one indication of registration before report of awareness. As we have seen for the group as a whole, this does *not* happen to any significant extent (Figure 8.2) and therefore offers no clear support for registration before report of awareness. (It may be worth noting that the nonsignificant increase, for all three measures, in fixations on the target areas in this early part of the curve from "something minus 3" [s − 3] to s − 1. Similarly, when extended back to the s − 4 level—before illumination increments—the curve begins even lower than at s − 3 (see Figure 8.2, dotted lines; the increase is still nonsignificant).

2. Accuracy of the "Something" Awareness Statement as a Function of Prior Fixations in the Target Areas

An intriguing correlation was discovered: The greater the accuracy and completeness of the "something" description, the more on-target looking has occurred on all exposures *before* the "something" level ($r = 0.51$, $p < 0.01$). Therefore, the looking that took place before a report of awareness must have involved some intake of information. The result is even more convincing after exclusion of the step before the awareness stage, since there might have been some unreported near-awareness at that point. Without the s − 1 exposure, the correlation remains significant ($r = 0.45$, $p < 0.05$).

3. Fixations in the Target Areas During Cheese vs. Blank Exposures

In the first exposures at illumination levels long before any awareness is reported or even faintly likely, two exposures were given of *cheese* and two of the blank. Registration before a report of awareness might be shown by greater concentration of fixations in the target areas during exposure of *cheese* (exposures 1 and 3) than during exposures of the blank (exposures 2 and 4). Mere inspection of a simple graph of the mean fixations-on-target scores for these four exposures reveals no major differences between them.[6] (Note the first four exposures in the curve, Figure

---

[6]Figure 8.4 represents the target concentration scores (measure 1) for all subjects *for each exposure.* (The presentation in Figure 8.4 differs from Figure 8.2 which gives percentage of fixations in the target area before, at, and after each subject "something" threshold.) The curves in Figure 8.4 start with a downturn, which may be explained by the tendency to first look at the upper or upper-right part of the screen. This common tendency to recognize more words in the right visual field than the left is noted by Buswell (1935) and Mishkin and Forgays (1952). The initial downturn (increased scatter) probably

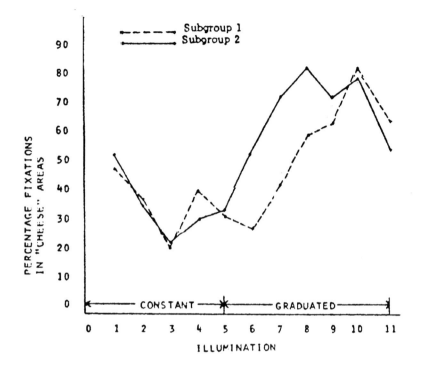

Figure 8.4. Percentage of fixations in target areas for each exposure of the slide. Subgroup 1 started one illumination step lower (5 volts) than subgroup 2. Pilot indicates *each step*, regardless of slight illumination difference between subgroups.

8.4.) For more exact analysis, a score was constructed for each subject of the difference between his fixation-on-target score for exposures 1 and 3 versus exposures 2 and 4. For the total group, a two-tailed t test of these differences is nonsignificant.

4. Fixations in the Target Areas in Relation to Recall of Cheese-Associated Words

After the first four exposures, the recall test for cheese associates was administered. Registration before awareness might be

appears after the preference is overcome by the subject's repeatedly being shown an apparently blank field. Concentration in the target areas increases until *cheese* is seen. By the seventh or eighth exposure the subject is aware of seeing something. The first report usually is of something in the upper-right quadrant before anywhere else, probably because of slightly more illumination on the right half of the field than on the left half

indicated if fixations in the target areas are associated with recall of cheese-associated words minus recall of words not associated with cheese. Table 8.1 lists correlations between fixations on target areas for the first two cheese exposures versus the two blank exposures, with the cheese-minus-control-word score. Some amazingly high correlations emerge between fixations on the target area scores and the recall of cheese-minus-control words. However, the comparable correlations for the blank exposures are almost as high. It is possible that all succeeding exposures in the series could have been contaminated by some stimulation from the initial exposure of the stimulus.

Control Group Exposures of Blank Slides

To control for this possibility, 14 new subjects were shown four exposures of the blank slide. Then, the list of words was given. With this group, if no correlation appeared between fixations in the target area and recall of cheese associates, it would support the interpretation that the experimental group's fixations in the target area correlated with recall of cheese associates because of subliminal exposure of *cheese*. No correlation existed (− 0.04) between fixations in the target area and recall of cheese associates. This absence of correlation in the control group suggests that in the experimental group, exposure of the word *cheese* was having an effect on the recall of cheese associates for those subjects who happened to look more in the target area. Greater looking in the target area was associated with recall of cheese associates because the eye would get more stimulation from the word *cheese.*[7]

5. Fixations in the Target Areas in Relation to Recall of Cheese-Associated Words for Subgroup 1 vs. Subgroup 2

Subgroup 2 was started with the very slight constant advantage over subgroup 1 of 5-v higher illumination, although the advantage made no difference in their initial reports describing what

caused by the slight skewedness in the angle of the slide's projection. Further impetus may come from the common preference for the upper-right quadrant. Only after *cheese* becomes perceptible is there more looking around again. Before the fourth or fifth exposures, any concentration of fixations *seems* to be a matter of chance or, at times, because the gaze is momentarily arrested by a brief after-image of the fixation point seen previously in the center of the screen.

[7]There is, in addition, some individual consistency in preference for looking at certain areas of the screen for both control and experimental groups. For the control group the

they saw. If the greater illumination on exposures 1 and 3 allowed more stimulation to get into the system, this extra stimulation nevertheless might increase the preference for recall of *cheese*-associated words. The number of *cheese*-control associates recalled it significantly greater ($p < 0.01$) for subgroup 2 than for subgroup 1. Correlation for each subject's recall preference with fixations in the target area further confirms this possibility: for subgroup 1, it is 0.39 (n.s.); for subgroup 2 it is 0.72 ($p < 0.05$).[8]

CONCLUSIONS

1. *Awareness and eye fixations: The stimulus intensity which produces the first awareness of "something" also produces the first concentration of the gaze on the stimulus area (Figure 8.2).* Our results reveal a great coincidence of first massing of eye fixations in the target area at the time of first report, "I see something." This first report of awareness is the only one which shows a significant increment in on-target looking. The association probably works as an orienting response in two directions: As soon as one is aware of something in an area of the field, one directs one's gaze there; one concentrates one's gaze to become more aware of what is there.

This main finding is subject to limits listed under "Future Directions for Research"; e.g., a more sensitive discrimination procedure might have revealed some tendency to concentrate fixations before first awareness of something. However, the prominent association of concentrating fixations with first awareness is likely to be replicated.[9]

2. *Registration before awareness and eye fixations.* The existence of registration before reports of awareness of the stimulus was

correlation of fixations in the target area for exposure 1 + 3 vs. 2 + 4 is 0.47 (which misses the 0.05 level, but it reaches a significant *rho* of 54). In the experimental group the similar correlation was 0.6 ($p < 0.01$).

[8]The slight advantage given subgroup 2 also could have made a difference in the first concentration of fixations in the *cheese* areas. The curves (Figure 8.4) for the two subgroups are shaped almost alike; at exposure 6, however, subgroup 2 is higher than subgroup 1 for fixations in the *cheese* areas. For subgroup 1, the upturn is first evident at exposure 7.

[9]An apparently analogous result has been discovered for pupil size response to near-threshold flashes of light (Hakerem and Sutton, 1966): "If the intensity of the light is adequate and it is reported as seen, there is pupillary response. If the same light is reported as not seen, there is no pupillary response" (pp. 485–486).

slightly supported—at least enough for the evidence to be glanced over. The lack of strong evidence may result from the small input. Studies of subliminal perception have typically concluded that indirect recovery effects are modest, and our results may be no exception. Of the types of evidence explored, the most likely to be substantial are (1) the higher the accuracy of the "something" awareness statement, the more the *prior* fixations had fallen in the target area; (2) the more fixations in the target area for the first two *cheese* exposures, the more recall preference for cheese-associated words; (3) the very slightly higher initial illumination given to one subgroup significantly increased the correlation referred to under (2) and the preference for recall of cheese-associated words.

A factor, therefore, that seems to facilitate registration before reports of awareness is greater concentration of the gaze upon an area, although one is not aware it is a target area. Such concentration enhances the chances of being affected by subliminal stimulation from that area. As we showed earlier, it is not the amount of looking around that counts,[10] but the amount of hitting the target.[11]

FUTURE DIRECTIONS FOR RESEARCH

For refining the findings on the relationship of awareness and eye fixations, further provision should be made for identifying the exact point in the 10-sec period when the first differentiation occurs. The subject might press a buzzer at the point of first

---

[10]An alternative hypothesis does *not* apply: Pure extensiveness of inspection (scatter) influences registration before reports of awareness. In Luborsky, Blinder, and Schimek (1965) the amount of scatter was significantly correlated with the conscious intake of information: The smaller the spread, the less the recall of sexual information in the pictures. In the present experiment, however, the correlations with scatter and scatter per fixation were insignificant.

[12]The tentative conclusion that greater concentration of the gaze on an area facilitates registration—even when one is not aware of it as a target area—may have an important implication for tachistoscopic experiments: *More perceptual intake should occur when a prior fixation point has been provided and the stimulus is flashed very near it.* Mackworth and Bruner (1965) take a position which has the same implication. They conclude that the clear field of view is much smaller than people have thought. The eyes must be carefully aimed, since only the area near the fixation point provides useful data input.

awareness of any differentiation. A testing of the limits would be useful—after each period of inspecting the screen, a "something–nothing" sequence of exposures would be presented to find if the subject is making any discrimination.

Ulrich Neisser (personal communication) proposes a design that would more directly find the relationship between awareness and the location of fixations. The experimenter would repeatedly flash an initially subliminal stimulus (perhaps at a constant rather than increasing exposure), but without requiring the subject to maintain a fixation point. One could then relate the point where the eye happened to be at the moment of the flash with the form of the awareness and the recall phenomena.

2. Recovery of faint registrations reported in experiments using a variety of indirect recall methods (the Pötzl-type, rebus-type [Shevrin and Luborsky, 1961] recall-of-associated-words type, etc.) depends upon a certain optimum level of stimulation having gotten into the perceptual system. The largest amount may be taken in at a point *moderately* below threshold, but not *far* below. We should examine the curve for the fixations at each exposure step to find the first evidence of registration—it may be only at the s − 1, s − 2, and s − 3 points (and not much below). A proposed design would entail repeating an indirect recall measure, such as recall of word associates after several illumination levels. The design calls for several groups, each to be given the recall words at a different point in the illumination series.

3. The degree of threat triggered by a stimulus may be a major factor influencing the lag between the first concentration of fixations on a target and the report of awareness of seeing something. Some recent work on thresholds and some of the perceptual defense studies support this view (Silverman and Silverman, 1964; Silverman and Luborsky, 1965). The response to threat may be a function of defense and cognitive style (Luborsky, Blinder, and Schimek, 1965). It may therefore be worth repeating the experiment, incorporating a threatening word in addition to the relatively neutral word *cheese*.

4. Other positions and sizes of the stimulus on the screen should be tried. A smaller target area covering less of the field would lessen the possibility of chance concentration of fixations in that area.

COMPARISON WITH SIMILAR STUDIES

No experiments in the literature are identical to our method of photographing and measuring fixation deployment during faint illumination. Instead of trying to set the stage for subliminal registration by the usual device of shortening the exposure to a brief flash, we have attempted it by low illumination, as was done by Miller (1939). A somewhat similar technique, first used by Urbantschitsch (1907), has been repeated recently with positive results by Friedman and Fisher (1960). In the Urbantschitsch method, the picture is covered by sheets of blank paper, so that the subject is not aware of any differentiation. He is then asked to close his eyes and report images.

Some subliminal research findings have points of comparability with our own. Goldberg and Fiss (1959) conclude that discrimination in a task which requires accurate perceiving necessitates at least partial awareness of the stimulus. Discrimination of geometric figures takes place only when the person is able to distinguish parts of the stimulus. Nevertheless, they also raised the possibility that before discrimination occurs, registration might be taking place which could only be shown by the indirect emergence of the registration (or activation) via certain media—for example, in waking images. This possibility was confirmed in a study by Fiss, Goldberg, and Klein (1963). They reported that a "low-level stimulus, too faint to be discriminated or even partially perceived, could exert marked and objectively measurable effects on another mode of conscious experience-imagery" (p. 43). In our present study, we have been able to show the simultaneity of directing one's gaze and concentrating one's fixations on an area, with awareness of something in that area. We also turned up some evidence for registration before reports of awareness. A probable reason for not finding more of these indirect recovery effects may have to do with the *position* of our instrument for indirect recovery—the recall words are presented at a point at which stimulation from the word *cheese* is so far below threshold that, if it gets through at all, only tiny effects can be expected. This applies especially to subgroup 1 subjects, who were started at a lower illumination point.

Block and Reiser's study (1962) is similar to our own in its main results. The task they posed to each subject was to decide whether a circle or a hexagon had been flashed and to make a random guess, even if little or nothing had been seen on the screen. A mild shock was administered after one of the two pictures was flashed. They found that at an experimentally specified low illumination level (minus 1 to minus 2 steps below threshold), registration was manifested in physiological discrimination and in psychological responses reflecting partial awareness. The partial awareness was inferred by the experimenter from the subject's choice of the response "unsure," rather than the response "a complete guess." At still lower illumination levels, they believe that no information gets into the brain's registration system. Our findings are probably similar to theirs: by giving our subject a set to report anything he sees as soon as he sees it, at whatever level of confidence he has in it, we are gearing him for fine discrimination. When the subject reports "something," he is probably giving his first faint impression, often an uncertain one, with partial awareness. What we refer to as our "something" response is probably close to the range of Block and Reiser's minus 1 or even minus 2 steps below threshold response. Just below our "something" response we may get only a little information in to the system, and further down, none.

SUMMARY

While eye fixations were being photographed for 10-sec periods, the word *cheese* was presented so faintly that no subjects could report seeing anything. After two exposures of *cheese* and two of a blank, a list of words was read once and recall tested. Half of the words were associates of *cheese,* and half were not. Graded increments of illumination were then given of the *cheese* slide.

We focused on two questions: (1) At what point in the increasing illumination series would the eye fixations begin to concentrate around the word *cheese*—before, or coincident with, report of awareness? (2) Could evidence be found for registration before the concentration of fixations and before the report of awareness (i.e., after the first two exposures of the *cheese* slide)? The answer to the first question was clear and simple. The stimulus intensity producing the first awareness of "something" also produces the first concentration of fixations on the stimulus. At the time of the first report, "I see something," there is the first massing of eye fixations on the target. Evidence was not as clear to answer the second question. Because of these findings, one cannot reject the possibility that registrations are getting into the system before the first concentration of fixations and before the report of awareness: (1) The higher the accuracy and completeness of the "something" report, the more the *prior* fixations had fallen on the target area of the screen, (2) the more fixations there were on the target area for the first two exposures of *cheese*, the more recall preference for cheese-associated words; and (3) the very slightly higher initial illumination given to one subgroup significantly increased the correlation referred to under (2) and the recall preference for cheese-associated words.

REFERENCES

Block, J. D., & Reiser, M. F. (1962), Discrimination and recognition of weak stimuli: I. Psychological and physiological relationships. *Arch. Gen. Psychiat.*, 6:25–36.

Buswell, G. T. (1935), *How People Look at Pictures: A Study of the Psychology of Perception in Art.* Chicago: University of Chicago Press.

Fisher, C. (1965), Psychoanalytic implications of recent research on sleep and dreaming. *J. Amer. Psychoanal. Assn.*, 13:197–319.

Fiss, H., Goldberg, F. H., & Klein, G. S. (1963), Effects of subliminal-stimulation on imagery and discrimination. *Percept. Mot. Skills*, 17:31–44.

Friedman, S. M., & Fisher, C. (1960), Further observations on primary modes of perception: The use of a masking technique for subliminal visual stimulation. *J. Amer. Psychoanal. Assn.*, 8:100–129.

Goldberg, F. H., & Fiss, H. (1959), Partial cues and the phenomenon of "discrimination without awareness." *Percept. Mot. Skills*, 85:22–26.

Hakerem, G., & Sutton, S. (1966), Pupillary response at visual threshold. *Nature*, 212 (5061):485–486.

Luborsky, L., Blinder, B., & Mackworth, N. (1963), Eye fixation and the recall of pictures as a function of GSR responsivity. *Percept. Mot. Skills*, 18:469–483.

———————— (1964), Eye fixation and the contents of recall and images as a function of heart rate. *Percept. Mot. Skills*, 18:421–436.

———————— Schimek, J. (1965), Looking, recalling, and GSR as a function of defense. *J. Abnorm. Psychol.*, 78:270–280.

Mackworth, N., & Bruner, J. (1965), Selecting visual information during recognition by adults and children. (Mimeographed.)

———— Kaplan, I. (1963), Points of view and lines of sight. *Ikon*, 13:45–60.

Miller, J. (1939), Discrimination without awareness. *Amer. J. Psychol.*, 52:562–578.

Mishkin, M., & Forgays, D. G. (1952), Word recognition as a function of retinal locus. *J. Exp. Psychol.*, 43:43–48.

Shevrin, H., & Luborsky, L. (1961), The rebus technique: A method for studying primary-process transformations of briefly exposed pictures. *J. Nerv. & Ment. Dis.*, 133:479–488.

Silverman, L., & Luborsky, L. (1965), The relationship between perceptual blocking and inhibition of drive expression. *J. Pers. Soc. Psychol.*, 2:435–436.

———— Silverman, D. (1964), A clinical-experimental approach to the study of subliminal stimulation: The effects of a drive-related stimulus upon Rorschach responses. *J. Abnorm. & Soc. Psychol.*, 68:158–172.

Spence, D., & Holland, B. (1962), The restricting effects of awareness: A paradox and an explanation. *J. Abnorm. & Soc. Psychol.*, 64:163–174.

Urbantschitsch, V. (1907), *Über subjective optische anschauungsbilder.* Leipzig: Deuticke.

Woodworth, R., & Scholsberg, H. (1954), *Experimental Psychology.* New York: Holt.

NAME INDEX

Abrams, R. L., 17
Allers, R., 16, 99–101, 126–127, 131, 133, 141, 143–146, 176, 251–252, 287, 294, 300
Allport, A., 14
Allport, F. H., 138, 139–140, 183, 195n, 241
Arlow, J. A., 23
Aserinsky, E., 345–346

Bach, S., 240, 284, 338
Bargh, J. A., 8, 14–15n
Barr, A. H., 238
Bender, M. B., 130
Berger, R. J., 348
Bernat, E., 248
Betlheim, S., 85–86, 87, 99
Bevan, W., 346
Bexton, W. H., 293
Blake, R. R., 88
Blinder, B., 361n, 368, 376n, 377
Block, J. D., 362, 370
Bond, J. A., 10, 12–13, 14, 24n, 32, 249
Boutwell, L., 345n
Brady, J. P., 361n
Brakel, L. A. W., 10, 11, 12–13, 14, 17, 21, 24n, 32, 34, 249
Brandt, R., 361n
Brech, E., 249
Brenner, C., 23, 188–189
Brewer, M. B., 14
Bruner, J., 88, 89, 138, 139, 376n
Bunce, S. C., 17
Bush, R. R., 315–317, 332, 333
Buswell, G. T., 372–373n

Colby, K. M., 185n

Dalbiez, R., 137, 186
Dement, W., 345–346
Derman, J., 361n
Dickman, S., 4, 8
Dixon, N., 2, 240–241, 243
Doane, B. K., 293
Draine, S. C., 17

Eagle, 240
Ehrenzweig, A., 231–232, 238
Erdelyi, M., 242–243
Eriksen, C., 248

Ferguson, M. J., 8, 14–15n
Fisher, C., 1, 2–7, 8–26, 29–34, 39, 62, 181, 196n, 201–202, 239, 241, 247, 248, 250, 300, 301, 341n, 345n, 346, 357, 361, 378
Fiss, H., 240, 378
Fliess, R., 72, 77
Forgays, D. G., 372–373n
Foulkes, W. D., 346, 354
Freud, S., 3–4, 6, 8, 18–19, 23, 33–34, 37–39, 72–74, 79, 82–83, 85, 86–87, 88, 90, 92–93, 94, 98–99, 129, 131–132, 134, 137, 175–176n, 178, 182, 186–191, 193, 242–243, 249, 256, 286, 347, 348
Friedman, S. M., 378
Frink, H., 137, 186
Fritzler, D., 244

Giddan, N. S., 346

383

SUBJECT INDEX

primary process and, 133–134
Unintentional recall, 288
Upright-light condition, 260, 261,
    269, 292–294

Verbal trace, 348
Verbalization, in cognition, 194
Visual acuity, 370n
Visual agnosia, 87–88, 99
    perceptual distortions in, 84–85
Visual discrimination, 180
Visual perception, 81–82
    preconscious, 38
    research on, 21–22
Visual percepts, 95
    in cognition, 194
Vital Lies, Simple Truths (Goleman),
    243
Voyeuristic-exhibitionistic dreams,

78–79
Voyeuristic-exhibitionistic wishes,
    49–50, 60–62, 170–174
Voyeuristic images, 163–164, 170

Waking subliminal stimulus, 345–357
Warm-up period, 304, 305–306
Wish fulfillment, 90
Word association tests, 143
    factors in results of, 128–129
    response time in, 127
    with tachistoscopic exposure,
        99–104, 106–107, 110–112,
        114, 117–119, 121–125
Word associations, 16
    tracking subliminal effects, 33
Word-stem completions, 32
Words, tachistoscopic exposure to,
    68–69, 73